GEORGE FARAH **no**
debate

How the Republican and
Democratic Parties
Secretly Control
the Presidential Debates

SEVEN STORIES PRESS
New York · London · Toronto · Melbourne

Seven Stories Press
140 Watts Street
New York, NY 10013
http://www.sevenstories.com/

IN CANADA
Hushion House, 36 Northline Road,
Toronto, Ontario M4B 3E2

IN THE UK
Turnaround Publisher Services Ltd.,
Unit 3, Olympia Trading Estate,
Coburg Road, Wood Green, London
N22 6TZ

IN AUSTRALIA
Palgrave Macmillan, 627 Chapel Street,
South Yarra VIC 3141

LIBRARY OF CONGRESS
CATALOGING-IN-PUBLICATION
DATA
Farah, George.
No debate : how the Republican and
Democratic parties secretly control the
presidential debates / George Farah.—
A Seven Stories Press 1st ed.
    p. cm.
Includes bibliographical references
and index.
ISBN 1-58322-630-3 (pbk. : alk. paper)
ISBN 1-58322-665-6(hc. : alk. paper)
1. Presidents—United States—Election.
2. Campaign debates—United States.
3. Television in politics—United States.
4. Political parties—United States.
I. Title.
JK524.F37 2004
324.7'3—dc22
                    2004003568

College professors may order
examination copies of Seven Stories
Press titles for a free six-month
trial period. To order, visit
www.sevenstories.com/textbook or fax
on school letterhead to 212.226.1411.

Jacket design by POLLEN, New York
Text design by India Amos

Printed in Canada

9 8 7 6 5 4 3 2 1

For my dad

The basis of our political systems is the right of the people to make and to alter their Constitutions of Government. But the Constitution which at any time exists, till changed by an explicit and authentic act of the whole people, is sacredly obligatory upon all. The very idea of the power and the right of the people to establish Government presupposes the duty of every individual to obey the established Government.

All obstructions to the execution of the Laws, all combinations and associations, under whatever plausible character, with the real design to direct, control, counteract, or awe the regular deliberation and action of the constituted authorities, are destructive of this fundamental principle, and of fatal tendency. They serve to organize faction, to give it an artificial and extraordinary force; to put, in the place of the delegated will of the nation, the will of a party, often a small but artful and enterprising minority of the community; and, according to the alternate triumphs of different parties, to make the public administration the mirror of the ill-concerted and incongruous projects of faction, rather than the organ of consistent and wholesome plans digested by common counsels, and modified by mutual interests.

However combinations or associations of the above description may now and then answer popular ends, they are likely, in the course of time and things, to become potent engines, by which cunning, ambitious, and unprincipled men will be enabled to subvert the power of the people, and to usurp for themselves the reins of government; destroying afterwards the very engines, which have lifted them to unjust dominion.

—*George Washington, in his farewell address,*
September 17, 1796

We are not afraid to entrust the American people with unpleasant facts, foreign ideas, alien philosophies, and competitive values. For a nation that is afraid to lets its people judge the truth and falsehood in an open market is a nation that is afraid of its people.

—*John F. Kennedy, on the twentieth anniversary*
of the Voice of America, February 26, 1962"

Contents

List of Cartoons

Acknowledgments

Thanks to Marty Plissner, Greg Ruggiero, and Christopher Shaw. Thanks also to Robert Riley, who taught me to be a better writer. And very special thanks to two people who made this book possible, who patiently worked with me night after night for no reason other than kindness and love: Michael Farah and Terra Schmookler.

1

Debate Cartel

THROUGHOUT EACH ELECTION season, in state after state, presidential candidates deliver rehearsed stump speeches in separate auditoriums. Candidates praise their own platforms and, from a safe distance, ridicule their opponents. The candidates rarely meet each other. But every four years for the past quarter century, for no more than a total of six hours, the leading candidates have come face-to-face in pivotal presidential debates, the quintessential political event of a televised democracy. For those six hours, grappling with the same questions, on the same stage, at the same time, the candidates confront each other.

And no matter how much or how hard they practice, debate participants may encounter a discomforting element of spontaneity. Professor Alan Schroeder, author of *Presidential Debates: Forty Years of High-Risk TV,* called presidential debates "a rare walk on the wild side."[1] During the debates, the candidates cannot huddle with their managers, advisors, or high-priced political consultants.

Most important, candidates are speaking before an audience in the tens of millions. Frank J. Fahrenkopf Jr., cochair of the Commission on Presidential Debates, dubbed the events "the Superbowl of politics."[2] No other forum provides candidates with simultaneous access to tens of millions of voters, and no electoral event has a greater impact on American voters. The Supreme Court of the United States described presidential debates as the "only occasion during a campaign when the attention of a large portion of the American public is focused on the election."[3]

Because of this audience size, presidential debates serve as critical introductions to the candidates for a majority of voters. The debates are the first and last time most eligible voters can witness substantive political discussion between the candidates. "After months of wondering 'where's the beef,' the debates are like a sixteen-ounce filet mignon," said Congressman Ed Markey (D-MA).[4] The debates allow voters, previously subject to an onslaught of thirty-second television commercials, to assess the candidates' policies and characters. Former presidential candidate John B. Anderson put it simply, "They've heard about these fellows, now they really are going to take the time to sit down for at least an hour or ninety minutes and hear what they have to say."[5]

The debates often make or break candidates. John F. Kennedy said he would never have reached the White House "if not for the 1960 debates."[6] Jimmy Carter attributed both his victory in 1976 and his defeat in 1980 to his respective debate performances. Candidates who refused participation in these public forums would likely relinquish the possibility of victory.

Likewise, candidates prohibited from participating in the presidential debates are never really introduced to most voters and never have a chance of victory. Professor Jamin Raskin, author of *Overruling Democracy*, explained that "excluding a candidate from a debate is almost always an electoral death sentence. While his opponents are validated in the public eye and given millions of dollars in free publicity, an excluded candidate receives a stamp of irrelevance, frivolousness, or marginality."[7] By extension, many of the issues espoused by an excluded candidate are dismissed along with his candidacy. John B. Anderson called his exclusion from the second 1980 presidential debate "absolutely crushing."[8]

The Power of the Sponsor

Ironically, what makes presidential debates so valuable to the electorate—confrontation, spontaneity, audience size, pressure—terrifies the Republican and Democratic candidates, and their campaigns therefore strive to control these critical election events. "The rationale is simple," wrote Sidney Kraus, the preeminent debate scholar. "More control over the events increases the probabilities of impressing the electorate, gaining advantages over the opponent, and winning the election."[9]

In 1960, Richard Nixon underestimated the power of televised debates. For the first presidential debate in American history, he showed up at the studio underweight, pale, and needing a shave. His light gray suit blended into the backdrop, and he refused a professional makeup job. Standing beside the tanned, done-up Kennedy, Nixon looked awkward and sweaty, and six weeks later he lost the election. Ever since, major-party campaigns have understood the significance of presidential debates, and risk-averse campaign managers have done everything in their power to exclude both challenging formats and popular third-party candidates. The result has frequently been minimal authentic debate on many critical issues—especially those issues on which the Republicans and Democrats already agree.

Campaign managers will do almost anything—avoid debates, bar candidates, select tame moderators, and so on—to protect their candidates. Consequently, the responsibility for producing fair, unscripted, and robust debates that maximize voter education rests squarely on the shoulders of the debate sponsor. Lawrence Noble, former general counsel of the Federal Election Commission, explained:

> The primary concern is getting the Republican and Democratic candidates to debate. Once you have that, then you have a situation in which the Democratic and Republican candidates have tremendous leverage over the debates. That's where you need the debate sponsor to issue rules, and say fine, you have tremendous leverage, but we're going to make sure that you don't foreclose valid third-party candidates and difficult questions just because of that leverage.[10]

Only the debate sponsor can ensure that American voters have the opportunity to watch real and informative debates rather than glorified news conferences between entrenched powers. The sponsor controls two of the most critical elements of the presidential debates: (1) who will participate in the debates, and (2) how the debates will be structured. To execute this power responsibly, only nonpartisan champions of democracy and voter education should sponsor presidential debates. The *Washington Post* editorialized that "the debates are a form of job interview, and the prospective employers deserve to ask the questions and set the rules."[11]

An effective debate sponsor must serve as a bulwark against the antidemocratic demands of the Republican and Democratic party campaigns. Unfortunately, that hasn't always been the case. Because of the influence of the major parties, the American people were deprived of presidential debates entirely for many years.

A Brief History

Presidential debates exist primarily because major-party candidates once considered them politically expedient. When deciding whether to debate, candidates have never been swayed by the desire to strengthen the democratic process. In fact, before presidential debates became institutionalized, most front-runners avoided debates at all costs. Throughout the 1940s, President Franklin Delano Roosevelt ignored invitations to debate over the radio, and during the 1950s, President Dwight Eisenhower, "notorious for his butchery of the English language,"[12] rejected repeated network offers.

By 1960, however, 88 percent of American homes had a television set, and both major-party candidates, Richard Nixon and John F. Kennedy, neither of whom were incumbents, eagerly anticipated the opportunity to debate. The networks, moreover, were under serious pressure to demonstrate greater civic integrity. CBS and NBC had been caught in quiz-show scandals that graced the front pages of every major newspaper; the game shows had been scripted and rehearsed from beginning to end, and according to Marty Plissner, former political director of CBS News, "there were calls on both Capitol Hill and Wall Street for heads to roll."[13] To clean up their image, the networks proposed giving up valuable hours of prime-time television to host presidential debates, but ironically they confronted a federal regulatory obstacle.

Section 315 of the 1934 Communications Act required broadcasters to give "equal time" to all political candidates seeking the same office. Televised presidential debates in 1960 would have violated the Communications Act unless all fourteen balloted candidates were invited to participate. Congress responded by temporarily suspending Section 315 of the Communications Act for the 1960 presidential election. Five weeks later, the networks simultaneously broadcast the first televised presidential debate, a legendary spectacle that revealed the political power of television and broke all viewership records.

Despite the tremendous success of the 1960 debates, the public was deprived of presidential debates for the next three elections. Had Kennedy lived to run for reelection, presidential debates could have been institutionalized decades earlier. Kennedy had promised to debate again in 1964, and he had even proposed legislation to suspend the equal-time rule. But President Lyndon B. Johnson had no intention of risking his lead against Barry Goldwater, and when the bill to suspend Section 315 came out of conference, the heavily Democratic Senate tabled it.

In 1968, when Democratic candidate Hubert Humphrey called Nixon "Sir Richard-the-Chicken-Hearted," the public's fancy was momentarily gripped.[14] But President Nixon, who had learned his lesson eight years earlier, adamantly refused to debate. When a Democratic Congress pushed a bill to suspend Section 315, Senate Republicans threatened a filibuster, and the bill never came to a vote. Four years later, in 1972, President Nixon predictably vetoed a campaign finance reform package that would have suspended Section 315.

In 1976, however, an unelected incumbent, Gerald Ford, needed to prove his legitimacy. Ford had never run in a national race before; his post-Watergate pardon of Nixon was unpopular; he had won his party nomination by the narrowest margin of any incumbent in history; and he was trailing the Democratic nominee by more than twenty points in the polls.[15]

Moreover, in 1975, the Federal Communications Commission (FCC) had announced a major regulatory decision that permanently removed the need for congressional action. In its *Aspen Institute* decision, the FCC ruled that televised presidential debates would be exempt from the equal-time requirement as long as they were not sponsored by broadcasters. (In 1983, hoping to increase televised debates at the local level, the FCC modified regulations again to allow broadcasters to sponsor exclusive political debates. Today, there are no longer any FCC regulations that require the inclusion of third-party or independent candidates in presidential debates.)

The *Aspen Institute* decision paved the way for the 1976 presidential debates, sponsored by the League of Women Voters, which had been holding local candidate forums for generations. League sponsorship prevented major-party candidates from covertly refusing participation. No longer could comfortable incumbents simply veto legislation or hide behind a compliant Congress. Major-party candidates would have to participate in debates or suffer public criticisms from the *nonpartisan* League of Women Voters. As a result, there have been presidential debates in every election year since 1976.

The League of Women Voters sponsored presidential debates again in 1980 and 1984. In 1988, the Commission on Presidential Debates (CPD) replaced the League as sponsor, and the CPD has hosted quadrennial presidential debates ever since.

The Bipartisan CPD

The CPD is a nonprofit, tax-exempt organization. It has eleven governing board members, four honorary board members, an executive director, and a small administrative staff. According to the CPD, it was created to institutionalize presidential debates and to educate voters. The organization's mission statement reads: "The Commission on Presidential Debates was established in 1987 to ensure that debates, as a permanent part of every general election, provide the best possible information to viewers and listeners."

The CPD proudly publicizes its independence from political parties and purports to objectively determine who will participate in the debates and under what conditions. Testifying before Congress, Frank J. Fahrenkopf Jr., cochairman of the CPD, said:

> Campaign staffs are legitimately interested in structuring the debates in ways that are advantageous to their candidates. But at the end of the day, the debates belong to

the voters. They are the ones who want debates, they are the ones who watch and learn from them, they are the ones who base their votes on debates. The CPD is in the business to represent the American people.[16]

The general counsel of the Federal Election Commission, Lawrence Noble, had a different view. In 1997, he accused the CPD of violating federal debate regulations at the expense of the public interest and recommended a full-blown investigation.

The CPD is not the honorable institution it claims to be. In fact, the CPD is a corporate-funded, bipartisan cartel that secretly awards control of the presidential debates to the Republican and Democratic candidates, perpetuating domination of a two-party system and restricting subject matters of political discourse. Through the CPD, the Republican and Democratic candidates exclude popular third-party candidates, eliminate challenging debate formats, and avoid addressing many important national issues. The presidential debates become exchanges of sound bites rather than exchanges of ideas. The CPD represents the Republican and Democratic nominees, not the American people.

Fahrenkopf testified that "the Commission on Presidential Debates has no connection with any political party."[17] But the cochairmen of the CPD—Fahrenkopf and Paul G. Kirk Jr.—are the former heads of the Republican National Committee and the Democratic National Committee, respectively. Fahrenkopf, who served as party chair longer than any other Republican in the twentieth century, and Kirk, who once served as chief political assistant to Democratic Senator Ted Kennedy, created the CPD in 1987 and have led the CPD ever since. Former presidents Gerald Ford, Jimmy Carter, Ronald Reagan, and Bill Clinton are the honorary cochairmen of the CPD.

The initial board members of the CPD selected by Fahrenkopf and Kirk constituted a list of who's who in the Republican and Democratic parties: Barbara Vucanovich, then a Republican congresswoman from Nevada; Pete Wilson, then a Republican senator from California; Kay Orr, then a Republican governor of Nebraska; David Norcross, then counsel to the Republican Party Chair (Fahrenkopf) and later general counsel of the Republican Party; John Culver, a former Democratic senator from Iowa; Vernon Jordan, then a Democratic strategist and later senior advisor to President Clinton; Richard Moe, former chief of staff to Vice President Walter Mondale; and the late Ambassador Pamela Harriman, founder of the first Democratic Political Action Committee and later chair of the 1992 Clinton-Gore presidential campaign.[18] Democratic Congressman John Lewis, the late Republican Senator Paul Coverdell, and former Republican Treasury Secretary Paul O'Neill replaced three of these board members.

To undermine criticisms of partisanship, Fahrenkopf and Kirk recently filled open seats on the board with less doctrinaire Republicans and Democrats. Currently, in addition to Kirk, four directors are Democratic Party loyalists: Caroline Kennedy Schlossberg, daughter of the late President John F. Kennedy; Newton N. Minow, who served as special assistant to Democratic presidential candidate Adlai E. Stevenson and was later appointed chairman of the FCC by President Kennedy; H. Patrick Swygert, who served as an assistant to Democratic Congressman Charles Rangel; and Antonia Hernandez, who served as counsel to the Senate Committee on the Judiciary, then chaired by Senator Ted Kennedy. In addition to Fahrenkopf, three directors are Republican Party loyalists: former senator John Danforth from Missouri, former senator Alan K. Simpson from Wyoming, and Congresswoman Jennifer Dunn from Washington.

Dorothy Ridings (president of the Council on Foundations) and Howard Buffett (son of billionaire investor Warren Buffett) were invited to the board in 1997 to counter accusations of partisanship following the exclusion of Ross Perot from the 1996 presidential debates. CPD officials claim that Ridings and Buffett are independents politically, but Ridings is a registered Democrat and Buffett was elected Republican commissioner of Douglas County in Nebraska and often makes contributions to Republican candidates. The *St. Louis Post-Dispatch* reported, "The nonprofit commission, founded by former chairmen of the national Republican and Democratic committees, has a board stocked with nothing but Democrats and Republicans."[19]

The six-to-five ratio of Democrats to Republicans on the CPD's board compensates for the party affiliation of Janet Brown, the executive director of the CPD, who is a registered Republican and once served as press secretary to then senator John Danforth.

The current CPD board members make no effort to disguise their partisanship during election years. Nine of the eleven members contributed to Republican or Democratic candidates in 2000. Jennifer Dunn was the master of ceremonies at the 2000 Republican National Convention, and she vigorously campaigned for George W. Bush. Caroline Kennedy Schlossberg gave a speech in support of Al Gore at the 2000 Democratic National Convention before introducing her uncle, Senator Edward Kennedy. Newton N. Minow served on the Gore Commission, a presidentially appointed body that reported to the vice president and attempted to define the public-service obligations of television stations. Alan K. Simpson energetically campaigned for George W. Bush, and after his election, the president appointed Simpson to the board of directors of the Federal National Mortgage Association. John Danforth was on the short list to become the Republican vice-presidential candidate in 2000, and Bush asked Danforth to represent the campaign in a federal challenge to the manual vote recount in Florida.[20] In 2001, President Bush appointed Danforth to be the special envoy to Sudan.

The CPD board members ardently believe in a two-party system. When the CPD was created, Paul Kirk declared, "As a party chairman, it's my responsibility to strengthen the two-party system." Framed on the wall of Frank Fahrenkopf's office, which is stocked with mementos of him and former president Ronald Reagan together, is the December 1983 issue of *American Politics*, and the cover article about him is titled "Managing and Building the Two-Party System." Even Dorothy Ridings enthusiastically supports the two-party system. "I certainly believe in a two-party system," she said. "It's a lot better than the France I knew when I was growing up, which had fifty-seven parties. . . . I've seen enough of the consequences of a huge multiparty system where government stability is often in question."[21]

Accordingly, the CPD perceives third parties as political and ideological threats, and it does not hesitate to exclude popular third-party and independent candidates from the presidential debates. In fact, CPD directors consider it their duty to the republic. "You can argue about third parties all day, but I come down on the side that the stability of the country depends on the two-party system," said Newton Minow, vice-chairman of the CPD.[22] CPD director Alan Simpson said, "You have a lot of thoughtful Democrats and Republicans on the commission that are interested in the American people finding out more about the two major candidates—not about independent candidates, who just mess things up."[23] Congressman John Lewis (D-GA), a former CPD director, explained:

> There's no question that having the two major parties in absolute control of the presidential debate process, and there's no question that they do, strengthens the two-party system. These are the most important events of an election, and if no other candidates are getting in the debates, the American people are just not going to hear about them, which means the two parties basically have a monopoly.[24]

The CPD, therefore, is not "nonpartisan" but rather "bipartisan," a crucial distinction that determines whether voters have the opportunity to see candidates they want to see and hear about issues they want to hear about. The *Boston Globe* described the CPD as "a Washington-based bipartisan body established in 1988 by the national Democratic and Republican parties."[25] Barbara Vucanovich, a former CPD director, praised Executive Director Janet Brown for being "extremely careful to be bipartisan."[26] David Norcross, former vice-chairman of the CPD, admitted, "It's really not nonpartisan. It's bipartisan."[27]

Not surprisingly, the CPD has consented to virtually every joint debate request of the two major-party candidates. "The commission does what you tell them to do," said Scott Reed, chairman of Bob Dole's 1996 presidential campaign.[28] CPD directors have no incentive to challenge the shared demands of Republican and Democratic debate negotiators. "The commission is a setup for the two-party system," said Professor Larry Sabato of the University of Virginia. "Its decision is being presented as if it were made by a group of Olympian gods. But this is a group of hard-bitten pols who play at the highest levels and have very clear motives."[29] Cochair Paul Kirk admitted, "It's not that easy, when one comes from a position of leadership of a particular political party, to then put on a hat and to be able to conduct the business of the commission in a nonpartisan way."[30]

Corporate Connection

In addition to their partisan ties, most board members of the CPD have close ties to multinational corporations. Five are partners of corporate law firms, and collectively, the directors serve on the boards of more than thirty companies, ranging from gambling to pharmaceutical to agricultural to insurance industries. John Danforth, for example, is a partner at Bryan Cave, one of the fifty largest law firms in the world, and he serves on the boards of the Dow Chemical Company, General American Life Insurance Company, GenAmerica Financial Corporation, Cerner Corporation, and Metropolitan Life Insurance Company. Danforth's grandfather founded the Ralston Purina animal food empire, and Danforth owns millions in company stock.

The CPD directors' ties to corporate boardrooms create an additional, albeit subtle incentive to exclude viable third-party candidates; for the past three decades, most third-party candidates on enough state ballots to win an electoral college majority have been sharply critical of growing corporate power. This additional incentive is not based on calculated financial losses due to the possible success of third-party challengers. Rather, it stems primarily from a broader ideological opposition to third-party candidates unremittingly critical of corporate power. David Norcross, former vice-chairman of the CPD, said, "I don't know whether Ralph Nader had retarded development somewhere or what, but he doesn't understand that corporations are nothing but people who employ people. That's why you don't need him in the debates."[31]

Nowhere is that conflict of interest more apparent and more relevant than with the cochairmen of the CPD. Fahrenkopf and Kirk, who totally control the CPD, don't just profit from Corporate America as partners of corporate law firms and directors of corporations. They are also registered lobbyists for multinational corporations, and their income as well as their clients' income is directly affected by who gets elected. Doug Ireland, columnist for *The Nation*, described Kirk as "a tough and cynical lawyer-lobbyist whose influence-peddling fortunes are umbilically tied to those of the Clinton White House."[32] Since 1996, Kirk has collected $120,000 for lobbying on behalf of Hoechst Marion Roussel, a German pharmaceutical company.

Kirk's lobbying practice, however, pales in comparison to that of his CPD cochair. As president of the American Gaming Association (AGA), Frank Fahrenkopf is the lead advocate for the nation's $54 billion gambling industry. He earns $800,000 a year lobbying on behalf of eighteen corporations directly involved in the hotel/casino industry—ITT, Hilton—as well as most of the major investment banking firms—Goldman Sachs, Merrill Lynch.[33]

As president of the AGA, Fahrenkopf is the fiercest proponent of gambling. His advocacy consists of directing enormous financial contributions to major-party candidates and saturating the media and academic world with "expert" testimony extolling gambling's "many benefits." Reverend Tom Grey, head of the National Coalition Against Legalized Gambling, said, "Frank Fahrenkopf has got the political leadership of both parties at the Las Vegas feeding trough."[34] Under Fahrenkopf's watch, the casino industry's contributions to national elections have increased from $3 million in 1994 to over $11 million in 2000.[35] "We're not going to apologize for trying to influence political elections," said Fahrenkopf.[36] He even commissioned the Las Vegas branch of Arthur Andersen to conduct an economic study of the impact of gambling while Arthur Andersen was a dues-paying member of the AGA.

What is really troubling about Kirk's and Fahrenkopf's roles as corporate lobbyists has little to do with ideological incentives to exclude third-party and independent candidates disparaging of corporate power. That Public Citizen, a civic organization founded by Ralph Nader, released reports in 2000 severely criticizing the pharmaceutical and gambling lobbies certainly didn't help Nader's chances of getting in the 2000 presidential debates. Nevertheless, Kirk and Fahrenkopf would have just as easily excluded a proponent of the pharmaceutical and gambling industries if that candidate posed a threat to the major parties. "They're not really interested in stifling us because of the issues we're raising, but simply because we're a threat to the two parties at all," said Ron Crickenberger, former political director of the Libertarian Party.[37]

The real concern is what Kirk's and Fahrenkopf's lobbying practices reveal about their civic priorities and conceptions of democracy. Their lobbying demonstrates a willingness to protect corporate prof-

CHART 1   National Sponsors of the CPD

1992	1996	2000
AT&T	Anheuser-Busch	Anheuser-Busch
Atlantic Richfield	Sheldon S. Cohen—Morgan,	The Century Foundation
Sheldon S. Cohen—Morgan,	Lewis & Bockius, LLP	The Marjorie Kovler Fund
Lewis & Bockius, LLP	Dun & Bradstreet	3Com
Dun & Bradstreet	Joyce Foundation	US Airways
Ford Motor Company	Lucent Technologies	
Hallmark	The Marjorie Kovler Fund	
IBM	Philip Morris Companies Inc.	
The Marjorie Kovler Fund	Sara Lee Corporation	
J. P. Morgan & Co.	Sprint	
Philip Morris Companies Inc.	Twentieth Century Fund	
Prudential		

its at the expense of the voters' wishes and the democratic process. It shouldn't come as a surprise, therefore, that the cochairs of the CPD protect major-party interests at the expense of the voters' wishes and the democratic process.

Corporate Carnivals

The CPD's intimate relationship with corporate boardrooms has also directly impacted the financing and character of the presidential debates. The debates are now primarily funded through corporate contributions.

Since 1980, corporations have helped pay for presidential debates, and under the appropriate circumstances, this is perfectly legal. Corporations and unions are prohibited from contributing to candidates running for federal office. In 1979, however, the Federal Election Commission ruled that "nonpartisan" debate sponsors could accept corporate contributions as long as they "use preestablished objective criteria to determine which candidates may participate." (Debate sponsors that raise corporate cash but fail to use "preestablished objective" criteria are illegally contributing to participating candidates.)

The League of Women Voters solicited corporate donations for the 1980 and 1984 presidential debates, and corporate donors were rewarded with favorable publicity and a few tickets to the debates. Corporations contribute to the CPD for free tickets and the public relations benefit as well. However, the League and the CPD have had very different relationships with corporate contributors. When the League requested corporate donations, they received next to nothing. By contrast, corporations flood the CPD with hundreds of thousands of dollars.

This discrepancy is partly a consequence of increased advertising benefits. Under the auspices of the CPD, debate sites have become corporate carnivals, where sponsoring corporations market their products and propaganda to influential journalists and politicians. In 1992, after providing some $250,000 in contributions to the CPD, cigarette manufacturer Philip Morris won the right to hang a large banner that was visible during postdebate interviews.[38] For the third 2000 presidential debate, Anheuser-Busch, which contributed $550,000 to the CPD, set up several information booths to distribute glossy pamphlets touting the benefits of consuming beer, denouncing "unfair" beer taxes and calling on the government to "avoid interfering" with beer drinking.[39] *Washington Post* reporter Dana Milbank described his experience at a presidential debate in 2000:

> The whole campus is closed—ostensibly to thwart terrorists, more likely to thwart Nader and Buchanan. Nader gets kicked out of the debate audience, even though he got himself a ticket from a student. He's threatening lawsuits. But I'm not worried about such things. I am inside the debate area, and I am delighted to find an Anheuser-Busch refreshment tent, where there is beer flowing, snacks, Budweiser girls in red sweaters, the baseball playoffs on television, ping-pong and fusbol.[40]

Corporations that donate to the CPD also gain greater access to power. Frank Donatelli, debate negotiator for the 1996 Bob Dole campaign, explained, "The Commission on Presidential Debates has been around for a while, and they have a very, very good program of making these sponsorships worthwhile to the sponsoring organization. They have a reception, they get to meet the candidates,

MORIN Salito
The Miami Herald

GET LOST, NADER! WE DON'T WANT YOU IN OUR DEBATES!!

RALPH NADER 2000

YEAH, SCRAM! YOU'RE NOT A REAL CANDIDATE, ANYWAY!!

AL

W.

CORPORATE INTERESTS

CARTOON A

and they get a lot of publicity. The debate commission does take care to listen to their sponsors."[41] CPD director Antonia Hernandez said, "Do donors think of it as a way of access and thereby getting some benefit? Well, I'm sure they do."[42]

But most important, by donating to the CPD, corporations make tax-deductible contributions that benefit both major parties simultaneously. Donations to the *nonpartisan* League were primarily considered civic charity. Corporations, however, perceive donations to the *bipartisan* CPD to be bipartisan political contributions. Nancy Neuman, former president of the League, explained:

> One of the big differences between us and the commission was that the commission could easily raise hundreds of thousands of dollars in contributions. They did it very quickly in 1988. Even though I would go to some corporations, I would be lucky to get five thousand dollars. Why? Because under the commission's sponsorship, this is another soft-money deal. . . . It is a way to show your support for the parties because, of course, it is a bipartisan commission and a bipartisan contribution. There was

nothing in it for corporations when they made a contribution to the League. Not a quid pro quo. That's not the
case with the commission.[43]

Many corporations relish the opportunity to shower Republican and
Democratic candidates with financial support, and there are several
distinct advantages, from the corporate viewpoint, to giving money to
the CPD. Unlike Political Action Committee and "soft money" contributions, donations to the CPD are tax-deductible (which means taxpayers are subsidizing the exclusion of popular candidates, challenging
formats, and important issues from the presidential debates). Unlike
contributions to political parties and conventions, which must be dis-
closed to the public, donations to the CPD can be kept private. Unlike
contributions to a candidate or her party, a single donation to the CPD
hits two birds with one stone. Stephen K. Lambright, vice president
of Anheuser-Busch, said spending money to sponsor the debates "is
a good way to do it because we don't have to choose sides."[44]

Political contributions, however, are not simply about influencing
potential lawmakers. They're also about keeping certain elected officials in power, and by supporting an exclusionary debate commission,
the corporate community helps sustain a business-friendly two-party
system and limit robust debate over corporate accountability issues.
(See cartoon A.) Corporate sponsors know that promoting the CPD
promotes the major parties and that the major parties are often more
likely to protect their profit margins. Nathan Johnson, reporter for
the *Press and Dakotan*, wrote:

> The corporations who sponsor the debates—3Com Inc.,
> Yahoo, Inc., Sun Microsystems Inc., AT&T Company
> and Anheuser-Busch Companies, Inc.—funnel millions
> of dollars into the two major parties every year. After
> making such major investments, they aren't very eager to
> allow a third party candidate the opportunity to ascend
> to the presidency and thereby render their investment
> less valuable.[45]

Talk show host Phil Donahue said, "Can you imagine how enthusi-
astic AT&T is to have Ralph Nader on that stage?"[46]

Corporate contributions to the CPD are one-of-a-kind; no other corporate donations simultaneously strengthen both major-party candidates, directly prevent ideas from entering the collective voter consciousness, improve the public image of the donor corporations, and result in tax subsidies for donor corporations. When Fahrenkopf was asked if there was anything wrong with beer and tobacco companies sponsoring the presidential debates, he said, "Boy, you are talking to really the wrong guy. I'm a guy who represents the gambling industry."[47]

Memoranda of Understanding

The CPD is dominated by loyal Republicans and Democrats who are deeply entrenched in their parties and the corporate structure that supports them. Yet the CPD denies ever yielding to major-party candidate demands and vigorously proclaims independence from candidate control.

According to the CPD, it establishes objective criteria to determine candidate participation and conducts comprehensive studies to select the most educational format. Fahrenkopf explained how it works:

> I'm just flat-ass telling you: We will not do a debate—we will not use the CPD to do a debate if the candidates come to us and they sit down and they negotiate and they say all right, we've agreed we're going to do three debates. We've agreed that so-and-so is going to be the moderator, we're going to do this thing. We'll say hey, we announced, we'll tell them, we announced a year ago what the criteria was going to be; we announced a year ago what our standards were going to be, what the format was going to be and how we're going to do it. Your proposal does not meet our criteria. We will walk.[48]

But they don't walk. On the contrary, the CPD readily endorses all the joint decisions of the Republican and Democratic candidates. Every four years, the CPD publicly proposes debate formats and a debate schedule and publishes candidate selection criteria. Questions concerning third-party participation and debate formats, however, are ultimately resolved behind closed doors, where Republican and Democratic negotiators draft secret debate contracts called Memoranda of Understanding. The Memoranda of Understanding dictate precisely how the debates will be run—from decreeing who can participate, to selecting compliant moderators, to stipulating the height of the podiums. The CPD, posing as an independent sponsor, implements the directives of the Memoranda of Understanding, shielding the major-party candidates from public criticism and lawsuits. Scott Reed, Bob Dole's campaign manager, explained how it really works:

> In 1996, we told the commission what to do. We agreed with the Clinton people when we were going to meet to talk about the debates. The commission gave us their conference room, but big deal. We could have met in anybody's conference room. They were really a neutral party. Once we agreed with the Clinton team what we wanted to do on the details, we handed it to the commission and they implemented it. We told them the cities. It wasn't the cities they wanted. We told them the dates. It wasn't the dates they wanted. We told them the format. It wasn't the format they wanted. But their job was to implement it and execute it and perform it, and they did a good job.[49]

Frank Donatelli, debate negotiator for Bob Dole, summarized the process: "The commission throws the party, the commission gets the food, hires the band, but as to who shows up, what the time is and what the dress is, those are the candidates' decisions."[50] *Washington Post* reporter David Von Drehle concluded that the CPD "is designed to let the major parties control the process."[51]

Each major-party campaign employs seasoned political operatives to handle the debate negotiations. The list of negotiators—from Commerce Secretary Mickey Kantor to DNC Chairman Ronald Brown to television producer Harry Thomason to Congressman Vin Weber to Labor Secretary Alexis Herman to Defense Secretary Donald Rumsfeld—reveals the gravity campaigns attach to debate negotiations, and understandably so. Professor Alan Schroeder wrote, "It is generally believed that Kennedy's team won the 1960 negotiations; Republicans and Democrats more or less tied in 1976; Reagan's handlers triumphed in 1980 and again in 1984; Bush's took the 1988 talks, and the Clinton staff prevailed in 1992 and 1996. In every instance the successful side in predebate negotiations has gone on to carry the vote."[52]

These Republican and Democratic negotiators have very significant ties to the CPD. Vernon Jordan was a CPD director before becoming Clinton's debate negotiator in 1996. Fahrenkopf appointed Fred Malek deputy chairman of the Republican Party before Malek became President Bush's negotiator in 1992. Scott Reed, Bob Dole's campaign manager, worked directly for Frank Fahrenkopf, his friend and mentor. David Norcross was vice-chairman of the CPD—Fahrenkopf called him "my consiglieri"—before becoming Dole's debate negotiator in 1996. Fahrenkopf said of Karl Rove, George W. Bush's campaign manager, "I've known Karl since he was this tall. We go back a long way, and we are very, very good friends."[53] Richard Moe even temporarily entered negotiations on behalf of Dukakis in 1988 while serving as vice-chairman of the CPD. Bob Teeter, President Bush's campaign manager in 1992, described the CPD: "You have someone there you know. They are all friends of mine."[54] Naturally, the incestuous relationship between campaign negotiators and CPD directors reinforces compliance with the demands of the major-party candidates. David Norcross acknowledged the apparent conflict of interest: "Vernon [Jordan] and I served together on the commission, and I must confess that I didn't have any particular problem sitting across the table from him negotiating for Dole, but yeah, it kind of puts the fox in the chicken coop."[55]

Under CPD sponsorship, secretly negotiated Memoranda of Understanding between the Republicans and Democrats have dramatically increased in length and depth. There were no Memoranda of Understanding in 1976 and 1980. In 1984, the League and the two major-party campaigns collectively negotiated a three-page Memorandum of Understanding. In 1988, the year CPD sponsorship began, the Bush and Dukakis teams surreptitiously drafted a seven-page Memorandum of Understanding—the first time a debate sponsor had been excluded from the negotiations. In 1992, 1996, and 2000, the Memoranda of Understanding, which were all written by Republican and

Democratic campaign officials without any input from the CPD, ran at least eleven pages long.

Since 1992, Memoranda of Understanding have been remarkably similar, all addressing in like fashion: candidate participation, format, staging details, podiums, audience placement, selection of moderators and panelists, dressing rooms, press seating, restrictions on camera shots, distribution of tickets, time limits on responses, opening and closing statements, role of the moderator, press passes, and even coin tosses. In fact, entire paragraphs, word for word, are included in the agreements year after year, which is why the American people are subject to the same charade year after year. Each Memorandum of Understanding begins with a statement such as:

> This memorandum of understanding constitutes an agreement between the Bush/Quayle '92 and Clinton/Gore '92 Committees regarding the rules that will govern any Presidential and Vice Presidential debates in 1992 ("debates"). This agreement shall be binding upon the Bush/Quayle and Clinton/Gore campaigns, as well as the campaign of any other candidate who participates in such debates and, if it agrees to sponsor the debates, on The Commission on Presidential Debates ("Commission").

Each Memorandum of Understanding includes the following absolute condition: "The debate will be sponsored by the Commission, provided that the Commission agrees to all provisions of this Agreement."

To conceal major-party manipulation, each Memorandum of Understanding stipulates, "All discussions, communications, lists, or other writings between the parties regarding the inclusion or exclusion of potential moderators and panelists shall remain confidential between the signatories of this agreement and their representatives." Professor Sidney Kraus described the secrecy surrounding the drafting of Memoranda of Understanding: "One who attempts to gain information about the negotiations as they proceed gets the impression that what 'gags' the negotiators is nothing less than the threat of punishment under a 'Debate Secrets Act.'"[56]

(The author has obtained a copy of the previously unpublished 1996 Memorandum of Understanding, which was jointly drafted by Senator Bob Dole and President Bill Clinton's rival presidential campaigns. The document, which can be viewed in Appendix A, has never been made public before. As will be shown in later chapters, the 1996 Memorandum of Understanding is particularly significant because it demonstrates how the Republican and Democratic candidates excluded a popular and taxpayer-financed third-party candidate from the debates, arranged a debate schedule that deliberately minimized audience size, and banned follow-up questions from the debate formats.)

The CPD approach—accepting unilaterally imposed and secret instructions from the major-party campaigns—drastically differs from the practices of previous sponsors. Marty Plissner, former political director of CBS News, testified before Congress in 1993:

> The networks in 1960 engaged in extensive negotiations with the candidates before the Nixon-Kennedy debates were put on and the networks were major participants. This was not put together between Nixon and Kennedy in the back room. The League of Women Voters in the days when it was sponsoring debates hand-wrestled very aggressively with the candidates and had real input. The sine qua non of the candidates getting together and producing by dictate the 36-page document deciding every element of the campaign is an innovation in the past two cycles.[57]

The public consequences of such unprecedented and covert major party manipulation are clear: debate formats are stilted and unrevealing; candidates who the American people want to see are excluded; pressing national issues are ignored; and, ultimately, voter education is diminished. In fact, most voters don't even bother watching the presidential debates anymore; 25 million fewer Americans watched the 2000 presidential debates than watched the 1992 debates, and only 30 percent of households watched the 2000 debates, compared to 60 percent in 1980. The Republican and Democratic candidates do not pay a political price for this undermining of voter education because the CPD shields them from public accountability.

Under the Radar

Public outrage over the composition, financing, and operation of the CPD is virtually nonexistent because most Americans know very little about the organization. Many assume that the Commission on Presidential Debates is a federal agency; the word "commission" allows the CPD to masquerade as a neutral government body. "The CPD is basically under the radar," said Janet Brown. "A lot of people, including the media, think that it is part of the federal government."[58]

Without visible public outrage, Republican-Democrat control over the CPD will not end. Although a plurality of voters now consider themselves independent, there are no internal plans to transform the ideological nature of the CPD's board, and there never have been. John Culver, a former U.S. senator and CPD director, said:

> When I was on the commission, I thought we ought to have greater turnover. These guys have run the commission from the beginning. There really is no official sanction. It is presumptive. But of course, that's what the nature of the commission is. Where did these people come from to be final arbiters of free speech?[59]

The CPD was created to eternally serve the Republicans and Democrats, regardless of and in opposition to the changing composition of the electorate.

THE AMERICAN PEOPLE want the presidential debates to consist of popular candidates discussing important issues in an unscripted manner. A nonpartisan sponsor willing to resist the leading two candidates' antidemocratic demands is needed to host such informative debates. But the CPD is bipartisan—not nonpartisan—and it is designed to secretly maximize joint Republican-Democratic control over the presidential debates. The result of CPD sponsorship is major party candidates discussing their favorite issues in an entirely scripted manner. This not only makes for three hours of disappointing television, it causes widespread damage to our democratic process.

2

Hostile Takeover

I N 1920, JUST months before Congress ratified the Nineteenth
Amendment and awarded women the right to vote, suffragist
Carrie Chapman Catt founded the League of Women Voters.
The League dedicated itself to inspiring the 20 million adult women
who had long been told that voting was "unladylike" to participate in
the political process. One of the League's major projects was to host
candidate debates, which had been missing from national political
discourse since 1860. By 1922, the League had sponsored senatorial
debates in Ohio and Indiana.

When it began sponsoring presidential debates in 1976, the League
was motivated by that same commitment to civic education and voter
turnout. In 1987, Grant P. Thompson, then executive director of the
League, explained, "It sounds old-fashioned, but we sponsor debates
because we believe in them. In many ways, the League of Women Voters stands for good, old-fashioned values, the power of the informed
voter. That looks pretty square in a society run by pre-packaged, 30-
second commercials, but it's something in our experience people
have valued."[1] Invariably, public opinion polls give the League one
of the highest credibility ratings of any organization.[2]

The League demonstrated its commitment to the public interest
at the negotiating table. When meeting with campaign officials, the
League always brought a team of experts to negotiate everything
from format to the distribution of tickets. Lee Hanna, producer of the
1980 League-sponsored presidential debates, said, "Most important

is to prevent the candidates in advance from being allowed to make decisions about the agenda of the debates—how many there are to be, under what circumstances, what the subject matter should be, what the format is. Once they are involved, what we end up with is something that evolves out of compromise."[3] Under League sponsorship, there were no secretly drafted Memoranda of Understanding.

Unlike the CPD, the League pushed for revealing debate formats, and unlike the CPD, the League made sure to include popular third-party and independent candidates. David Norcross, former vice-chairman of the CPD, said, "They would pick the dates and say, 'Take it or leave it.' They would pick the panel and say, 'Take it or leave it.' They would pick the format and say, 'Take it or leave it.' It was their way or the highway."[4] Election after election, the League worked on behalf of the American people and, in the process, infuriated the major parties.

1980

The League invited independent candidate John B. Anderson to participate in the first 1980 presidential debate. President Jimmy Carter, however, refused to debate Anderson, who was expected to attract moderates that would otherwise vote for Carter. The president publicly degraded Anderson to keep him out of the debates. "I believe that John Anderson, as far as a presidential candidate, is primarily a creation of the press," said Carter. "He doesn't have a mandate from the American people."[5] But the League insisted that Anderson be included if he managed to draw 15 percent in the polls. League president Ruth Hinerfeld said that if Carter disagreed with the arrangements, "we would go ahead with two people."[6]

On September 21, 1980, the League hosted a presidential debate between John B. Anderson and Republican nominee Ronald Reagan that attracted over 55 million viewers. Nothing demonstrates the significance of nonpartisan sponsorship more than the League's willingness, despite enormous political opposition, to host a Reagan-Anderson debate absent President Carter. The *Christian Science Monitor* editorialized that "the public interest is served by the League of Women Voters' decision to invite independent candidate

John Anderson to participate."[7] The League had even planned to place an empty chair on stage to illustrate Carter's "cowardice," but their lawyers advised against it. (Johnny Carson, then host of *The Tonight Show*, said, "What bothers me is, suppose the chair wins."[8]) The CPD would never, in its wildest dreams, even consider sponsoring a presidential debate without a major-party candidate.

After that first debate, Anderson climbed from 15 to 19 percent in most national polls, and the *New York Times* editorialized, "Whatever [Reagan's] immediate motives, he and the sponsoring League of Women Voters deserve credit for setting a valuable precedent of including independent candidates."[9] The inclusion of Anderson, however, was the beginning of the end of League sponsorship. Newton Minow, vice-chairman of the CPD, said, "The parties lost confidence in the League, especially after 1980. . . . The League did try to dictate terms, and the parties wanted some flexibility."[10]

1984

In 1984, the major-party campaigns tried to expand their control over the debate negotiation process, and the League made them pay a price for it. The League didn't care about campaign squabbles over the color of the backdrop curtain—Reagan wanted royal blue, Mondale wanted something darker. Nor did the League care about the angle of the podium—Reagan wanted to face the audience, Mondale wanted to face Reagan. But when it came to the composition of the panelists, something that would affect the content of the debate discourse, the League vigorously resisted the demands of the campaigns.

The League had always prohibited candidates from selecting the panelists outright. Instead, the campaigns could submit a list of fifteen suggested questioners. After eliminating some names and adding others, the League would send back a shortened list of proposed panelists, and, if absolutely necessary, the candidates could veto a biased or incompetent reporter. That procedure produced no vetoes in 1976 and only one veto in 1980. In 1984, however, all twelve names on the list were rejected. By the end of the process, the League had submitted seventy-one more names, of which sixty-eight were vetoed, in roughly equal numbers by both camps. The two campaigns never agreed on a fourth questioner, and on October 7, 1984, the first presidential debate aired with only three panelists: Diane Sawyer, Fred Barnes, and James Weighart.

Despite angry threats not to participate from the major-party candidates, the League held a news conference and lambasted the campaigns for having "totally abused" the process. "It got ridiculous," said Nancy Neuman, former president of the League. "They just got rid of panelists who would ask intelligent questions."[11] When the League publicized the campaigns' manipulation of the format, leading media outlets prohibited their reporters from serving as panelists. "When I found that they were picking and choosing, blackballing some and anointing others after they'd passed some kind of litmus test, I decided we shouldn't participate," said Bill Kovach, former Washington bureau chief of the *New York Times*. CBS announced that its news personnel would "not be available for any further participation unless a more acceptable procedure is developed for the selection of future panelists."[12] Rushworth M. Kidder of the *Christian Science Monitor* wrote:

> The politicians perhaps thought that by vetoing their sometime critics they could avoid adversarial questions. Perhaps they thought that by rejecting some better-known journalists they could contrive to produce a pool of less-seasoned questioners incapable of pressing them hard on the issues. Or perhaps they simply sought to punish individual journalists or news organizations which they felt were not giving them a fair shake. Whatever the motive—fear, manipulation, or vengeance—it is sad commentary on both parties.[13]

As a result of the criticism, the panelist selection process for the second debate was entirely different. Not a single journalist was rejected; the candidates were too afraid of the public outcry. "Nobody really wanted to exercise veto power and we were able to work it out through consensus," said Karen Lebovich, spokeswoman for the League.[14] Possessing the courage to criticize the candidates, the League was able to protect the integrity of the format. Nancy Neuman concluded, "The League's experience with the campaigns in negotiating panelist selection for the 1984 debates is convincing evidence that backstage manipulations of the debate ground rules do occur and that the public's interest is best served by a sponsor willing to blow the whistle on such abuses."[15]

Republican-Democratic Party Collusion

What the League offered is pure and simple: mobilization of public opinion to pressure the candidates, efforts to objectively determine third-party participation, protection of the integrity of format, rejection of excessive candidate control, and transparency. With that formula, the nonpartisan League served the public interest well.

And it's precisely because the League served the public interest so well that the CPD was created. The Republican and Democratic parties didn't want a debate sponsor that limited their candidates' control; they wanted presidential debates entirely under their control. David Norcross described why he helped create the CPD: "The League of Women Voters was too dictatorial and took pleasure in ignoring or avoiding the politics of the whole situation. So I thought it was time for the parties to step in, provide a service, and I saw the debate commission as that service. I accepted the assignment with relish."[16] John Buckley, communications director of the Dole campaign, said, "The League of Women Voters lost sponsorship because they did not keep the interests of the two parties in mind."[17] When asked what was wrong with the way the League had sponsored debates, Janet Brown, executive director of the CPD, said, "The League had gotten quite dictatorial. Before a debate, one of the candidates asked me when I would put the pads on the podiums. The League had made the candidates use cards. We didn't care."[18] But this was not just about pads and cards. The major parties wanted a sponsoring organization willing to exclude independent candidates like John B. Anderson, willing to allow the major-party candidates to veto as many panelists as they wanted, and willing to implement secretly negotiated agreements.

The bipartisan motives and objectives of the CPD are apparent in the organization's formation. The CPD was created by the major parties as an extension of the major parties. In fact, the Democratic

CHART 2   Sponsors of the Commission on National Elections

Archer-Daniels-Midland	John M. Olin Foundation
Chicago Pneumatic Tool Company	NBC, Inc.
The Ford Motor Company Fund	MCA, Inc.
Hallmark Cards, Inc.	Martin Marietta Corporation Foundation
Xerox Foundation	Benton Foundation
R. J. Reynolds Industries Inc.	Capital Cities Communications, Inc.
Merchant Sterling Corporation	CBS, Inc.
Young & Rubican Inc.	Dayton Hudson Foundation
The Washington Post Company	The Henry Ford II Fund
Times Publishing Company	Foote, Cone, & Belding Foundation
Science Applications International Corporation	

and Republican parties initially planned to directly sponsor the presidential debates themselves. In 1984, Democratic National Committee Chairman Charles Mannat and Republican National Committee Chairman Frank Fahrenkopf met several times to discuss joint party sponsorship of the debates. "I am a believer and I think chairman Mannat is, that the two major political parties should do everything in their power to strengthen their own position," said Fahrenkopf. "We're party builders."[19]

The next year, Fahrenkopf and Kirk (who replaced Mannat) participated in the Commission on National Elections, a private study of the election process to which the CPD attributes its creation.[20] The study—funded by multinational corporations, newspaper companies, and television networks—was cochaired by Melvin Laird, a former Republican congressman and secretary of defense, and Robert S. Strauss, a former chairman of the Democratic National Committee and ambassador to the Soviet Union. Strauss had also been the chairman of President Jimmy Carter's reelection campaign in 1980, when John B. Anderson was included in the presidential debates over Carter's objections. Strauss had vociferously criticized the League's decision to include Anderson, claiming that it would "dilute" President Carter's ability to challenge Reagan.

Although the Commission on National Elections was purportedly formed to correct "major flaws" in presidential election campaigns, the panel concluded, according to Strauss, "that the system had served the nation well."[21] In fact, the Commission on National Elections only made one significant recommendation—that the major parties usurp control over the presidential debates:

> The commission therefore urges the two parties to assume responsibility for sponsoring and otherwise ensuring that presidential candidate joint appearances are made a permanent and integral part of the presidential election process. If they do so, the commission believes that the parties will strengthen both the process and themselves. . . .
>
> Major questions remain regarding the equal time requirements for television coverage of [major] party versus independent or third-party candidates. Yet in the commission's judgment, the importance of television forums argues for erring on the side of favoring the party nominating processes rather than the rights of other candidates.

On November 26, 1985, six months after the publication of the Commission on National Elections study, Frank Fahrenkopf and Paul Kirk, still chairmen of their respective parties, authored a one-page Memorandum of Agreement on Presidential Candidate Joint Appearances:

> It is our bipartisan view that a primary responsibility of each major political party is to educate and inform the American electorate of its fundamental philosophy and policies as well as its candidates' positions on critical issues. One of the most effective means of fulfilling that responsibility is through nationally televised joint appearances conducted between the presidential and vice-presidential nominees of the two major political parties during general election campaigns. Therefore, to better fulfill our parties' responsibilities for educating and informing the American public and to strengthen the role of political parties in the electoral process, it is our conclusion that future joint appearances should be

principally and jointly sponsored and conducted by the
Republican and Democratic National Committees.[22]

Nothing so succinctly describes what would become the CPD approach
to presidential debates as this document of intent written by the heads
of the major parties and soon-to-be cochairmen of the CPD. The
presidential debates are not debates but "joint appearances," and
the candidates are not qualified candidates but the "nominees of the
two major political parties." There it is plain and simple, before the
party chairs understood the illegality of corporate-financed party
sponsorship or anticipated public outrage.

In 1986, the Democratic National Committee and the Republican
National Committee actually ratified an agreement between Fahrenkopf and Kirk "for the parties to take over presidential debates."[23]
Fifteen months later, Fahrenkopf and Kirk held a news conference
announcing the incorporation of the CPD: "We have no doubt that
with the help of the Commission we can forge a permanent framework on which all future presidential debates between the nominees of the two political parties will be based."[24] That same day, the
Democratic and Republican Parties issued a press release calling the
CPD "a bipartisan, non-profit, tax-exempt organization formed to
implement joint sponsorship of general election presidential and vice-
presidential debates, starting in 1988, by the national Republican and
Democratic committees between their respective nominees."[25] (See
Appendix B) For the next eighteen months, Fahrenkopf and Kirk
served as cochairmen of their parties and cochairmen of the CPD
simultaneously, and they made no effort to conceal their dislike of
third-party candidates. The *New York Times* reported:

> In response to questions, Mr. Fahrenkopf indicated that
> the new Commission on Presidential Debates, a nonprofit
> group made up of representatives from each party, was
> not likely to look with favor on including third-party
> candidates in the debates. He said the issue was a matter
> for the commission to consider when it worked out the
> format, timing and other details of the debates with the
> candidates. Mr. Kirk was less equivocal, saying he per-

sonally believed the panel should exclude third-party candidates from the debates."[26]

These published accounts were the last sincere statements from Kirk and Fahrenkopf concerning the real intentions and controlling authority of the CPD. They soon learned about FEC debate regulations and the potential public outcry against having the major parties overtly exclude third-party candidates, and they began disguising the objectives of the CPD. "It very quickly changed from bipartisan to nonpartisan, and it changed that way for legal reasons," said Fahrenkopf.[27] Currently, the CPD describes itself as "a nonpartisan, nonprofit, tax-exempt corporation not affiliated with any political party"[28]—a stark contrast from the definitions of sixteen years ago.

Some reporters immediately criticized the creation of the CPD. NBC News anchor Tom Brokaw warned, "Debates could become self-serving organs of the political parties."[29] Mary McGrory, columnist for the *Washington Post*, wrote:

> Would somebody care to tell me what was wrong with the way the League of Women Voters ran the presidential debates? Something called the Commission on National Elections, which was run by Robert S. Strauss and Melvin R. Laird, two old pros I never thought of particularly as reformers, has come forward and fixed something that wasn't broke.[30]

The League of Women Voters also denounced the formation of the CPD. In 1987, League president Nancy Neuman wrote:

> The most recent entrant in the debate sponsorship competition—the Democratic and Republican national committees—may well provide the candidates with the safest, most risk-free debates option yet. If the political parties have their way, the presidential debates could be little more than political pillow fights, with no referee—no honest broker—representing the public. . . . In response to reporters' questions about how they would deal with non-

major-party candidates, party chairs Paul Kirk and Frank
Fahrenkopf answered that party-sponsored debates would
involve only the nominees of the two major parties. The
League knows from experience just how inadequate and
short-sighted this response is. There is a clear public interest in seeing a serious independent candidate debate.[31]

Battle for Control

The CPD made its move to take over in 1988. But when Fahrenkopf
and Kirk announced that the two parties would jointly sponsor the
1988 presidential debates "to strengthen the role of political parties
in the electoral process," the League reacted. Hours later, Nancy
Neuman held a news conference to confirm that the League would
sponsor the 1988 debates, thereby escalating the war with the Democratic and Republican parties.

After prolonged negotiations, James Baker of the Bush campaign, Paul Brountas of the Dukakis campaign, the League, and the
CPD reached a simple compromise: The CPD would sponsor the
first Bush-Dukakis debate, and the League would sponsor the second Bush-Dukakis debate. (Vice President Bush was not attracting
enough female voters, and the last thing James Baker wanted to do
was further alienate the gender by completely rejecting the League
of Women Voters.[32])

But just as the League was gearing up for debate negotiations on
format and production, the Bush and Dukakis campaigns handed
the two sponsors a secretly negotiated Memorandum of Understanding—a script dictating every detail of the debates, ranging
from the selection of panelists to the color of timer lights on the
podiums. The agreement banned follow-up questions, and even
required the League to disinvite civic group leaders and replace
them with a handpicked partisan audience. The existence of the
CPD allowed the campaigns to privately negotiate and deliver a
Memorandum of Understanding; if the League withdrew, the CPD
could simply take over.

The CPD immediately accepted the Memorandum of Understanding. Executive Director Janet Brown said, "The commission is

delighted to respond positively to the invitation and regards it as a vote of confidence in the commission's approach to the debate."[33]

The League immediately rejected the Memorandum of Understanding. "The issue," said Nancy Neuman, "is who's in control of the debate." After sponsoring presidential debates for three consecutive elections, the League refused to let Republican and Democratic operatives dictate the terms of debate. "I asked that the campaigns open the door to the League," said Neuman. "I was certain that the voters' interest would be better served if there were a third party in the room keeping campaign manipulations in check."[34] But the campaigns rebuffed her requests to negotiate.

"The League has two choices," concluded Neuman. "We could sign their closed-door agreement and hope the event would rise above the manipulations, or we could refuse to lend our trusted name to this charade." On October 2, the League's fourteen trustees voted unanimously to pull out of the presidential debates, and on October 3, they issued a blistering press release:

> The League of Women Voters is withdrawing sponsorship of the presidential debates . . . because the demands of the two campaign organizations would perpetrate a fraud on the American voter. It has become clear to us that the candidates' organizations aim to add debates to their list of campaign-trail charades devoid of substance, spontaneity and answers to tough questions. The League has no intention of becoming an accessory to the hoodwinking of the American public.[35]

More important, Nancy Neuman made public the secret Memorandum of Understanding—the detailed blueprint drafted by the two campaigns. This last act of defiance infuriated the major-party candidates. "This will put them out of the debate business forever," said Paul Kirk. Even while losing sponsorship, the League fought for the voters by exposing candidate collusion and manipulation. "Score one for the truth," editorialized the *Chicago Tribune*.[36]

Professor Sidney Kraus concluded, "The League was the victim of a strategy designed to eliminate it from debate sponsorship

entirely."[37] The CPD conducted the 1988 debates on the same terms
that the League had deemed fraudulent, and ever since, most popular
third-party candidates have been excluded, debate formats have been
choreographed, and significant issues have been ignored.

Tactical Advantages

If the major parties simply wanted the debates under their control,
they could have sponsored the debates themselves. But there are several clear benefits to awarding sponsorship to a seemingly independent nonprofit organization. FEC regulations, for example, prohibit
corporations from financing presidential debates unless hosted by a
"nonpartisan" organization using "preestablished objective criteria."
Because the parties are partisan organizations, they cannot use corporate contributions to pay for the debates. Instead, the sponsoring
parties would have to pay for the debates themselves. Scott Reed, Bob
Dole's campaign manager, explained, "Events like this are very expensive. For the debate commission to be able to raise the money to pay
for it is just a huge relief of a burden on the campaign because we're
operating under spending limits in the general elections. We don't
want to have to waste a couple million bucks on a debate, which is
what it costs to set a room up properly."[38] The Republican and Democratic parties use the CPD to circumvent FEC regulations and funnel
corporate contributions into bipartisan-controlled debates.

More important, the CPD allows the major parties to divert
media criticism, public outrage, FEC complaints, and lawsuits onto
an external and unaccountable organization. If the voting public
believed that the Republican and Democratic parties were excluding engaging formats, popular third-party candidates, and difficult
questions from the presidential debates, Republican and Democratic
candidates would likely pay a price in the polls (and in the court-
room). Consequently, although major-party candidates and their
negotiators dictate the terms of the televised forums, they publicly
claim to have merely participated in debates constructed by the CPD.
Bobby Burchfield, debate negotiator for President Bush in 1992, said,
"The candidates would much rather let the commission be the bad
guy on keeping Ralph Nader out than take the heat themselves."[39]

The CPD shields the Republican and Democratic candidates from public accountability. John Buckley, communications director for the Dole campaign, called the CPD "a very convenient mechanism for insulating the parties from third-party challengers."[40] George Stephanopolous said, "The debate commission can provide cover if the two candidates don't want a third candidate in.[41] Bob Neuman, former spokesperson of the CPD, said, "You could always blame the commission for excluding a third-party candidate."[42] The CPD is a potent and effective instrument of deception for major party candidates who want to sanitize the debates without offending voters.

The CPD also spares the major parties from worrying about time-consuming details such as renting auditoriums, finding production crews, and press credentialing. Scott Reed said, "If you're a campaign manager, you're focused on getting your candidate ready and your campaign ready for the event. You don't want to have to be worried about the carpet and lighting, and all the other detailed things which are very important and have to be done in a fair manner. That's the beauty of the Fahrenkopf commission."[43]

And by creating the CPD two years before the expiration of their respective terms, Fahrenkopf and Kirk guaranteed themselves prestigious positions in the political world. Although they receive no monetary compensation, the title of chairmen awards them power, access, and the spotlight. James A. Baker, former secretary of state and perennial campaign manager, said, "In my view, the chairmen jumped into this because they wanted to have a role for themselves."[44] When asked why the CPD allows major-party candidates to dictate the terms of the debates, Marty Plissner, former political director of CBS News, said, "Because they want to keep sponsoring the debates. Paul Kirk is a Boston loghead who hasn't had any role in politics since the 1980s, and Frank Fahrenkopf is the chairman of the U.S. gaming institute. These guys want to still feel important."[45]

Unlike the League of Women Voters, which has dozens of other civic responsibilities and 130,000 members, the CPD exists only as long as it sponsors the debates. If the candidates were to choose another sponsor, Fahrenkopf and Kirk would lose some of their political status. The ideological incentive to submit to the major parties is significantly furthered by the CPD's battle for self-preservation.

The Institutionalization Myth

The CPD claims that it was primarily created to "institutionalize the debates." Professor Richard Neustadt, former chair of the CPD's Advisory Committee, said, "Putting these things in charge of representatives of national parties added somewhat to the likelihood that the candidates would be forced to participate."[46] Indeed, the CPD has helped institutionalize presidential debates. Placing the debates in the hands of major-party chairs has increased public expectation of the debates and brought greater pressure to bear on the candidates to participate. Establishing a national organization solely focused on presidential debates has channeled more resources toward the presentation of debates. Promoting the CPD as lone credible sponsor has prevented the candidates from debating on cable channels or off prime time.

But the institutionalizing effect of the CPD has been greatly exaggerated. Fahrenkopf claimed that without the CPD "it is unlikely that there would be presidential debates."[47] Presidential debates, however, were already substantially institutionalized before the CPD was created. "The League institutionalized the debates," said CPD director Dorothy Ridings. "There was no way they could back out after 1980."[48] Richard Moe, former vice-chairman of the CPD, said, "The critical thing was with Ronald Reagan as the incumbent president, who, virtually certain of reelection, agreed to debate [in 1984]. That really sealed it, that did more than anything to institutionalize the debates."[49] Marty Plissner said, "Who needs the debate commission? They could hold those debates on an aircraft carrier in the Taiwan Straits and it would be carried on every network. They could hold it in a submarine that's about to surface and they'd find a way of getting it."[50] Public expectations are now such that any candidate seen dodging the debates will suffer significantly in the polls, and that alone ensures candidate participation.

More important, the CPD's contribution to the institutionalization of the debates has come at a great cost. The League had several flaws. It lacked the financial resources to secure debate sites comfortably ahead of time. Its candidate selection process relied on unreasonable or ambiguous criteria. It used the press panelist format too often. But it was open to reform. Its primary goal was voter education, and it had no vested interests. It strived to include viable independent candidates and confrontational formats without losing the participation of both major-party candidates. The public had great confidence in the League; 61 percent of registered voters preferred the League over the CPD to sponsor the 1988 presidential debates.[51]

The CPD's takeover has produced excessive candidate control, the loss of transparency, the exclusion of popular candidates, the manipulation of formats, and silence on many important national issues. Paul Taylor, executive director of the Alliance for Better Campaigns, said, "A twofold dynamic happened when debates were transferred from the League to the CPD. Having the parties play an institutional role has institutionalized the debates. The CPD has ensured that major-party candidates participate every four years. But the price of that has been far too much candidate control, and, by extension, third-party exclusion."[52] Expecting full accommodation from the CPD, major-party campaigns now make demands considered unthinkable under League sponsorship, and such unprecedented bipartisan manipulation generates public apathy and cynicism. Kay Maxwell, president of the League, said, "The perception of corruption, which exists with the Commission on Presidential Debates in charge, dissuades participation in the political process."[53] Republican presidential candidate Alan Keyes explained:

> I believe, in fact, that good arguments can be made as to why the two-party system may be better or worse or this or that. But if the two-party system cannot defend itself on a truly fair playing field, then it does not deserve to exist. And if it then erects all kinds of corrupt and limiting mechanisms in order to try to defend itself against that true test, at the end of the day, we all know what this feeds. It feeds cynicism. It feeds distrust. It feeds a sense on the part of many people in this country that in fact our elections are a sham that have no significance, but are in fact a manipulated outcome dictated in the end by those who already have the power and the money. That sense

of cynicism will destroy our political system—no, it is
destroying our political system.[54]

Further institutionalizing presidential debates did not have to
come at such a terrible price. A diverse debate commission could
have been created, with Kirk, Fahrenkopf, the president of the League,
and third-party enthusiasts all playing leadership roles.

CANDIDATES AND SPONSORS both have power. The candidates
don't have to debate, and the sponsor can always embarrass the candidates. A healthy predebate dynamic involves the candidates and
the sponsor capitalizing on their powers—the candidates pushing
for debates that maximize their chances of victory, and the sponsor
pushing for debates that maximize voter education. The League played
this role well, taking risks even when public expectation was virtually
nonexistent. The CPD, however, has performed the opposite function,
eliminating the sponsor's role as public-interest advocate. Despite
greater public expectation, which has significantly strengthened the
sponsor's leverage vis-à-vis the candidates, the CPD regularly and
deliberately capitulates to major-party interests.

3

Candidate Exclusion

"**T**HERE IS NOTHING I dread so much as the division of the Republic into two great parties, each under its leader," said John Adams, one of the framers of the Constitution.[1] The Constitution even contemplates the possibility of multicandidate presidential races; under the Twelfth Amendment, if no candidate receives a majority in the Electoral College, the House of Representatives must choose a president from the candidates with the top *three* Electoral College vote totals.

Nevertheless, the board members of the CPD ardently believe in a two-party system and are unabashedly contemptuous of third-party and independent candidates. Jimmy Carter, honorary cochair of the CPD, said, "The proper debate that would be interesting to the American people is the debate between the two men who have a chance to be elected president and who have gone through the process of a two-party system and been nominated by our parties."[2]

David Norcross, former vice-chairman of the CPD, also opposes the inclusion of third-party and independent candidates in presidential debates. "I think extra candidates just usually end up being tools for one of the two so I don't like the idea," said Norcross.[3] He described what would have happened if Ralph Nader and Pat Buchanan had been invited to the 2000 presidential debates (they were not):

> It would have been great entertainment, terrible education. Nader would have gone on one of his Naderite flings,

Buchanan would have had his Pitch Fork troops coming
in from the right, and Gore and Bush would be left with
serious, non-funny stuff to talk about. Having done that,
having been through that, the major-party candidates
start rolling their eyes at each other waiting for the time
to be over so these guys having their moment in the sun
can stop making jackasses of themselves. . . . We don't
need third parties.[4]

Richard Moe, former vice-chairman of the CPD, concurred:

Unlike a lot of other democracies, we are traditionally a
two-party system. And third-party candidates come and
go, and they play important roles, and we ought to recognize that and honor that role, but I'm not convinced
that you should lower the threshold where you encourage
the proliferation of third, fourth, and fifth parties. I don't
think that's a useful thing for democracy.[5]

For four decades, Newton Minow, former chairman of the FCC
and now vice-chairman of the CPD, has advocated free television
airtime so that citizens can regularly hear from candidates. When it
comes to the presidential debates, however, Minow has no problem
censoring candidates. In a *New York Times* op-ed piece, he wrote:

Because debates are political events, responsibility for
them should rest with the political system—with the
Democratic and Republican Parties. . . . Although entrust-
ing such debates to the major parties is likely to exclude
independent and minor-party candidates, this approach
is consistent with the two-party system. Moreover, if the
Democratic and Republican nominees agreed, other candidates could be included.[6]

In 2000, former senator Alan Simpson replaced Paul O'Neill on
the board of the CPD, after President George W. Bush appointed
O'Neill Treasury Secretary of the United States. Simpson, one of the

latest additions to the CPD, explained his newfound responsibility during an interview in 2002:

> It is a two-party country. It seems to work better when you have the embracing of the two-party system. I'd like to preserve that. I have seen enough in my time, in my lifetime, with three very capable people—Anderson, Perot, and Nader—who have messed things up, who have ruined the cake mix. Whichever side you're on, they hurt or helped and made a significant difference. I do not believe in independent party status. People who often are independent are people who are disgruntled. Many of them are quite zealous in their causes, and I think those people sometimes are a bit turbulent in the political waters. . . . The purpose of the commission, it seems to me, is to try to preserve the two-party system that works very well, and if you like the multiparty system, then go to Sri Lanka and India and Indonesia and get picking around it instead of all this ethereal crap.[7]

Simpson went on to argue that independent and third-party candidates should "not be included in the debates" because "it's obvious that independent candidates mess things up."

Mickey Kantor, chairman of Clinton's 1992 and 1996 presidential campaigns, concluded, "The CPD is basically opposed to the inclusion of third-party candidates."[8] The CPD is relieved when the major-party candidates demand the exclusion of third-party challengers in secretly drafted Memoranda of Understanding. Lawrence Noble, former general counsel of the Federal Election Commission, summarized the process, "If the debates are sponsored by the debate commission, when neither candidate wants a third party in there because it's not in their interests, the debate commission is not going to allow it."[9]

Most voters, however, want to see well known third-party candidates, such as Ross Perot and Ralph Nader, included in the presidential debates, and they are very often disappointed. (See cartoon B.)

CARTOON B

1988

The CPD established a candidate selection process in 1988 to comply with FEC regulations and to publicly legitimize third-party exclusion. "In order for us to be able to withstand further litigation and so forth, we have criteria in place," said Paul Kirk.[10]

The 1988 candidate selection process, which was used again in 1992 and 1996, automatically invited the Republican and Democratic candidates to participate in the presidential debates. To determine which, if any, third-party and independent candidates would also be invited to the debates, the CPD created an advisory committee comprised of two professors and one civic leader: Professor Richard Neustadt of Harvard University, Diana Carlin of the University of Kansas, and Vernon E. Jordan Jr., longtime civil rights leader and Washington power lawyer.

The Advisory Committee was charged with deciding which third-party candidates had a "realistic chance of being elected." According to the CPD, if the reputable academics of the Advisory Committee determined that a third-party candidate was viable, that candidate would be invited to the debates.

The CPD ensured that the Advisory Committee served the interests

CHART 3   1988 Criteria

1. *Evidence of National Organization.* The Commission's first criterion considers evidence of national organization. This criterion encompasses objective considerations pertaining to the eligibility requirements of Article II, Section 1 of the Constitution and the operation of the electoral college. This criterion also encompasses more subjective indicators of a national campaign with a more than theoretical prospect of electoral success. The factors to be considered include: (a) satisfaction of the eligibility requirements of Article II, Section 1 of the Constitution of the United States, (b) placement on the ballot in enough states to have a mathematical chance of obtaining an electoral college majority, (c) organization in a majority of congressional districts, (d) eligibility for matching funds from the Federal Election Commission or other demonstration of the ability to fund a national campaign, and endorsements by federal and state officeholders.

2. *Sign of National Newsworthiness and Competitiveness.* The Commission's second criterion endeavors to assess the national newsworthiness and competitiveness of a candidate's campaign. The factors to be considered focus both on the news coverage afforded the candidacy over time and the opinions of electoral experts, media and non-media, regarding the newsworthiness and competitiveness of the candidacy at the time the Commission makes its invitation decisions. The factors to be considered include: (a) the professional opinions of the Washington bureau chiefs of major newspapers, news magazines, and broadcast networks, (b) the opinions of a comparable group of professional campaign managers and pollsters not then employed by the candidates under consideration, (c) the opinions of representative political scientists specializing in electoral politics at major universities and research centers, (d) column inches on newspaper front pages and exposure on network telecasts in comparison with the major party candidates, and (e) published views of prominent political commentators.

3. *Indicators of National Enthusiasm or Concern.* The Commission's third criterion considers objective evidence of national public enthusiasm or concern. The factors considered in connection with this criterion are intended to assess public support for a candidate, which bears directly on the candidate's prospects for electoral success. The factors to be considered include: (a) the findings of significant public opinion polls conducted by national polling and news organizations, and (b) reported attendance at meetings and rallies across the country (locations as well as numbers) in comparison with the two major party candidates.

of the Republican and Democratic parties by hand-picking individuals to serve on the Advisory Committee who were ideologically committed to a two-party system. Professor Richard Neustadt, who chaired the Advisory Committee, was a consultant to Presidents John F. Kennedy and Lyndon B. Johnson and served on the platform committee of three Democratic National Conventions. "I believe that the two-party system is an inevitable consequence of the way the Constitution was structured through the states," said Professor Neustadt. "Nobody wants to be listening to third-party candidates in June or July."[11]

Professor Diana Carlin, a steadfast Democrat, said, "The inclusion of one or more fringe candidates might prevent major-party candidates from appearing, or would diminish the effectiveness of the debates with too many voices."[12] She contributed five hundred dollars to Clinton's 1992 presidential campaign while serving on the Advisory Committee.

Vernon Jordan served as President Clinton's advisor, chaired Clinton's 1992 presidential transition team, turned down the nomination for attorney general, and was accused of assisting President Clinton's cover-up of the Monica Lewinsky affair. The *Washington Post* called Jordan "President Clinton's closest confidant, a man with whom the leader of the Free World spends time on the links, on vacation on Martha's Vineyard, in workaday conversation, at Christmas Eve dinners with just the two men and their wives, and most of all, at moments of crisis."[13]

The Advisory Committee would never have included another John B. Anderson over the objections of another Jimmy Carter. Professor Neustadt said, "I think that if someone wishes, which would be quite difficult, they could find a means for third-party candidates to present their cause over television. But that is not the commission's mission. We have to put the major-party candidates on the air. Otherwise, we fail to fulfill the mission of the CPD."[14] A source who worked in the CPD's office and spoke on the condition of anonymity called the Advisory Committee "a bipartisan committee created by a bipartisan commission to protect the Republican and Democratic parties."

To further comply with FEC regulations, Professor Neustadt developed criteria for the Advisory Committee to interpret. Neustadt, however, did not establish objective thresholds, such as ballot access standards or poll results, that would have produced unambiguous results. Instead, he crafted entirely subjective criteria that could theoretically justify the exclusion of any candidate. The CPD explained:

"The criteria contemplate no quantitative threshold that triggers automatic inclusion in a Commission-sponsored debate. . . . Judgments regarding a candidate's election prospects will be made by the Commission on a case-by-case basis." In other words, the 1988 criteria were anything but "preestablished objective."

The Neustadt criteria relied on vague factors susceptible to infinite interpretation, like "the professional opinions of the Washington bureau chiefs of major newspapers, news magazines, and broadcast networks." Did the Advisory Committee actually contact Washington bureau chiefs? Which ones? Were they all Republicans and Democrats? Dr. Diana Carlin testified, "I know from having been a member of the Neustadt Committee in 1988 and 1992, it would have been very easy to apply objective criteria. The subjective criteria, however, puts one in a position of being similar to a Supreme Court Justice and interpreting some things, and that is what I felt like during that process."[15]

The criteria, if actually applied, also irrationally awarded the established media unwarranted power to determine the legitimacy of a presidential candidate. "Who elected the media?" asked American University law professor Jamin Raskin.[16]

Moreover, the criteria were created to determine an entirely premature hypothesis—"a realistic chance of winning the election." Professor Raskin explained that in a rational democracy "the debate among candidates comes first, and *then* voters decide who they think should be elected."[17] Predicting potential winners in the middle of the campaign to validate the exclusion of "likely" losers from an event intended to *change* public opinion shortchanges voters. It also forces third-party candidates into a fatal catch-22: they cannot demonstrate their legitimacy without first presenting their platforms, but they cannot present their platforms without first demonstrating their legitimacy. Ira Glasser, former executive director of the ACLU, wrote:

> This is a curious criterion in a democracy. It means that people with different ideas that have not yet gained wide support will be denied the opportunity to gain that support by being denied access to the relevant audience. Applied years ago, it would have excluded all minor-party

candidates and robbed America of many policies they first
voiced and which only later gained wide acceptance.[18]

Knowing the criteria in advance would not, in any way, have clari-
fied the goals for third-party and independent candidates. The criteria were just fluff to disguise partisan agreement over the exclusion
of an external threat. But having a *bipartisan* advisory committee
interpret subjective criteria still does not guarantee compliance with
major-party demands. If some of the Advisory Committee members
were seized by the spirit of democracy or persuaded by public opinion, they could have concluded that certain third-party challengers
had realistic chances of victory. So, the CPD instituted two structural
procedures to ensure that the Advisory Committee interpreted the
subjective criteria in the desired manner.

First, Advisory Committee members were sometimes told, before
they made their recommendations, exactly what the major-party candidates wanted. They often knew that the candidates had submitted
ultimatums in the form of Memoranda of Understanding, and they
knew that disagreeing with the demands of the major-party candidates could undermine CPD sponsorship.

Second, the CPD prepared briefing books for the Advisory Committee that were designed to correspond with the eleven criteria. The
briefing books included financial and polling data, samples of news
coverage, transcripts of interviews, party platforms, indications of
grassroots support, and a listing of qualified state ballots. The Advisory Committee members didn't have to do any research or contact
any reporters; they merely matched the information in their briefing
books to the criteria, and voilà, the decision was already made.

Even if, somehow, the ideologically and structurally biased Advisory Committee interpreted the subjective criteria in a manner dis-
pleasing to the CPD, Fahrenkopf and Kirk could reject the *nonbinding*
conclusions of the Advisory Committee. "I never thought we should
dictate anything," said Professor Neustadt. "They were free to do as
they please. We didn't want any more influence. We just wanted to
give our advice. Nothing more."[19] In short, the candidate selection
process employed in 1988, 1992, and 1996 consisted of individuals
selected by the major-party chairmen using materials prepared by

a bipartisan commission to interpret subjective criteria, and if they had come up with the "wrong" conclusion, Fahrenkopf and Kirk would have just rejected it.

This layered candidate selection process was designed to disarm the potential critic.

QUESTION: Why isn't a particular third-party candidate in the debates?

ANSWER: *He does not have a "realistic chance of victory."*

QUESTION: How do you know that he doesn't have a realistic chance of victory?

ANSWER: *We used multifaceted, comprehensive criteria that you can neither test nor clearly articulate.*

QUESTION: Who measured whether that third-party candidate met the criteria?

ANSWER: *An independent committee of distinguished professors and civic leaders.*

Scott Reed, Bob Dole's campaign manager, called the Advisory Committee "very good public relations."[20]

For three election cycles, parallel processes took place to determine candidate inclusion. In one room, major-party debate negotiators drafted Memoranda of Understanding. In another room, the Advisory Committee met to make recommendations. The former was decisive, and the latter relevant only to disguise major-party manipulation, appease federal regulators, and avoid public criticism. Professor Kenneth Thompson, who joined the Advisory Committee in 1992, said, "We may have operated under illusions. But we thought just the opposite—that we could influence the parties in some way or another. That we had some leverage and that we ought to be totally independent. But it was probably a delusion."[21]

In 1988, only four candidates were on enough state ballots to win an electoral college majority: Vice President George H. Bush of the Republican Party, Governor Michael Dukakis of the Democratic Party, Dr. Lenora Fulani of the New Alliance Party, and Ron Paul (who is now a congressman) of the Libertarian Party. On October 1, the Bush and Dukakis campaigns submitted a seven-page Memorandum of Understanding to the CPD, which invited only Bush and Dukakis to the debates, and the Advisory Committee delivered a recommendation to exclude all third-party and independent challengers.

Lenora Fulani and Ron Paul were destined for debate exclusion, and thus for marginal success. Ron Paul led third-party candidates with only 432,000 votes, less than 0.5 percent of the popular vote. Former presidential candidate John B. Anderson concluded, "The two parties had stolen the democratic process from the American people, and nobody much cared."[22] The major media criticism of the CPD focused on the stilted format. The lack of public outrage was primarily due to the relative dominance of the major parties at the time and the failure of a third-party candidate to attract significant attention. That soon changed.

1992

On February 29, 1992, Ross Perot said that he would spend between $50 million and $100 million if volunteers got his name on the ballot in all fifty states. A month later, he led polls in Texas, California, and Colorado, and on May 17, a CNN/Time poll put Perot ahead nationally for the first time. On July 16, however, Perot stunned his supporters and quit the race.[23]

On September 9, with Perot out of the race, the Advisory Committee convened. The committee, still chaired by Professor Neustadt, had been expanded. Vernon Jordan had left to work on Bill Clinton's presidential campaign, and three new advocates of a two-party system— Professor Kenneth Thompson of the University of Virginia; Eddie Williams, president of the Joint Center for Political and Economic Studies; and Dorothy Ridings, president of the Council on Foundations—joined the committee.[24]

The Advisory Committee unanimously concluded that no third-party or independent candidate had a realistic chance of victory. But again, the Advisory Committee's recommendations served only to disguise, through semantic ambiguity, the decisions of the Republican and Democratic candidates. Immediately afterward, Fahrenkopf wrote a letter to Samuel Skinner, White House chief of staff, stating, "The question as to whether debates will be held, how many, where, when, format, etc., is a matter that will not be finally resolved until the nominees and/or their representatives have an opportunity to meet and discuss same following the two nominating conventions."[25]

To get the ball rolling and raise money, the CPD held a news conference and laid out a proposal for three debates. The Clinton campaign promptly accepted the CPD's proposal and announced that it would "work out the details" with President Bush's reelection campaign as long as the CPD participated in the negotiations. The Bush campaign ignored the CPD's proposal and announced that it would only negotiate privately with the Clinton campaign. Bob Teeter, chairman of the Bush campaign, wrote to the CPD:

> I will not be attending any meeting involving the Commission on Presidential Debates until the two campaigns have agreed on the terms and conditions under which they will debate, have selected the Commission as the sponsor, and the Commission has agreed to sponsor the debate or debates in accordance with those terms and conditions.[26]

Mickey Kantor, Clinton's campaign manager, used the CPD to publicly assume a pro-democracy image. "We believe any discussion ought to be held under the auspices of the commission and in public," said Kantor on CNN. "We think this ought to be done in the sunshine." There was significant deadlock, and the first two presidential debates were canceled.

The CPD, however, did not care to participate in the negotiations. "We have never demanded to be at the table," said Fahrenkopf. "If a private meeting is what's necessary, that's fine with us."[27] Kantor's rhetoric had less to do with wanting transparent negotiations and more to do with strategy. "We knew [the Bush campaign] would never allow the debate commission in the room," said Kantor. "We just wanted to upset them."[28]

President Bush's refusal to accept the CPD's debates undermined his campaign. A New York Times/CBS News poll found that 63 percent of registered voters believed that Bush was avoiding debates. Clinton showed up at a canceled debate site in East Lansing, Michigan, and told a massive crowd, "I guess I don't blame him. If I had the worst record of any president in 50 years, I wouldn't want to debate either."[29] Bush was the subject of protests at nearly every stop on his campaign trail. Costumed chickens taunted him in city after city. On *The Late Show*, David Letterman ridiculed the president by listing the "Top Ten Debate Conditions Demanded by George Bush."

Tired of his dropping poll numbers, President Bush suddenly challenged Clinton to four Sunday debates beginning October 11. "Let's get it on," Bush told a roaring crowd. Bob Teeter then faxed Mickey Kantor: "Why is Gov. Clinton continuing to hide behind the commission? Why are you ducking direct discussions?" Later that afternoon, the Clinton camp acquiesced and arranged a private meeting.

On September 30, debate negotiators for President Bush and Governor Clinton met until midnight at Kantor's law firm. The next day, Ross Perot announced that he was reentering the race. He immediately polled at 7 percent nationally.

The Bush campaign was delighted with Perot's return. Bush's advisors no longer believed that their candidate could win a plurality of votes, and they wanted Perot in the presidential debates to tip the election in their favor. When Perot had quit the race, Clinton had shot up fourteen points in the polls, whereas Bush had climbed only three points. If Perot was allowed to debate, the Bush campaign reasoned, he could diminish Clinton's support. Bobby Burchfield, debate negotiator for the Bush campaign, explained what happened next:

> We, the Bush campaign, made it a precondition for the debates that Mr. Perot and Admiral Stockdale be included in the debates. Mr. Perot stood at less than 10 percent in every national poll, and few, if any commentators gave him a chance of winning. Under the CPD's criteria for determining whether a non-major-party candidate would be included in the debates, it was far from clear that Mr. Perot would qualify. . . . Therefore, the Bush campaign insisted and the Clinton campaign agreed, that Mr. Perot and Admiral Stockdale be invited to participate in the debates.[30]

Clinton did not want Perot in the presidential debates, but he couldn't oppose Bush's demand without losing public support. "We did not want to alienate Perot voters," said Kantor.[31]

On October 3, after twenty-four hours of negotiations, Bob Teeter and Mickey Kantor held a news conference to announce that they had reached a tentative agreement. On October 4, Perot received a take-it-or-leave-it invitation from the major-party candidates to participate in the presidential debates. That same day, the major-party negotiators submitted a detailed thirty-seven-page Memorandum of Understanding to the CPD. The document, which was concealed from the public, described exactly how the debates would be carried out, covering everything from the length of opening statements to the selection of panelists to Perot's inclusion.

The CPD, however, did not want Perot invited to the debates. "The debate commission expressed concern about the requirement that Mr. Perot be included," said Bobby Burchfield. The CPD was worried about two potential consequences of Perot's inclusion. First, if the CPD simply accepted the demands of the major-party candidates without proof of another Advisory Committee review, it could lose its tax-exempt status and the right to host future debates. Ironically, other minor-party candidates were poised to file lawsuits against the CPD if it arbitrarily reversed its decision on Perot. Two other third-party candidates, Andre Marrou of the Libertarian Party and Lenora Fulani of the New Alliance Party, were on enough state ballots to win an electoral college majority. Marrou had matched Perot's achievement of qualifying on the ballot in all fifty states and had raised more money in donations than the self-financed Perot campaign. Clay Mulford, Perot's senior advisor, understood the problem:

> We were afraid the commission would have difficulty developing a calculus that would show how we were different from the Libertarians and the New Alliance Party and so forth. And if we're at 7 percent and we're not making campaign appearances, we're not buying TV time, we're not visible, we could be marginalized and they'd have a difficult time getting us in.[32]

Second, CPD directors did not want to promote the growth of any third parties. Arthur Block, an attorney for the New Alliance Party, described Perot's campaign as "exactly the type the CPD was designed to screen out."[33] If Perot was let on stage, third-party politics and the CPD would never be the same. Future third-party candidates could always point to Perot's 1992 predebate poll numbers to justify the inclusion of anybody at 7 percent in the polls. "The commission was worried about the precedent of third-party candidates always being included," said Mickey Kantor.[34] Including Perot undermined one of the CPD's two principal functions—strengthening the two-party system and submitting to the demands of the major-party candidates. Ironically, at this particular juncture, these functions were in conflict; the short-term wishes of the candidates threatened the long-term interests of the two-party system.

On October 5, 1992, at the request of the CPD, the Advisory Committee reconvened. After what Professor Neustadt called "a long, puzzled afternoon," the Advisory Committee recommended that Perot be included in the first debate, but that his inclusion in the second and third debates be subject to further review after that first debate. "We knew that if we decided not to recommend Perot's inclusion, the two campaigns were likely to seek another sponsor that would," wrote Professor Carlin.[35] The CPD adopted the Advisory Committee's recommendation and, for the moment, rejected the major-party candidates' request that Perot be included in *all three* debates at the outset. By including Perot in only one debate, Fahrenkopf and Kirk hoped to appease the major-party candidates, protect the two-party system, and demonstrate that Perot's inclusion was based on Advisory Committee review.

But it was all a bluff. Under no circumstances would the former party chairmen defy the shared demands of the Republican and Democratic candidates. The Bush and Clinton campaigns rejected the CPD's proposal, and accordingly, the CPD caved in. At a post-election symposium, Professor Neustadt explained:

> Mr. Verney [Perot's campaign manager] says that his understanding is that the two candidates invited them

to debate. That I believe is correct, that's what I was told. The candidates then presented the commission with an ultimatum—Frank [Fahrenkopf] put it nicer than that, a contract. I understand that to be the case. The commission, I know, took the position that it had to go through its procedures; that is what its lawyers told it to do and that's what it did. I and my committee were part of its procedures so we were assembled. . . . The commission did not accept our recommendation.[36]

On October 7, the CPD informed Bob Teeter and Mickey Kantor that Perot would be invited to all three presidential debates.

Fahrenkopf has repeatedly said, "The candidates have never told us who was going to be included."[37] Janet Brown wrote in a deposition to the FEC, "Neither the major parties nor any CPD sponsor had any input or influence on CPD's candidate selection process." Paul Kirk described the power of the Advisory Committee: "If they say Perot in, Perot in. If they say Perot out, Perot out. And if you don't like it, either campaign, then you'll have to find another sponsor."[38] In reality, however, the CPD rejected the Advisory Committee's recommendation, and Perot participated in all of the 1992 presidential debates only because President Bush wanted him there. "If not for the candidate's agreement that Perot be included in 1992, he wouldn't have been included," said Bobby Burchfield.[39] Pat Choate, Perot's running mate in 1996, said:

> Mr. Perot was in the debates in 1992 not because of criteria but because George Bush insisted that Ross Perot be in those debates, and indeed, the commission opposed Ross Perot being in the debates, and the campaigns of Bill Clinton and George Bush had to insist and threaten the commission to take the debates away from them before they would actually permit Ross Perot to be in the debates.[40]

When asked if the composition of the CPD prevents it from measuring the viability of third-party and independent candidates objectively, Fahrenkopf said, "1992 is the proof of the pudding."[41] Janet Brown said, "We wouldn't have included Perot if we weren't serious and nonpartisan."[42] But it's precisely because the CPD is partisan that Perot was included in the first place. Would the CPD have accepted a proposal to exclude Perot? "Sure," said Bob Teeter. "If the candidates agree on a proposal, they would accept it."[43] Mickey Kantor said, "Perot's inclusion or exclusion was up to the debate negotiators, not to the debate commission."[44]

Although Perot was invited to the debates, he was deliberately barred from the discussions concerning format, staging details, schedule, and so forth. "The terms we agreed upon were that he would be invited as a guest," said Ron Brown, chairman of the Democratic National Committee. "He wouldn't participate in the rulemaking, in the scheduling, or in the site selection, but he would be invited to participate in the debates."[45] Perot's exclusion from the negotiations put him at a distinct disadvantage. For example, his advisors could not make sure that the town hall audience included Perot supporters. Nor, after the debate, could they run an already produced commercial using a line from the debates—"I agree with Ross"—because of restrictions in the Memorandum of Understanding prohibiting the rebroadcasting of debate footage.

Still, Perot was universally deemed the winner of two (out of three) presidential debates, and he rapidly climbed from 7 percent in predebate polls to 19 percent on Election Day—the largest demonstrable gain for any candidate in the history of presidential debates.[46] Primarily due to his inclusion, 70 million Americans watched the final 1992 presidential debate, the largest debate audience since 1980, and 55.24 percent of eligible voters went to the polls, a greater percentage than had voted since Kennedy's election in 1960.

The 1992 presidential debates were hailed as a stunning success— the inclusion of a popular third-party candidate, a mixed array of formats, one of the most widely watched political events in American history—and the CPD received all the credit. The media lavished praise on the CPD even though every laudable (and deplorable) characteristic of the 1992 debates was secretly decided by the presidential candidates and their negotiators.

1996

In 1996, six candidates were on enough state ballots to win an electoral college majority: President Bill Clinton of the Democratic Party,
Senator Bob Dole of the Republican Party, Ross Perot of the Reform
Party, Harry Browne of the Libertarian Party, John Hagelin of the
Natural Law Party, and Howard Phillips of the U.S. Taxpayers Party.
Seventy-six percent of eligible voters wanted Perot included in the
1996 presidential debates, and many pundits and newspapers supported his inclusion. Senator Sam Nunn (D-GA) came out in favor
of Perot's inclusion:

> Four years ago, Ross Perot almost single-handedly forced
> the nation to focus on issues both political parties usu-
> ally ignore—a full discussion of the budget deficit and
> reform of entitlement spending, including Social Secu-
> rity. The American people want more—not less—of this
> sort of debate. If we miss this year's opportunity to give
> them what they want, I am not sure how much longer the
> American voters will support the two-party system.[47]

Former Democratic presidential candidate Jesse Jackson said, "No
small group of ten people who are pro–two party and anti–third
party have the moral authority or the right to deny him access to be
a factor in this debate." Marty Plissner, former political director of
CBS News, wrote:

> Perot's 19 percent of the popular vote in 1992 had been
> the best showing by a minor-party candidate in eighty
> years. Theodore Roosevelt aside, it was the best since the
> current two-major-party system was forged in 1856. It not
> only won Perot a place in the record books, it also entitled
> him to federal funding for the current campaign. When
> the U.S. Treasury wrote Perot a check for $30 million,
> Perot assumed that, along with his twenty million votes
> in the last election, it assured him a place in the debates.
> Federal funding was one of the "objective criteria" in the

commission's published guidelines for judging "viability."
Perot had been ruled viable without it in 1992. How could
he be rejected now?[48]

This time, the Republican and Democratic candidates wanted Perot
out of the debates.

The hypocrisy of the CPD and of the major-party candidates
reached unprecedented levels in 1996. Both Senator Dole and President Clinton feigned lack of authority in deciding who could be in
the debates. "I'm not on the commission," said Dole, when asked
whether Perot would be included.[49] The Clinton campaign even
made public statements supporting Perot's inclusion. "We have
always assumed Ross Perot would be in the debates," said Peter
Knight, Clinton's campaign chairman.[50] But behind the scenes, Dole
and Clinton decided Perot's fate. Political commentator George Will
wrote, "Exclusion actually was a deal struck by the Dole and Clinton
campaigns."[51]

The press described the events leading up to the 1996 presidential
debates with a uniform narrative: Bob Dole desperately wanted Perot
out of the debates, Clinton emphatically wanted Perot in the debates,
and after objectively determining that he did not have a "realistic
chance of victory," the CPD excluded Perot. This narrative paints
the CPD as a powerful decision-making body that independently
resolved a crucial dispute between the Clinton and Dole campaigns.
The CPD even comes off looking courageously nonpartisan for defying the demands of the incumbent president.

But this narrative is inaccurate. Yes, Dole did want Perot out of
the debates. Scott Reed, Dole's campaign manager, explained:

> We went into the debate process with a very specific strategy: We didn't want Perot in the debates. Nothing else
> really mattered. The timing, all that crap, it doesn't matter to me. What mattered was the fact that if Perot was
> on the stage, he would get a lot of votes. The presidential
> debates have become the defining event of the presidential election, and it's the first time that the country really
> gets to take an unfiltered look at the candidates. Because

after the conventions, with all the balloons, the hoopla, and the partisanship, it is really the defining event of the fall. So obviously we thought it would be important that Perot be excluded, and outside of that we didn't care a lot about the negotiations and the details and all of that. We made sure Perot wasn't going to be in the debates.[52]

Dole had calculated that Perot would take more votes away from him than from Clinton. "We felt that it was probably to our advantage to have Perot excluded, and we proceeded accordingly," said Frank Donatelli, debate negotiator for the Dole campaign. "We set that as our number one goal."[53]

Meanwhile, the Clinton campaign continued to publicly support Perot's inclusion. Mickey Kantor, then commerce secretary and lead negotiator for the president, said on CNN, "In 1992, President Bush and then governor Clinton had no problem with having Ross Perot in the debates. I don't understand why Senator Dole and his handlers have a problem with it—I'm mystified by it."[54] In truth, however, Clinton didn't want Perot in the debates any more than Dole did. Clinton was winning by twenty-six points, and he didn't need a wealthy wild card changing the dynamic of the race. George Stephanopolous explained, "Basically, the economy is doing well. Clinton is ahead. We just don't want anything to shake up the race."[55]

Then why did Clinton say, over and over again, that Perot should participate in the debates? Because it was politically advantageous. By telling the public that he favored Perot's inclusion, Clinton convinced voters sympathetic with Perot that he was the good guy. For the rest of the campaign, Perot and his supporters would blame Dole for their fatal exclusion. On *Meet the Press,* Perot said that Dole was responsible "for throwing us out of the debates. He's the one who did it, no, ifs, ands, and buts." The Reform Party candidate even accused Dole of "poisoning the attitudes of millions of independent voters."[56] A postelection panel conversation at Harvard University briefly focused on the Clinton strategy:

GEORGE STEPHANOPOLOUS: We didn't want Perot in either.

NEWS ANCHOR CHRIS MATTHEWS: You didn't?

STEPHANOPOLOUS: No.

MATTHEWS: Well, why did you make us think you did?

STEPHANOPOLOUS: Because we wanted Perot's people to vote for us. How's that for candor. [Laughter][57]

The board members of the CPD knew that Dole wanted Perot excluded from the debates, and the Republican board members proceeded accordingly. Scott Reed, Dole's campaign manager, wrote in an e-mail, "I had a high level of confidence the Commission would not include Perot—and had a source that confirmed that [on the Commission]. . . . In my eyes, the Commission was to execute what the two campaigns had agreed to. Period."[58] When asked if the composition of the CPD facilitated the achievement of his objectives, Reed said:

Yeah, I used to work for [Fahrenkopf]. He was the chairman of the Republican National Committee when I was a fieldboy and I was in charge of the New England region. Politics is about relations, being able to pick up the phone and have a discussion that is not on the front page of the newspapers the next day. Doesn't mean you're doing anything malicious or anything, but you need to be able to have an open discussion. That's why the idea that it's a bipartisan commission makes sense.[59]

The Clinton campaign made no similar effort to convince the CPD to exclude Perot. They assumed that the CPD would bar Perot regardless of any external influences, and in any case, Perot's inclusion would largely disadvantage Dole. "We let the commission make their own decision," said Mickey Kantor. "If Perot was included, we knew it could help us politically, and we would have been happy if he was excluded. The Republicans were so focused on making sure the commission excluded Perot because they were so at risk politically. So they spent an awful lot of time and energy. I just assumed the commission would exclude Perot."[60]

Fahrenkopf and Kirk didn't have to twist any arms to ensure that the Advisory Committee excluded Perot. In fact, the Advisory Committee didn't even implement the criteria.[61] The Washington bureau chiefs of the *New York Times,* the *Wall Street Journal,* the *Los Angeles Times,* the *Chicago Tribune, Time, Newsweek,* the *Atlanta Constitution,* NBC, CNN, and ABC said that they were never interviewed by the Advisory Committee.[62]

On September 17, 1996, the Advisory Committee unanimously recommended inviting only Dole and Clinton to the presidential debates, and the board of the CPD unanimously approved the Advisory Committee's recommendation.

"The commission has spoken," said a senior Dole official.[63] But the CPD's ruling did not terminate discussion about Perot. In fact, negotiations over Perot's participation had only just begun. Clinton had successfully convinced Perot supporters to focus their attacks on Dole, but what really made his strategy so clever materialized behind the scenes, after the CPD excluded Perot. On September 21, four days after the CPD announced that Perot did not have a "realistic chance of victory," major-party negotiators met to draft a Memorandum of Understanding. During those debate negotiations, Perot's potential inclusion was actually used as a bargaining chip. Despite the CPD's ruling, Clinton proposed that Perot be included in the first debate. Clinton had every intention of participating in two-man debates, but he wanted to milk Perot's exclusion for all it was worth.

Dole was terrified by Clinton's proposal. He knew that Clinton could force Perot into the debates; the candidates certainly didn't have to participate in CPD-sponsored forums, and other organizations were more than willing to host inclusive presidential debates. To avoid that nightmare scenario, Dole awarded Clinton the right to dictate the terms of the debates (schedule, format, etc.) as long as he agreed to exclude Perot entirely.

In short, President Clinton and Mickey Kantor, the masterminds behind the Democratic debate strategy, destroyed Dole's negotiating team. They were able to convince the Dole campaign that they wanted Perot included, use that threat as negotiating leverage, and determine critical elements of the debates. George Stephanopolous, senior advisor to President Clinton, said, "[The Dole campaign] didn't have leverage going into negotiations. They were behind. They needed to make sure Perot wasn't in. As long as we would agree to Perot not being in it, we could get everything else we wanted going in. We got our time frame, we got our length, we got our moderator."[64] David Norcross, debate negotiator for Dole, admitted that Clinton got "pretty much everything he wanted."[65] Mickey Kantor explained:

> We knew that we would get whatever we wanted out of the debate negotiations because the Dole campaign, frankly, would give almost anything, any advantage they had, in order to keep Perot out. . . . Once we realized just how strongly they felt about this, the situation was fairly easy to take advantage of.[66]

Unfortunately, what Clinton wanted was entirely detrimental to the public interest. To preclude substantive discussion, he eliminated follow-up questions from the debate formats and restricted the candidates' responses to a mere ninety seconds. More important, because of his twenty-six-point lead, Clinton desired the smallest possible audience for the debates. The CPD had proposed three debates. Dole requested four. No way, said Clinton, and there were only two presidential debates. The 1996 Memorandum of Understanding stipulated:

> There will be two (2) Presidential debates and one (1) Vice Presidential debate before live audiences. The parties agree that they will not (1) issue any challenges for additional debates, (2) appear at any other debate or adversarial forum with any other presidential or vice-presidential candidate, or (3) accept any network air time offers that involve a debate format or otherwise involve the simultaneous appearance of more than one candidate.

David Broder of the *Washington Post* wrote:

> As questionable as was the commission's decision to exclude Perot from the debate, even more disturbing was its silent acquiescence in President Clinton's cancellation

of the first debate, scheduled for tonight in St. Louis. . . .
It is especially galling to see a commission so macho in
barring the door to Perot so meekly bowing to an edict
from Clinton, who blithely scheduled a fund-raiser in
Philadelphia on the night set for the first debate.[67]

Even worse, Clinton's debate schedule reduced the size of the television audience for the remaining two debates. He deliberately scheduled both debates opposite the major league baseball playoffs. After the election, Chris Matthews asked representatives of the Clinton campaign, "Why didn't you have the debates when people were watching the election?" With cynical candor, George Stephanopolous replied, "Because we didn't want them to pay attention. And the debates were a metaphor for the campaign. We wanted the debates to be a nonevent."[68]

The significance of manipulating the debate schedule was so great that when Tony Fabrizio, Dole's pollster, was asked what it would have taken to achieve victory, he said, "I think if we could have had the debates scheduled under our terms."[69] Dole lost considerable ground as a result of Clinton's strategy, but more important, the voters lost. Because of Clinton's negotiating tactics, millions of Americans chose to miss the presidential debates. There was an orchestrated plan to bore the public into electoral apathy, and since fewer than half of all eligible voters turned out in 1996, the first time voter turnout in a presidential election had dipped below 50 percent since 1952, the Clinton strategy was a rousing success.

The major-party candidates submitted a Memorandum of Understanding encompassing all of Clinton's autocratic format and scheduling demands, and again, the CPD gladly implemented the agreement. "The CPD would have sponsored the debates regardless of the outcome of the negotiations," said Mickey Kantor. "We wanted them to sponsor it. We had confidence in them. It's bipartisan. Janet, Paul Kirk, and Frank Fahrenkopf are people we trusted—Republicans and Democrats."[70] The 1996 Memorandum of Understanding, which stipulated that "the participants in the two Presidential debates will be Bill Clinton and Bob Dole," was concealed from the media and the general public. (See Appendix A for a copy of the previously unpublished Memorandum of Understanding.)

However, trying to justify Perot's exclusion to voters proved difficult for the CPD. In a letter defending their rejection of Perot, the Advisory Committee listed only three factors: (1) Perot's 1996 poll numbers were lower than his 1992 poll numbers, (2) none of the academics or journalists consulted found Perot to have a realistic chance of election, and (3) Perot could not spend his personal fortune because he had accepted federal matching funds.

The Advisory Committee misled the public.[71] Although Perot garnered more excitement in 1992, partly due to his novelty, he was polling at virtually the same level before the 1996 debates as he had in 1992. In fact, because of Dole's lackluster numbers, Perot had a greater chance of beating a major-party candidate in 1996. "If you go by the criteria, you can make an argument that he should be in," admitted George Stephanopolous.[72]

In 1992, from the time Perot reentered the race to the day the Advisory Committee made its decision, national polls showed that Perot's support ranged from 7 to 9 percent, with an average of 8 percent.[73] In 1996, for the week preceding the Advisory Committee's decision, Perot's support ranged from 6 to 10 percent, with an average of 7.7 percent, just 0.3 percent lower than in 1992.[74]

Moreover, the decision to exclude Perot in 1996 partly because he accepted federal matching funds positioned the CPD against democratizing functions of the federal government. To stem the influence of special-interest contributions, the federal government distributes matching funds to political parties that earned at least 5 percent of the vote in the previous election. The government requires candidates who receive matching funds not to spend more than $50,000 of their personal wealth. Because Perot captured 19 percent of the vote in 1992, he was offered $29 million in federal matching funds for his 1996 campaign. Perot accepted the $29 million and waived his right to spend from his massive fortune, but remarkably, the CPD used that decision against him. The Advisory Committee's letter justifying Perot's exclusion argued, "In 1992, we concluded that his prospect of election was unlikely but not unrealistic. With the 1992 results and the circumstances of the current campaign before us, including Mr. Perot's funding limited by his acceptance of a federal subsidy, we see no similar circumstances at the present time."

9-25-96 THE PHILADELPHIA INQUIRER. UNIVERSAL PRESS SYNDICATE.

CARTOON C

The Advisory Committee's rationalization for Perot's exclusion was shameful, especially considering that one of the CPD's criteria for inclusion was "eligibility for matching funds from the Federal Election Commission." The *Boston Globe* editorialized:

> Perot is on all 50 state ballots, and because of the 19.7 million votes he won in 1992, he has qualified for $29 million in federal campaign funds. This was twisted into a negative by the cochairman of the debate commission, Paul Kirk, because it limits Perot to using only $50,000 of his own money. Kirk said Perot's bottomless pockets would have been a stronger argument for debate participation. This puts the commission on record as valuing dollars over votes—a sad commentary on politics today. Indeed, it has been argued that the people running the commission are Washington lobbyists and insiders who have an interest in resisting the very changes Perot's Reform Party is pushing. What is not arguable is that with cochairmen who are former chairs of the Democratic and Republican national committees, the commission has an innate

bias against third parties because they challenge the two-party system.[75]

Before the CPD announced Perot's exclusion, the Reform Party was regularly touting the $29 million in federal funds; it was the first time a third party had received public funds for a general election. Little did they know that the CPD would turn this asset into a liability. Indeed, had Perot known, he would not have accepted the public funds, which were unquestioningly accepted by both major-party candidates. The Perot campaign even asked the Federal Election Commission to waive the $50,000 limit on personal spending. Pat Choate, Perot's running mate, said, "If they want Ross Perot to spend a great deal more money, if that's the criteria, he's willing to spend it."[76] (See cartoon C.)

In 1992, ironically, the major-party candidates democratized the debates by requiring Perot's inclusion. But in 1996, the Republican and Democratic nominees excluded the most legitimate third-party candidate since John B. Anderson—a third-party candidate who was on the ballot in all fifty states, who had won two of three debates just four years earlier, who captured an astounding 19 percent of the popular vote during his first presidential run, who was wanted in the debates by 76 percent of the American public, and who had received $29 million of taxpayer money. Yet he was reduced to nothing more than Clinton's bargaining chip. "There's something that stinks about this," said former Democratic presidential candidate Jesse Jackson. "It's fundamentally undemocratic. It's awfully close to corruption. There's something unhealthy about this. If this group can arbitrarily rule that a billionaire who gets 20 million votes and qualifies for $30 million in election funds can't participate then God help the rest of us."[77] The League of Women Voters would not have allowed this to happen. Nancy Neuman, former president of the League, said, "We probably would have let Perot in in 1996."[78]

The CPD received a barrage of criticism for Perot's exclusion. David Broder of the *Washington Post* wrote:

> Never again should a candidate such as Ross Perot—who
> is as widely known as the major-party nominees, who

qualifies for public financing and who is on the ballot in all fifty states—be barred from the forums that are so useful to prospective voters in making up their minds. . . . Putting the commission in charge automatically biased the system toward the two parties that have dominated our politics. The commission charter explicitly recognizes the legitimacy and importance of the two-party system, and the co-chairmen, Paul Kirk and Frank Fahrenkopf, are there as former chairmen of the Democratic and Republican national committees. The two-party system has served this country well and is worth protecting—but only up to the point that it does not conflict with other values important to the electorate. In an era when increasing numbers of voters are discarding old party loyalties, significant independent candidates have a claim on participation in the debates. This year, the commission overreached in protecting the major-party nominees, while failing—as has often been the case—to keep incumbent presidents from unilaterally dictating the rules of the game.[79]

The *New York Times* editorialized:

By deciding yesterday to exclude Ross Perot from this year's debates, the commission proved itself to be a tool of the two dominant parties rather than guardian of the public interest. This commission has no legal standing to monopolize debates, and it is time for some more fair-minded group to get into the business of sponsoring these important events.[80]

Perot's goal had been to draw more than 25 percent of the vote in order to win major-party status for the Reform Party. By doing so, Perot said, "we will have created an institution that can give people a voice."[81] Instead, Perot's exclusion shattered his campaign. Hours after a federal judge denied a request that Perot be allowed in the debates, FOX television abruptly canceled a Perot appearance on one of its morning shows. On Election Day, Perot received only 8.4 percent of the popular vote.

Most pundits got it wrong. The real story in 1996: Dole excluded Perot, Clinton made the debates a nonevent, and voters were short-changed.

2000

The exclusion of Ross Perot in 1996 unmasked the CPD's bipartisan nature, prompting a brief public outcry. It also brought the CPD closer to losing a legal battle. In 1996, Perot filed suit after the CPD announced his exclusion, and although Perot lost his case, District Judge Thomas Hogan was very critical of the CPD. "It is my hope that there is a different arrangement for these debates in the future," said Judge Hogan.[82] The legal threat was severely magnified when Lawrence Noble, the general counsel of the FEC, issued a scathing thirty-seven-page report requesting a full-blown investigation of the CPD. "The general counsel's report showed the debate commission that it might be crossing the line," said FEC commissioner Scott E. Thomas.[83]

After the 1996 election, the CPD underwent a makeover to conceal its blemishes. It replaced members of Congress on the board with civic leaders. It convinced Dorothy Ridings, former president of the League of Women Voters, to join the board. It constantly touted its "nonpartisan" status. But these changes were largely cosmetic; Fahrenkopf and Kirk still ran the show. "I would be surprised if their predominant concern still wasn't the two parties," said Lawrence Noble.[84] Nancy Neuman, former president of the League, said, "The CPD has evolved a bit. In the beginning, they said they would never ever include third-party candidates. It changed its rhetoric. But it is pretty unlikely for those on the CPD to change their direction."[85]

The final touch of the makeover was transforming the subjective criteria into a more "preestablished objective" threshold, as FEC regulations require. In 1999, Newton Minow coauthored a report that recommended a modification of the criteria. While carefully avoiding open acknowledgment of major-party manipulation—after all, Minow is vice-chairman of the CPD—the report criticized the subjective criteria:

The ultimate criteria should be straightforward, transparent and not subject to pretextual manipulation (either in appearance or reality). Accordingly, we believe that reliance on the contemporaneous judgment of historians, journalists, and pundits—as under the current Commission on Presidential Debates criteria—should be rejected. ... We also believe that the "wisdom-of-the-cognoscenti" standard reflected in the CPD's criteria arrogates far too much power over a critical national issue to an aristocracy of unelected analysts and observers.

But Professor Neustadt cautioned, "If the new criteria make it easier for more than two candidates to get into the debates, the major-party nominees may just refuse to participate, and then you've lost your best tool for informing the public."[86]

To neutralize accusations of partisanship while still ensuring third-party exclusion, on January 6, 2000, the CPD announced that third-party and independent candidates would have to reach 15 percent in predebate polls to receive an invitation to the presidential debates. In 1988, 1992, and 1996, the subjectivity of the long-winded criteria enabled the CPD to rhetorically justify the exclusion of any candidate. The advantage of the 2000 criterion is that it forces some transparency—candidate participation is less subject to the backdoor manipulations of Republicans and Democrats. "We in effect wiped away what Mr. Perot had complained about," said Fahrenkopf.[87] CPD director Antonia Hernandez said, "You might not like the 15 percent threshold, but it's clearly articulated, and if a person meets it, then that candidate gets in."[88]

However, setting the criterion at 15 percent was an improvement in method but not in outcome. "Anyone that has any experience in the civil rights area knows that something can be objective and still discriminatory," said Harry Kresky, a First Amendment attorney. Exclusion had merely been shifted from behind-the-scenes negotiation to an overt numerical obstacle. In fact, many pundits and political consultants thought the 15 percent criterion was more exclusionary. Bob Neuman, former spokesperson for the CPD, said, "The previous criteria allowed more flexibility for third-party candidates to get in."[89] Scott Reed, Dole's campaign manager, said that the 15 percent threshold "is a much greater barrier to third-party candidates" than the previous criteria.[90] The *Bismarck Tribune* called the 15 percent threshold a "third-party killer." The *Fort Lauderdale Sun-Sentinel* editorialized:

> In dictatorships, it's common for political insiders to hinder or even silence non-establishment challengers. To do that in America, which supposedly champions open elections, is outrageous and intolerable. But that is just what the Commission on Presidential Debates has done. On Thursday, it announced an unfair, unreasonable and unjust rule almost guaranteeing that only the Republican and Democratic nominees will be admitted to nationally televised presidential debates this fall.[91]

This certainly was intentional. Public outrage and FEC regulations were not the only impetuses for changing the criteria. Republican Party officials were tired of third-party candidates undermining their nominee, either as a source of leverage during debate negotiations or in the actual debates themselves. They believed that Perot partly cost Bush the election in 1992, and that Perot's potential inclusion significantly weakened Dole in 1996. In 2000, Pat Buchanan, appreciably to the right of Perot, had emerged as the Reform Party nominee, and he had $12.6 million in federal matching funds. To prevent Buchanan from undermining their candidate during negotiations or, worse, in the debates, Republicans advocated new criteria that would automatically exclude third-party and independent candidates long before negotiations began. Scott Reed, Dole's campaign manager, explained:

> The Republicans, Fahrenkopf, recognized the incredibly huge impact Perot had on the 1992 debates. The guy got 19 percent of the vote. There is no question about it, if he didn't go to those debates he wouldn't have gotten that many votes and Bush might have won. So I think the Republicans recognized that the third-party type

candidates were hurting them more, and there ought to be a halt to it.[92]

The CPD viewed the new criteria as benefiting both major parties; it would help prevent the short-term political interests of major-party candidates from ever again undermining the two-party system. In 2000, five third-party candidates were on enough state ballots to win an electoral college majority: Ralph Nader of the Green Party, Pat Buchanan of the Reform Party, Harry Browne of the Libertarian Party, John Hagelin of the Natural Law Party, and Howard Phillips of the Constitution Party. Two of these candidates—Nader and Buchanan—are well known public figures who attracted substantial media coverage and popular support, and 64 percent of likely voters wanted them in the debates. Nader and Buchanan focused much of their predebate campaign on creating public pressure that would propel them into the debates. They wrote letters to the CPD, the major-party candidates, and the television networks; appealed to labor unions, civic organizations, and religious groups to set up alternate debates; filed lawsuits; broadcast political advertisements; and collected tens of thousands of petition signatures. They managed to attract support in varied political circles. On August 6, 2000, the following conversation took place during CNN's *Late Edition with Wolf Blitzer*:

> CALLER: I'd just like to know why the Republicans and Democrats are both so afraid to let Ralph Nader and Pat Buchanan into the debates.
>
> WOLF BLITZER, CNN ANCHOR: Well, let's ask Leon Panetta that question first. What do you say about that?
>
> LEON PANETTA, GORE SUPPORTER AND FORMER WHITE HOUSE CHIEF OF STAFF UNDER PRESIDENT CLINTON: . . . I have to agree with the caller. I'm a little concerned that when somebody is getting as much attention as Ralph Nader is and when somebody's getting as much attention as Pat Buchanan has always gotten, the reality is the American people, I think, are entitled to

hear all of these candidates debate. You know, it would be healthy for the country and healthy for the discussion of the issues that are going to confront this country if you have all of those key players involved in a debate.

BLITZER: You agree with that, John Kasich?

CONGRESSMAN JOHN KASICH, BUSH SUPPORTER AND HOUSE BUDGET CHAIRMAN: Yes, Wolf, I really do. I think Leon's really hit it and that's a fact. You know, we shouldn't be afraid to hear other people's opinions and these are legitimate candidates.[93]

How would the major parties exclude such viable third-party candidates without infuriating voters? The 15 percent threshold meant that the major-party nominees, Al Gore and George W. Bush, didn't have to address the issue. The criteria spared them. The *Seattle Times* editorialized:

> Ralph Nader and Patrick Buchanan will not be allowed into this year's presidential debates. They should be, for at least one debate. . . . In the seven presidential elections in which we've had debates, in only one year, 1992, were there more than two candidates in any debate. That year, Ross Perot went into the debates with 5 to 6 percent support. He went on to win 19 percent of the vote. The two parties didn't like that. That is why they excluded Perot in 1996 and it is the reason for their 15 percent threshold now. The 15 percent threshold suits the two parties. It unduly restricts the American people.[94]

Major-party negotiators focused on the schedule and format instead of third-party participation. The Gore campaign immediately accepted the CPD's proposal. Following in the footsteps of his father, Bush summarily rejected the CPD's plan and publicized the forty-two other invitations he had received to debate. "There's more than just the commission debates," said Bush. On September 3, Bush essentially bypassed the CPD and proposed a total of five debates: a debate on

CARTOON D

Meet the Press, a debate on *Larry King Live,* a CPD-sponsored debate at Washington University, and two vice-presidential debates. Bush justified the alternate proposals by claiming that he wanted forums with less rigid formats. From the start, however, the CPD made it clear that the candidates could unilaterally negotiate a suitable format.[95]

In reality, Bush was terrified of the electoral consequences of real debates. Less articulate and less informed than his opponent, Bush wanted to dismiss presidential debates altogether. But he was unable to avoid debates without a severe public backlash, and Bush's team proposed substitute debates that minimized audience size, eluded prime time, and maximized the participation of Bush's formidable vice-presidential candidate, Dick Cheney. (See cartoon D.)

The Bush camp misread the American voter. After significant media coverage on the debate over the debates, Bush's poll numbers began to drop; voters could see right through his subterfuge. Remarkably, Bush had made the same mistake as his father. "It just seemed like he hadn't read the history very well," said Elaine Kamarck, senior policy advisor to Gore.[96]

On September 14, 2000, CPD directors Paul Kirk, Frank Fahren-kopf, John Danforth, Clifford Alexander, Dorothy Ridings, and Janet Brown met at the law firm of Ross, Dixon & Bell. They had a two-hour strategy session and agreed to take a hard line on debate sites and dates. Later that day, when they met with representatives of the Gore and Bush campaigns, Fahrenkopf stated that the CPD would allow the candidates to negotiate format and other details, but not the schedule and venues.[97] Don Evans, chairman of the Bush campaign, interrupted Fahrenkopf to announce that Governor Bush had dropped his objections and would accept the CPD's proposal. Over the next forty-eight hours, debate negotiators drafted a thirty-one-page Memorandum of Understanding in conformity with the CPD's schedule.

Although the 15 percent criterion excluded all third-party challengers, Bush and Gore could have invited anybody to join them. When asked who decides third-party participation, Marty Plissner, former political director of CBS News, said, "The candidates. You don't believe this crap about the criteria? If Gore and Bush wanted Buchanan and Nader in, they'd be in."[98] A week after the CPD announced the criteria, when a reporter asked Bush if he favored letting Nader and Buchanan in the debates, he said, "I don't know. I haven't figured out the impact yet." The reporter then asked if Bush was saying he would let them in only if it would help his presidential bid. Bush replied with a grin, "I am trying to win, aren't I?"[99]

However, the circumstances surrounding the 2000 election created perfect bargaining parity; if Bush pushed for Nader's inclusion, Gore could try to include Buchanan. "That was mutual assured destruction," said George Stephanopolous. "You knew that if one of them was in, both of them were in."[100] William Daley, Gore's campaign chairman, wrote in an e-mail, "Nader and Buchanan checked each other in their own way and no one really wanted either in the debates."[101]

With Nader and Buchanan on the sidelines, Gore and Bush participated in three presidential debates. The dreary events, which the public perceived as pitting a smiling bumbler against an arrogant policy-wonk, attracted the smallest audience in the history of televised presidential debates. Ronald K. L. Collins and David M. Skover, authors of *The Death of Discourse*, wrote, "Without a Jesse Ventura, Ross Perot, or Ralph Nader to jazz things up, the debates were predictable snoozers of sound bites, poll-tested blandness, and wooden affect. Both Gore and Bush recited their pat responses against the other's pat responses, and then played the 'I Love America' hit jukebox tune a few times so viewers could follow along." The only real excitement took place outside the debate hall, where helicopters swarmed over twelve thousand protesters outraged with third-party exclusion and where Ralph Nader was barred from entering a television viewing room even though he had a ticket. John Vezeris, a representative of the CPD, told Nader, "It's already been decided that whether or not you have a ticket you are not welcome."

Illusory Autonomy

To its credit, the CPD is becoming more autonomous with each election cycle, insisting on a particular debate schedule with increasing authority. Peter Knight, chairman of Clinton's 1996 campaign, said:

> [The CPD] doesn't operate totally independently, but I think that it is growing in influence as an institution. If you go back to 1988 and 1992, you find that the parties have a fair amount of influence over the process. But over time, the parties are having less influence over the process, although they still, between themselves, are having the ability to make decisions on it. Republicans are saying that they were able to influence the debate commission's decisions. There's some truth to that, but it's not pronounced. Might have been true in 1992, slightly less so in 1996, and less so in 2000. It's a just a maturation of the process.[102]

The CPD's autonomy, however, is largely illusory. The independent decisions of the CPD are almost always made in the best interests of the Republican and Democratic parties. That the major parties do not continually deliver marching orders to the CPD is reflective only of the parties' confidence in the organization's ideology and operation, not of any real distance between the political entities. The autonomy of the CPD is growing, therefore, because Fahrenkopf and Kirk have usurped campaign functions and executed them in the long-term interest of the two major parties. For example, the CPD replaced secret negotiations over third-party participation with an unreachable 15 percent threshold. John Buckley, communications director of the Dole campaign, said, "Is it convenient for the parties that the debate commission sets it up the way they do and they have a formula that means it's unlikely that a third-party candidate is going to shoot into national prominence? Yes, it is quite helpful to the major parties."[103]

Whenever the CPD does actually challenge the immediate interests of the major-party candidates—to preserve, for example, a particular debate schedule—the challenge is only temporary. The CPD quickly acquiesces if the major-party candidates jointly refuse to heed its meek protests. Mickey Kantor said, "The debate commission almost makes certain that there will be debates because I don't think any candidate, incumbent or not, can run away from their entreaties. Yet they've been very flexible in allowing the major-party candidates to set the debate process itself and the procedures governing the debates."[104] Congressman John Lewis, a former CPD director, said, "In the end, the final decisions about the presidential debates—on who participates, on the format—are really made by the candidates. And the debate commission will not oppose the decisions of the candidates."[105]

EVERY FOUR YEARS, the CPD unilaterally provides a forum that is designed to exclude third-party and independent candidates. If the Republican and Democratic campaigns desire the inclusion of a particular third-party candidate, the CPD may register momentary and private protest, if only to protect its tax-exempt status and remind the campaigns of the potential damage to the two-party system. The CPD, however, will ultimately submit to the major party candidates' demands and prepare for immediate implementation of a confidential Memorandum of Understanding drafted by Republican and Democratic negotiators. "The only way you can reach tens of millions of American voters is by having the major parties invite you," said Ralph Nader.[106]

4

Stilted Formats

I N 1991, THE television networks devised their own plan to host
the presidential debates. The presidents of CBS News, NBC News,
ABC News, and CNN proposed three presidential debates and
one vice-presidential debate between the major-party candidates on
the four weekday nights with the largest audiences. They would hold
the debates in Los Angeles, New York, Chicago, and Atlanta—"the
chief population centers of the four regions of the country."[1] They
would exclude all third-party and independent candidates. There
would be no live audience "because the on-site audiences in past
years had turned into a partisan cheering section." Candidates would
ask each other questions "to promote the freest possible exchange."[2]
There would be no panel of journalists, just a single moderator, who
would be present only to change subjects, clarify points, and keep
some kind of order. "We're trying to erase some of the errors of the
1988 campaigns that produced debates that weren't really debates,"
said Lane Venardos, vice president of CBS.[3]

Moreover, the debates would "be held at the networks' own
expense in their own facilities."[4] The networks would pay for the
entire series of presidential debates to the tune of $2 million. In a
letter addressed to the major parties, to the cochairmen of the CPD,
and to the president of the League of Women Voters, network executives wrote, "This proposal guarantees that time periods and facilities for the debates will be available. It eliminates any need to solicit
funds, and it provides professional staff and state-of-the-art studios

at no cost to any party, candidate or outside organization."[5]

The networks also expected to eliminate debate negotiations. Hal Bruno, political director of ABC News, said, "We're willing to offer our studio, the production facility, and our technical skills. The one thing we absolutely do not want to do is negotiate with candidates."[6] The League of Women Voters embraced the network plan, noting that it would be more likely to produce an "unscripted debate."

But the network proposal was rejected. Fahrenkopf and Kirk responded by actually criticizing the networks for lacking objectivity. In an op-ed piece published in the *Washington Post*, they wrote:

> ABC, NBC, and CBS are parts of giant corporate con-glomerates with many legislative and regulatory inter-ests in Washington. They, as well as CNN, have major issues pending before federal agencies and Congress. Do these interests enable the networks to act impartially and objectively as debate sponsors with no real or potential conflict of interest? We doubt it.[7]

The networks may not be ideal sponsors, but Kirk and Fahrenkopf— who have their own financial interests as registered lobbyists, who have their own political interests as former party chairmen, who are unaccountable to the public—are clearly in no position to criticize conflicts of interest. Marty Plissner, then political director of CBS News, rebutted with his own *Washington Post* op-ed piece:

> Yet, to what masters does the commission itself answer? Scanning the blue chip corporate donors, replete with leg-islative and regulative interests, proudly displayed in the commission's own literature, one finds: "Archer Daniels Midland, Atlantic Richfield, AT&T, Bankers Trust, Bell South . . . Morgan Guaranty, Mutual of Omaha, Nissan, Peoples Natural Gas . . . Prudential, Pfizer . . . Union Pacific, USAir."[8]

Eventually, Fahrenkopf and Kirk sat down with the network execu-tives, and they agreed on the number of debates, the format, and the exclusion of a live audience. After six months of negotiations, however, Roone Arledge, the president of ABC News, abruptly backed off. Plissner wrote, "Arledge, we were told, had been reminded (by Kirk and/or Fahrenkopf, we all assumed) that he had been part of that mid-1980s study group from which the debates commission claimed its origin."[9] On the very same day, the CPD pulled out of the negotiations. "The networks wanted to take over the debates," said Fahrenkopf. "We told them to get screwed."[10]

The CPD rejected the network offer to finance the debates, even though the networks agreed to exclude all third-party candidates. The CPD wanted major-party candidates to retain absolute control over structural elements of the debates—the schedule, the format, and staging details. David Norcross, then vice-chairman of the CPD, explained, "I saw nothing to be gained and much to lose in giving up all leverage over content, time, panelists and so forth. . . . Where, whether and when to debate is a matter properly left to the campaigns and I did not want to see the networks have any additional leverage over the candidates."[11] The CPD would rather raise corporate cash and allow major-party candidates to unilaterally select the panelists than accept conditional network contributions. The major parties believe that the debate schedule, format, and staging details are too critical to be left in the hands of uncontrollable news organizations.

The CPD purports to select debate formats based on the recommendations of symposia filled with campaign managers, reporters, and academics. But these symposia are ornamental. Behind the scenes, major-party negotiators hammer out the details concerning the format, schedule, and stage, and these details make up the majority of text in Memoranda of Understanding. Robert Asman, a former NBC producer hired by the CPD, said, "Working with the Commission on Presidential Debates, I had an inside look at how the two campaigns steamrolled all the proposals we had made based upon studies."[12] Negotiations over the schedule, format, and staging are usually as fierce as and more time-consuming than negotiations over third-party participation. "We have seen the candidates argue over the temperature in the hall," said Fahrenkopf.[13]

Ultimately, the 1992 debates bore very little resemblance to what the networks had proposed. There was an on-site audience and varied formats. Every aspect of the 1992 debates was decided by the candidates and delivered to the CPD on a take-it-or-leave-it basis.

Schedule

Every four years, the CPD holds a news conference and lays out a schedule for three ninety-minute presidential debates and one vice-presidential debate that, if implemented, would serve the electorate well. The directors of the CPD know that the proposed dates are subject to negotiation between the candidates, but the early announcement is necessary to attract corporate contributions. The following exchange took place at the Harvard Institute for Politics after the 1992 election:

> **CHARLIE BLACK, BUSH POLITICAL CONSULTANT:** I said right then, don't go out there and schedule a bunch of damn debates and just expect candidates to show up, because our philosophy is that once the nominees are chosen, they should talk to each other about what the debate format and schedule are going to be. Then maybe the commission would be an appropriate sponsor, but do not, I mean, we begged you three years ahead not to do what you did.

> **ED FOUHY, PRODUCER OF THE 1988 AND 1992 DEBATES:** It was the money, Charlie. We had to go out and raise the money.

That's not to say that the CPD appreciates the candidates changing its schedule. After selecting dates suitable to the television networks and raising funds for debate sites, the CPD wants the major-party candidates to accept its proposed schedule. In fact, scheduling is the only significant element of the debates that the CPD would rather have under its exclusive control, shielded from the influence of Republican and Democratic campaign managers. The major-party candidates, however, often end up negotiating a different debate schedule at the expense of voter education.

The public wants several debates, but for some major-party candidates, particularly bad debaters and front-runners, the fewer debates the better. In 1988, Bush wanted one debate, and Dukakis wanted as many as he could get. "There's no reason to think we'd need more than one," said Roger Ailes, Bush's senior media advisor. They agreed to two. (In 1996, frontrunner President Clinton also agreed to only two debates.)

The public interest is best served when debates are scheduled on nights likely to attract the widest possible audience. Major-party negotiators, however, have deliberately scheduled debates opposite major television events to shrink audience size, with networks complicit in the refusal to broadcast the debates. In 1988, when NBC planned on skipping the first debate to broadcast Olympic coverage, heads of both political parties complained. "A network has never refused to cover a general election debate between the two major-party nominees," wrote Senator Ernest Hollings (D-SC) and Rep. John Dingell (D-MI). NBC changed its mind because of the political backlash. But in 1992, no one pressured CBS when it opted for baseball play-offs because the debate schedule had been established at the last minute. "The blame is on the Bush campaign," said Rep. Edward Markey.[14] Ever since, the networks have brazenly avoided broadcasting debates if too costly, thus undercutting debate ratings and placing the onus of maximizing audience size on major-party negotiators.

The public also benefits from lengthy debates, which test the resilience of participating candidates. "In all debates, there is a witching hour that comes 60 to 70 minutes into the debate," said Michael Sheehan, who helped prepare Clinton in 1996. "Every stupid mistake comes then. The Jack Kennedy line came at 61 minutes. Ford's line about communist domination, the same thing. It's the clubhouse turn where the horse falls."[15] Afraid of stumbling, some candidates, particularly less articulate candidates, have negotiated for shorter debates. In 2000, George W. Bush proposed sixty-minute debates.

Scheduling is one of the few negotiable elements of the presidential debates in which the voters' interests and the CPD's interests are, at least initially, the same. Instead of publicly criticizing candidates that deviate from a set schedule, however, the CPD often acquiesces to the demands of the major-party nominees.

Format

Televised debate formats radically departed from untelevised debate formats. The seven 1860 Lincoln-Douglas debates ran three hours without a break, and the entire series was focused on a single topic: extending slavery to the territories. One candidate led with a sixty-minute speech, the other responded for ninety minutes, and then the candidate who spoke first concluded with a thirty-minute rebuttal. There were no moderators or panelists—instead, the candidates asked each other questions. In 2000, by contrast, the three Bush-Gore debates ran ninety minutes, and the series was focused on a multitude of topics. The candidates answered questions from a reporter, and their responses were restricted to two minutes. There was a moderator at each debate, and the candidates were prohibited from asking each other questions. Yet who's to say one format is better than another? Professor David Birdsell wrote, "The formats must be wide-ranging but probing, engaging but never merely entertaining, revealing of character but not at the expense of policy discussion, and short but thorough. . . . No format can attend to all of the legitimate questions about a candidate, so some critics are bound to walk away unhappy."[16]

Indeed, even in 1960, critics assailed the format of the first televised presidential debates. The networks had pushed for "real debates"—no moderators or panelists, just long opening statements and candidates questioning each other. But Kennedy and Nixon rejected this proposal because neither candidate wanted direct confrontation.[17] Instead, they insisted on the safest possible format, which hardly deviated from other campaign experiences: the *press panelist format*. Rather than talk to each other, Nixon and Kennedy answered questions from a seated panel of reporters. Professor J. Jeffrey Auer, author of *The Counterfeit Debates*, called the "so-called debates" a "double public press conference for simultaneous interviewing" and said they "created the illusion that the public question of great moment can be dealt with in 180 seconds."[18] Historian Daniel Boorstin called the 1960 debates a "clinical example of the pseudo-event."

While reporters tend to be informed questioners, the disadvantages of the press panelist format are many: the candidates never speak to each other; panelists steal the spotlight with "gotcha" questions;

panelists deliver mini-essays before they get to their questions; questions reflect the interests of the panelists rather than the interests of the public; panelists are sometimes hostile to the candidates; and so on. *Washington Post* columnist Mary McGrory wrote:

> The professional training that encourages reporters to sharpen their questions and tighten their prose deserts them on the set. Somehow the encounter is not so much to elicit information from the questioned but to display the erudition of the questioner. It is to reveal one's sophistication, one's truly impressive range of knowledge, one's exquisitely calibrated appreciation of the nuances of a question that clods might ask in two seconds.[19]

The League of Women Voters fought hard to create genuine debates. They required follow-up questions, provided comparatively lengthy response times, and prohibited the candidates from selecting the panelists. Armed with greater public expectations, a nonpartisan successor to the League would probably have modified debate formats to elicit more confrontational discourse. The history of presidential debate formats would likely have been a history of positive, incremental reform. Still, the League failed to fundamentally alter the format of the debates; for every single debate it sponsored, the press panelist format was employed. "We always tried to get rid of those damn press panelist formats," said Nancy Neuman. "But we couldn't do it."[20]

The CPD, however, managed to escape the restrictive press panelist format and employ two other formats in 1992, 1996, and 2000: the *single moderator format* and the *town hall format*. The town hall format, which consists of voters in the audience posing questions to the candidates, is particularly popular with viewers because it raises issues that the public wants addressed and asks about them in terms accessible to everyday Americans. Moderator Carole Simpson recounted her exchange with the town hall audience minutes before the 1992 debate:

> "I just want to know the subjects that you're interested in, okay?" So they start yelling out—health care,

crime, education, gun control, abortion, trade deficit, the breakup of the Soviet Union, poverty, all domestic issues. Except for the trade deficit and the Soviet Union, they were domestic issues. The economy, the budget deficit. All the gamut of domestic issues. They're just shouting it out.

So I said, "Isn't anybody interested in Iran contra?" And people started, "No!" I said, "What about Iraq-gate?" "No!" They get louder and louder. I said, "What about the Jennifers, with a J and a G?" And they're all laughing, "No! No!" And somebody stood up and said, "That's you all. That's what the media cares about. We don't care about that. We want to know if we're going to have jobs. We want to know if we're going to have health care and stuff like that."[21]

The CPD accomplished what the League and the networks failed to accomplish: more diverse debate formats. However, a historical narrative that paints the CPD as the Great Format Reformer misattributes credit and ignores major format deficiencies unique to CPD-sponsored debates. The CPD never developed the "new" formats. The major-party candidates, for various reasons, chose to break from the press panelist format. The CPD took credit for the popular town hall format, falsely advertising it as a product of extensive study, but in reality, Governor Clinton proposed the format in 1992 because it paraded his interpersonal skills. Paul Begala, senior advisor to President Clinton, remembered:

It was Bill Clinton's idea. When we realized there would be more than two debates, the Governor told Bruce Lindsey to interrupt the negotiating meeting and say if there were going to be more than two, we wanted at least one of them to be real people asking questions, like a town hall meeting. When the word came back that the President's folks had agreed to it, we were hooting and hollering. We couldn't believe it.[22]

The CPD has never seriously lobbied for any formats on behalf of the public, as the League did. In fact, no other element of the debate negotiations involves less resistance from the CPD. The candidates call the shots concerning format, and the CPD does not much care. A source who worked in the CPD's office and spoke on the condition of anonymity said, "Kirk and Fahrenkopf only care about sponsoring the debates and protecting the two parties. They don't give a damn about what formats the candidates use."

As a result, while the basic formats have changed for the better, the structure and the rules governing them have become much worse. Candidates have extensively manipulated the details within the selected formats, however diverse, to eliminate the remaining shreds of spontaneity.

PANELISTS AND MODERATORS

Panelists and moderators have tremendous influence over what is talked about during the debates. Whether or not an issue is discussed depends almost entirely on the questions they pose. Scott Reed, Dole's campaign manager, said that the choice of moderator "is incredibly significant. The moderator sets the tone for the whole evening."[23]

In 1980, the League selected Bill Moyers ("the conscience of American journalism") to serve as moderator after consulting with the Nieman Foundation, Pulitzer Prize authorities, the Radio and TV News Directors Association, Newspaper Publishers' Association, American Society of Newspaper Editors, and the producers of *Face the Nation, Meet the Press, Issues and Answers,* and *Washington Week in Review.*[24] Moyers was no lapdog, and he wasn't particularly enthralled with the Republican and Democratic parties. A week before the 1980 election, he said:

> If you don't like any of the major candidates, one way to use your vote for a positive statement is to vote for some alternative candidate—minority parties need 5 percent of the vote on election day to qualify for retroactive federal funds. I think our political system needs other parties to keep the major parties honest, to force the major parties to think about ideas they would normally disavow out

of hand, and to bring into the system those people who feel they have no particular stake in the process anymore. Strong, as opposed to weak, minority parties will be like yeast in the bread of American politics.[25]

It is unlikely, however, that someone like Moyers will ever moderate a CPD-sponsored debate. Although Bob Neuman, spokesperson for the CPD, said that "candidates don't have much influence over the selection of moderators and panelists," the CPD allows the major-party candidates to handpick every single panelist and moderator. The 1992 Memorandum of Understanding stipulated:

> Representatives of each candidate will submit a list of at least six (6) and not more than ten (10) possible panelists to each other, but in any event such lists shall be submitted no later than by noon Tuesday 6 October 1992, Washington, D.C. time. Each side will then have the opportunity to approve or delete names from the other's proposed list. If necessary, this process shall be repeated until the agreed-upon number of names is submitted to the Commission.

David Norcross, former negotiator for Dole, described the process, "You get a list, you knock off the ones you don't want, I knock off the ones I don't want, you knock off the ones I don't want, and if there is nobody left, then you gotta put new names and start again."[26] Some notable reporters have refused to participate in debates governed by such a political panelist selection process. "I just feel very uncomfortable with the candidates selecting the reporters," said Tim Russert, host of *Meet the Press.*[27]

True to form, the candidates usually select moderators and panelists who ask safe and predictable questions. When Jon Margolis, a columnist for the *Chicago Tribune,* was chosen for the 1988 vice-presidential debate, he told his fellow panelists, "Well, we've all been cleared, which means at best that we're equal opportunity bland."[28] In 1996, George Stephanopolous proposed that Oprah Winfrey moderate a debate.

For the past three election cycles, the candidates have selected Jim Lehrer, host of PBS's *NewsHour*, to moderate every presidential debate, except for the 1992 town hall debate. Lehrer is an unbiased moderator, and he makes every effort to focus the debate on the candidates, rather than on himself. "I think Jim Lehrer does an excellent job," said Kay Maxwell, president of the League. "He tries to make the candidates' words more memorable than his own."[29]

Lehrer is effective at what he aims to accomplish, but viewers pay a price for his humility. He doesn't believe in challenging the candidates. "Many people think Jim Lehrer is fair-minded, objective, evenhanded, which he is, but he is also sedate," said Jon Margolis. "He does not ask difficult questions."[30] Lehrer only sparingly uses follow-up questions, which allow moderators to get past rehearsed answers and contest evasive or misleading responses. In 2000, Pat Caddell, former Democratic pollster, said that Lehrer was "running the debates as though they were some kind of sherry hour at the Institute for Politics at Harvard."[31] After the 2000 presidential debates, Massachusetts Senator John Kerry said, "You could have picked 10 people off the street who didn't know Jerusalem from Georgia and they would have had better questions."[32]

The position of moderator should be rotated among experienced journalists with varying styles. The public would welcome debates moderated by more aggressive anchors. With Lehrer serving as moderator since 1992, the debates have become passive events that sideline many of the voters' questions and criticisms. Even CPD director Howard Buffett recognized the problem: "I think candidates get off the hook. When they're allowed to do that, you don't accomplish as much as you could with the debates. You need moderators other than Lehrer who are also professional and yet don't pull all the punches." Buffett added without the slightest hint of irony, "I would love to see Tim Russert."[33]

CROSS-QUESTIONING

In 1976, the League tried to convince Jimmy Carter and Gerald Ford to question each other during the debates, but the candidates refused. However, the three panelists for the final 1976 debate—Robert Maynard of the *Washington Post*, Jack Nelson of the *Los Angeles Times*, and syndicated columnist Joseph Kraft—secretly met before the event and agreed that when the broadcast reached the sixty-minute mark, whoever had the floor would ask the candidates to break from the format and directly question each other. The panelists did not inform the moderator, Barbara Walters, of their plan until five minutes before airtime because they were afraid she would stop them. Unfortunately, the panelists were unable to pull it off. "Walters didn't try to scotch it," said panelist Jack Nelson, "but what happened was we didn't get the time cue."

In 1980, after vigorous lobbying from the League, Ronald Reagan and John B. Anderson agreed to question each other in the first debate. But during last-minute negotiations, candidate-to-candidate questioning was eliminated from the format. Lee Hanna, producer of the 1980 debates, said, "The candidates' representatives were pathetic in their desire to protect what they saw as their candidates' interests. The negotiations were exercises in frustration and hilarity."

For the second 1980 debate, however, the League came even closer to having the candidates question each other. The agreed-upon format permitted a candidate to follow up, question, rebut, or comment on his opponent's response to a panelist's question. Unfortunately, the candidates never asked each other a single question. To be effective, cross-questioning must be required, not merely permitted during short surrebuttals.

The CPD quietly dispensed with the advances of the League. Never in the history of televised presidential debates have candidates questioned each other, and through Memoranda of Understanding, risk-averse candidates keep it that way. The 1988 Memorandum of Understanding stipulated, "There will be no direct candidate-to-candidate questioning." The 1992 Memorandum of Understanding stipulated, "There will be no direct candidate-to-candidate questioning." The 1996 Memorandum of Understanding stipulated, "No cross-questions by the candidates or cross-conversation between the candidates will be allowed under these rules." The CPD's so-called debates explicitly prohibit the candidates from actually talking to each other.

In 1988, during a predebate meeting, panelist Peter Jennings of ABC News lobbied the other panelists to ignore the restrictive rules and force the candidates into direct confrontation. But moderator

CHART 4   Minutes allowed for each candidate's response

Sponsor	Year	Response Time
League	1976	3.5
	1980	4
	1984	4.5
CPD	1988	3
	1992	1.67
	1996	1.5
	2000	2

Jim Lehrer—who is selected not only for his compliance onstage but also for his compliance backstage—protested. "There was some discussion there about 'to hell with the rules, we can do any damn thing we want to,'" said Lehrer. "I kept saying we had made an agreement to come and do something. I felt it just as a matter of function, a matter of giving your word."[34] Jennings eventually acquiesced: "You got hired by the rules and you get played by the rules."[35]

RESPONSE TIMES

Restrictive time limits reduce the candidates' responses to memorized sound bites. Professor Stephen Coleman wrote, "How many university vivas, held to determine the qualification of a candidate for a doctorate, would ask a question about, say, the causes of inflation, and insist upon two-minute answers? Why should the public expect less when hearing the arguments of those seeking their votes?"[36]

According to polls and focus groups, the general public prefers debates that give candidates more time to answer questions. Under CPD sponsorship, however, response times have been gradually whittled down.

During the 1984 League-sponsored presidential debates, the candidates were collectively allotted a total of nine minutes per question sequence: 2.5 minutes to each candidate for an initial response, followed by a one-minute rebuttal for each candidate, followed by a one-minute response to a follow-up question for each candidate. During the 1996 CPD-sponsored debates, the candidates were collectively allotted a mere three minutes per question sequence: ninety seconds for Candidate "A," followed by a one-minute rebuttal for Candidate "B," followed by a thirty-second surrebuttal for Candidate "A" (follow-up questions were prohibited). Roger Simon, chief political correspondent for *U.S. News & World Report*, wrote, "In 1988, answers began to get shorter until they shrunk at one point to just 90 seconds. . . . Debates became theater."[37]

TOWN HALL FORMAT

Viewers and pundits have praised the town hall format for maximizing spontaneity and citizen participation, but with no opposition from the CPD, major-party negotiators transformed the popular format into a staged charade. In 1992, audience members could ask anything they wanted, including follow-up questions. In 1996, follow-ups and questions seeking clarification were banned. In 2000, the questions actually had to be written down on index cards and screened by moderator Jim Lehrer before the debates.

Janet Brown explained the changes with two words: "candidate fear."[38] William Daley, chairman of the Gore campaign, wrote in an e-mail, "The Bush campaign had a great concern over the possibility of a question out of left field and one that could be embarrassing."[39] Consequently, the major-party candidates turned a promising debate format into a farce. Mitchell McKinney, a University of Missouri speech communication professor, said, "Those citizens are there as props."

AS A RESULT of candidates handpicking panelists and moderators, the sparse use of follow-up questions, the prohibition on candidate-to-candidate questioning, overly restrictive response times, and the distortion of the town hall format, CPD-sponsored debates are not really debates. Despite the seeming diversity of format, the public is left with glorified bipartisan news conferences. The only difference from joint news conference to joint news conference is who asks all the questions—a panel of reporters, Jim Lehrer, or a prescreened group of undecided voters. The candidates never speak to each other, and because they are peppered by a succession of disparate questions, they merely recite prepackaged sound bites that fit sixty-second response slots and avoid discussing many important issues. "I'm trying to forget the whole damn experience of those debates," said former president George H. Bush. "'Cause I think it's too much show business and too much prompting, too much artificiality, and not really debates. They're rehearsed appearances."[40] In 1988, Dan Rather introduced the first presidential debate with the following remarks:

> This will not be a debate in the sense the word is often used in the English language because all of this is so tightly controlled by the candidates themselves and their managers. These things have developed over the years into what some people believe can more accurately be described as a joint campaign appearance or an orchestrated news conference.[41]

CPD director Howard Buffett said, "As a member of the public, sitting there watching the debates, sometimes I get extremely frustrated with the way you have these prescribed answers the candidates use and they sometimes don't answer the questions and they say what they want to say. But that's not the commission's responsibility."[42] Buffett is mistaken; in many respects, it is the commission's responsibility. No other sponsor has allowed the major-party candidates to negotiate exclusively. No other sponsor has implemented, without protest, Memoranda of Understanding that eliminate spontaneity, accountability, and confrontation from the debates. For example, the 1988 Memorandum of Understanding stipulated:

> The question-and-answer sequence will be as follows:
> 1. The moderator will indicate the topic, such as "arms control."
> 2. A panelist will ask a question of Candidate "A." (NOTE: The questions asked by the panelists will not exceed 45 seconds in duration.)
> 3. Candidate "A" will have 2 minutes to respond.
> 4. Candidate "B" will have 1 minute to rebut.
> 5. The same panelist will then ask a question on the same subject of Candidate "B."

6. Candidate "B" will have 2 minutes to respond.

7. Candidate "A" will have 1 minute to rebut.

The moderator will then indicate a second topic for questioning and the process will continue.

Format rules are necessary to maintain order and to address multiple issues, but these and other rigid format requirements implemented by the CPD seem designed to stifle, rather than inspire, actual debate between the candidates. "It's the two campaigns," said Tim Haley, campaign manager for Buchanan in 2000. "They try to sanitize the debates. These high-priced PR consultants making $10,000 a month don't want their candidates to look like a deer in the headlights. The more boring the debate is, the less of chance their guy is going to look bad."[43] In 1998, Walter Cronkite, former anchor of CBS News, wrote:

> The debates are part of the unconscionable fraud that our political campaigns have become. . . . Here is a means to present to the American people a rational exposition of the major issues that face the nation, and the alternate approaches to their solution. Yet the candidates participate only with the guarantee of a format that defies meaningful discourse. They should be charged with sabotaging the electoral process.[44]

Although there is no perfect format, a variety of simple changes can radically improve contemporary debate formats. Academics, pundits, civic leaders, and journalists recognize that permitting follow-up questions, increasing response times, prohibiting candidate selection of moderators, requiring candidates-to-candidate questioning, and employing a mixed array of formats would greatly enhance the quality of debate discourse. And there are a variety of formats available to debate sponsors willing to challenge participating candidates:

- **LOOSE SINGLE MODERATOR FORMAT:** A moderator merely introduces topics to spark discussion. The candidates may question each other, ask follow-up questions, and voice lengthy rebuttals.

This less structured format guarantees spontaneous conversation, where interruptions are possible and where the candidates, not their handlers, are responsible for content. The press has recommended a loose single moderator format for decades. In 1980, the *New York Times* editorialized, "Get rid of the clock and the fussy 'Time's up!' warnings; get the reporters out of the way. Keep it simple, flexible and open—a moderator, two chairs and maybe a coffee pot. Sparks should fly."[45]

- **TRADITIONAL COLLEGE DEBATE FORMAT:** A proposition is read, followed by opening statements and rebuttals concerning that proposition. This is a fitting format when a dominant policy issue is gripping the nation, such as the Vietnam War, but in more tranquil time periods, it may preclude discussion of other pressing topics.

- **MODIFIED LINCOLN-DOUGLAS FORMAT:** Professors David Birdsell and Kathleen Hall Jamieson support a modified return to the Lincoln-Douglas format—a series of eight-minute statements, six-minute rebuttals, and four-minute elaborations. Viewers would get an earful of substantive rhetoric, but partly at the expense of spontaneity.

- **AUTHENTIC TOWN HALL FORMAT:** An *authentic* town hall format prohibits the screening of questions, permits follow-up questions, and includes a representative sampling of Americans in the audience. This format minimizes the predictability of questions, and often addresses issues of concern to the electorate.

- **DIVERSE PANELIST FORMAT:** The traditional panelist format is employed, but with nonreporters, such as civic group leaders or students, asking most of the questions. Professor Sidney Kraus proposed this innovative version of the panelist format:

  If we must have panels of questioners, why must they be exclusively journalists and television personalities? Journalists are trained to ask questions, but they are not the only ones able to construct them. . . . Nonjournalists may bring a new and useful dimension to televised debates. Some historians, poets, novelists, and professors may add questions with perspectives more germane to the qualities of presidential leadership than some we have had in past debates.[46]

Staging

Major-party campaign officials consider seemingly minor staging details—such as backdrop and lighting—to be critical. "You will never persuade the negotiators that all of that is not determinative of the future of the Republic," said Bobby Burchfield, debate negotiator for the 1992 Bush campaign.[47] There are hundreds of staging details, the most important of which include audience composition, camera reaction shots, and, surprisingly, height of the podium. James A. Baker, former secretary of state and campaign manager, said:

> In 1988, when we were negotiating the debate arrangements with Dukakis, we got everything agreed to right down to the very end, and then they told us that they wanted to put a box, a little stand, underneath his, you know, where he would be. I said, "What? You want to put a box?" I said, "Your guy is running for president of the United States. What are you going to do when he meets with Gorbachev, bring out a little box for him to stand on so that he's eye level with Gorbachev?" And they couldn't respond to that. We finally let him have his box.[48]

Candidates have used staging details as effective visual tactics. In 1992, George H. Bush was caught looking impatiently at his watch during a town hall debate. It reinforced the notion, propagated by Democrats, that he "didn't care about the people." But it was no accident that Bush was captured on camera. Harry Thomason, senior media advisor to Clinton, explained, "We laid out the stage in a grid. We told Bill, 'Here is where the cameras will be. So if you will take 10 paces to this point, Perot will be over this shoulder and Bush will be over that shoulder.' We showed him where to go. And I mean he hit the marks exactly." Former President Bush described the hoopla created when he was caught looking at his watch, "They made a huge thing out of that. Now, was I glad when the damn thing was over? Yeah, and maybe that's why I was looking at it, only 10 more minutes of this crap."[49]

That same year, the Clinton debate team picked oversized stools for the candidates so that when diminutive Perot sat down, he looked ridiculous. "It was designed to make Perot look like a kid," said a Clinton aide. "And it worked."[50]

But to voters, most staging details are irrelevant. Who really cares what the color of the backdrop is? Who cares how high the podium is? The only staging detail that seems to upset the viewing public is the composition of the audience. Not only has the CPD invited corporate executives to the debates, but it has also allowed candidates to flood auditoriums with their supporters. The 1988 Memorandum of Understanding stipulated, "Each candidate shall have the first four rows for his personal use and succeeding rows will be made available for supporters of that particular candidate." For the 1988 vice-presidential debate, more than three hundred Democrats were flown in to raucously root for Lloyd Bentsen. "We told people when to cheer and when to applaud and when not to," said Thomas Donilon, a senior advisor to Michael Dukakis.[51] Professor Kathleen Jamieson called audience composition "a serious problem in debates" because the reaction of "audiences controlled by the candidates . . . mediate the reactions of the larger audience at home."[52] In 1996, the Dole campaign even put Bill Dale, the head of the White House Travel Office until he was fired amid allegations of financial misconduct, in the front row to fluster President Clinton.

Meanwhile, the press has been relegated to the back of the hall. The 1988, 1992, and 1996 Memoranda of Understanding stipulated, "Any press seated in the auditorium can only be accommodated in the two (2) rows of the auditorium farthest from the podiums." Nancy Neuman, former president of the League, called this demotion of the press a "detrimental First Amendment violation."[53]

Corporate executives and loud partisans didn't always get the prime seats at presidential debates. In 1980, the League wrestled with

"angry politicians" over the question of who got how many tickets.[54]
For each debate, the League distributed dozens of tickets to labor
organizations and civic groups, including the Urban League, the
National Association for the Advancement of Colored People, and
American Jewish Women.

One staging detail rarely discussed in the media and unknown to
the majority of voters is particularly appalling. Since the CPD began
sponsoring presidential debates in 1988, major-party campaigns
have required direct phone lines to the production office during the
debates. The danger is that campaigns may be able to manipulate
the topics discussed in a live debate. During the second 1988 debate,
for the first time in presidential debate history, there was a conversation between the moderator and the producer. Ed Fouhy, the CPD's
executive producer, asked Jim Lehrer, who was wearing an earpiece,
"When are you getting to foreign policy?" James Baker had used the
telephone line mandated in the Memorandum of Understanding to
contact Fouhy and complain about the exclusion of foreign policy
topics.[55]

Preparation

Major-party candidates spend an enormous amount of time preparing for presidential debates. They study massive briefing books put
together by campaign staff, lawyers, think tank scholars, and congressional aides. They study video footage of their opponent. They
learn where to stand, where to walk, and where to look. They undergo
a series of competitive rehearsals. Geraldine Ferraro explained her
preparation for a single vice-presidential debate in 1984:

> We spent a week going over questions and answers, try-
> ing to hone them down to where they were two-minute
> responses. And then spent a couple days at a hotel in
> New York again practicing and simulating the debate
> and standing at a lectern again being peppered with the
> questions from people who were playing moderator, and
> playing reporter and playing George Bush. And then we
> went into a studio and duplicated the whole thing.[56]

Candidates also manipulate predebate public expectations. Each campaign lavishes praise on its opponent in order to lower the threshold of victory for its own candidate. In 1992, Clinton called Bush "the most experienced debater since Abraham Lincoln." In 1996, John Buckley, Dole's communications director, called Clinton "the greatest debater since the days of the Roman Senate."[57] In 2000, Karl Rove, George W. Bush's campaign manager, said Gore was "the world's most preeminent debater." The Gore campaign joked that as a consequence of depressed expectations, "if he doesn't drool, Bush will be declared the winner."[58]

Most candidates should prepare for presidential debates. The significance of the events almost demands rigorous preparation. However, preparing for CPD-sponsored debates is like studying for a test after you've created the exam for the teacher. After dictating format, the major-party candidates spend weeks memorizing answers to predictable questions from the panelists they selected. Preparation has become a natural extension of format manipulation. "In modern politics, if you ever get a question that you didn't anticipate, somebody didn't do a very good job," said Scott Reed, Dole's campaign manager.[59] Former president George H. Bush described the preparation process:

> You prompt to get the answers ahead of time. Now this guy, you got Bernie Shaw on the panel and here's what he's probably gonna ask you. You got Leslie Stahl over here and she's known to go for this and that. I want to be sure I remember what Leslie's going to ask and get this answer, no, that answer's not quite concise and that's always—there's a certain artificiality to it, lack of spontaneity to it.[60]

Moreover, because formats are structured to eliminate spontaneity, candidates and their handlers spend preparation time inventing cute slogans that fit perfectly into sixty-second response slots. From Reagan's "there you go again" to Perot's "I'm all ears," debate punch lines circulated through the media are some of the few spoken words remembered by voters on Election Day. Professor Alan Schroeder, author of *Presidential Debates: Forty Years of High-Risk TV*, wrote, "The savvy debater does not wait for the high points to occur naturally; he manufactures them, polishes them, and finds a way to deploy them."[61] The finished product is a series of hollow sound bites.

This is not what the American people deserve. They deserve substantive discussion and unscripted confrontation. They deserve to understand the policies of the candidates for the most powerful office in the world. "The American people are the losers because the real issues never are aired by the candidates," said Congressman Ed Markey.[62] Former vice president Walter Mondale said, "I think the American people are looking for decency, for substance, for values. They're not looking for the slick answer."[63]

Perot's experience in 1992 confirms Mondale's hypothesis. While Bush and Clinton practiced emotional reaction shots, Perot was campaigning. He believed that preparing for the debates was a form of selling out—no more sincere than teleprompters and focus groups. He spent less than an hour preparing, and his refreshing "straight talk" during the debates virtually tripled his public support.[64] Professor Alan Schroeder wrote, "Perot's straightforward self-possession should serve as a model for other candidates, who too often approach debates like actors at a casting call, willing to twist themselves into pretzels in order to land the part."[65]

IN A CAMPAIGN era dominated by mass media and political consultants, candidates habitually deliver rehearsed slogans during stump speeches, news conferences, and interviews. The presidential debates are supposed to provide voters with an informative break from these canned answers. But the CPD ensures continued Republican-Democratic control and therefore continued packaging. Everything concerning the structure of the debates, even the color of timer lights on the podiums, is privately negotiated by Republican and Democratic officials. Except for its meager defense of the schedule, the CPD wholeheartedly endorses this major-party micromanagement; podiums are constructed, to the inch, according to Memoranda of Understanding.

5

The 15 Percent Fiction

I N 2 0 0 0, T H E CPD required candidates to reach 15 percent in predebate polls to receive an invitation to the presidential debates. The CPD announced that it will use the same criterion for the 2004 presidential debates.

At first glance, the 15 percent threshold seems fair. The clarity, transparency, and objectivity of the criterion are attractive. However, closer examination shows that the 15 percent threshold is the greatest obstacle to informative and democratic presidential debates.

Unnecessarily High

The CPD's primary defense of the criterion is, according to Janet Brown, that "over two hundred candidates run for president every four years. We can't let all of them onstage. We have to distinguish between serious and not-so-serious candidates."[1] Paul Kirk said, "Two hundred people file for the president of the United States. The question that the commission is left with is: Where do you draw the line?"[2] Kirk, Fahrenkopf, and Janet Brown present these figures to every reporter they encounter, and most pundits internalize them. In 2000, on *The Early Show*, Bryant Gumbel asked actor and Nader supporter Tim Robbins, "There are about two hundred people who are basically running for president. Should they all be allowed to debate?"[3] Deborah Mathis, columnist for the *Chicago Tribune*, depicted her conception of inclusive debates: "The nightmare scenario requires a few hundred lecterns, a few hundred microphones and shift changes for the moderators. And the only television air-time available for the big event is on a public access channel in Duluth. Not even C-Span will commit."[4]

Talking of two hundred candidates, however, is entirely misleading. Granted, numerous people file presidential candidacy forms with the FEC, and yes, many of them are, to use a favorite word of the major parties, "fringy." In 1996, candidates from 160 parties officially ran for president, including Frank Barela III of the People's Revolutionary Continental Army, Curtis Zar of the Committee to Ensure Curtis Zar as Pharaoh of the Federal Government, Jack B. El-Hai of Americans for a Hyphenated President, and Billy Joe Clegg of Clegg Won't Pull Your Leg for President. In 2000, 211 people officially ran for president, including Clay Hill of the Populist-Democratic Viking Party, Caesar Saint Augustine of the Get Even with the State-Federal and Local Level Committee, Freddy Irwin Sitnick of the Messiah for President Party, Jeff Costa of the Crustacean Liberation Party, and Mike of Mike's Party.

But to lump these candidates with the likes of Perot, Nader, and Buchanan is absurd. Only a handful of them were on enough state ballots to mathematically have a chance to capture the White House. In 1988 only two third-party candidates, in 1992 only three third-party candidates, in 1996 only four third-party candidates, and in 2000 only five third-party candidates were on enough state ballots to win an electoral college majority. How many third-party candidates were on the ballot in all fifty states and the District of Columbia? In 1988 only one third-party candidate, in 1992 only one third-party candidate, in 1996 only two third-party candidates, and in 2000 no third-party candidates were on all fifty state ballots. The *Las Vegas Review-Journal* editorialized:

> The commission itself is controlled by the major parties—and they obviously have no interest in advertising any alternatives to business as usual in Washington. Third party candidates must already navigate a maze of onerous and expensive requirements to appear on state ballots. A party that demonstrates it has the support and

organization to reach ballot status in most states deserves the opportunity to participate in the presidential debates. That condition alone would ensure the number of participants remains easily manageable.[5]

Political commentator George Will concurred:

> Debates should be open to any candidate with a mathematical chance to win the necessary electoral votes—any candidate who is on the ballots in states with a cumulative total of 270 electoral votes. Some people justify excluding from debates candidates not from the major parties in order to prevent "cacophony." But a high decibel level can betoken democratic vigor.[6]

A 15 percent threshold is entirely unnecessary to eliminate the bulk of candidates. It even contradicts the CPD's own history. During an interview in 2000, Fahrenkopf said, "We felt it was right for Perot to be included, and we still think it was right."[7] But in 1992, Perot was registering only 8 percent in predebate polls. When told that the 15 percent criteria would have excluded Perot in 1992, Fahrenkopf became flustered. "That's exactly right, it would have," Fahrenkopf said. "But it was he who attacked the criteria. You know, '92 was a weird year."[8]

If a 15 percent criterion was applied to all the presidential debates of the twentieth century, every third-party and independent candidate would have been excluded except for John B. Anderson. (Anderson was polling anywhere from 13 to 18 percent because of a twenty-year career as a respected Republican congressman and his participation in televised Republican primary debates.) Even a 10 percent criterion would have excluded every third-party and independent candidate except for Anderson. A 5 percent criterion applied to all previous presidential debates would have excluded every third-party and independent candidate except for Anderson and Perot. In fact, so formidable are the barriers to third-party voices; a 2 percent criterion applied to all previous presidential debates would have included only three third-party and independent candidates: Anderson in 1980, Perot in 1992 and 1996, and Ralph Nader in 2000. Richard Marin, pollster for the *Washington Post*, wrote, "The objection to the 15 percent cut point is exactly right. It's absurdly high."[9]

The CPD didn't establish the 15 percent threshold to prevent two hundred third-party candidates from participating in the debates. It established the 15 percent threshold to prevent the few popular third-party candidates on most state ballots from participating in the debates.

Excluding Potential

Six weeks before the 1998 gubernatorial election in Minnesota, the *Star Tribune* pegged Reform Party candidate Jesse Ventura at 10 percent in the polls. Three debates later, on October 20, he was at 21 percent. Remarkably, Ventura's cash-strapped campaign had not yet aired a single television advertisement. On Election Day, Ventura captured 37 percent of the vote and became the governor of Minnesota. Governor Ventura explained his astounding victory: "I was allowed to debate. I proved that you could go from 10 percent to 37 percent and win if you're allowed to debate. Rest assured these two parties don't want to ever see that happen again."[10]

Minnesota public radio and the Minnesota chapter of the League of Women Voters, which alternated sponsorship of the eight gubernatorial debates, insisted that Ventura be allowed to participate because he was on the ballot. Law professor Jamin Raskin described what happened next:

> The candidate who had been declared by the establishment, not serious, not viable, unelectable, proceeded to lay out a series of policy positions that were original and serious and substantive and he ended up defeating the Democrats and Republicans in the debates and going on to kind of wipe up the floor with them in the actual election itself. . . . Had Governor Ventura been excluded from the debates on grounds of viability, as Ross Perot was in 1996, not only would his political views and ideas have been suppressed, but he would have lost the elec-

tion. There's almost no doubt about that. That is if he had been declared nonviable, not having a serious chance of winning, he would have remained nonviable, and thus we see the perfectly tautological and self-fulfilling nature of the viability test.[11]

The CPD's criterion would have excluded Ventura. It requires candidates to prove their viability before the general public knows much about them. Congressman Jesse Jackson Jr. (D-IL) said that the 15 percent threshold "excludes non-major-party candidates on the basis of polls from a public who has not yet had an opportunity to hear from those candidates."[12] Alan Keyes, former Republican presidential candidate, said:

> We are right now faced with kind of a fiction in a lot of our politics. It is one that is promoted by the media and others, in which they do these phony polls and they come before the American people and say, see these are the ones who have support. Now it turns out that because of their censorship and the censorship of the process, a great many of the folks that are being polled aren't even aware of what the alternatives are.[13]

The CPD is essentially predicting, from premature and fluctuating poll numbers, who will *not* win the election, and is excluding those candidates. But aren't the voters, not the polling sample or the CPD, supposed to determine who will and will not win the election? "When I ran for governor, there wasn't one poll that said I would become the governor," said Ventura.[14] The CPD is usurping one of our most important public prerogatives: the ability to determine which candidates are "electable" by electing them. The CPD has no justification to intervene in election campaigns and preselect winners and losers; these predictions of defeat become self-fulfilling prophecies. In 1996, a CNN/*USA Today* poll found that 10 percent of adults "were less likely to vote for Perot" immediately after the decision by the CPD to exclude Perot from the debates. On a PBS program titled *Should Perot Debate?* Clarence Page of the *Chicago Tribune* said:

> Why do we keep trying to manipulate the outcomes of elections ahead of time? That's really what we get into here when we start trying to determine who's popular, who's viable, who's crazy, who isn't. This is a continuing question in this country. On the one hand, we give federal matching funds to Perot, but then we say, well, you're really too out of mainstream to be on the stage. We really ought to stop trying to manipulate history before it's happened.[15]

The experience of Ventura and Perot suggests that third-party candidates polling below 15 percent can surge in the polls if included in the debates, and possibly even win the election. In a country where the plurality of voters are independent, where routinely only half of the electorate votes, and where the two major parties are increasingly converging as their funding sources overlap, compelling third-party candidates allowed to fully participate may have "a realistic chance of victory."

Imagine a three-way race in which 37 percent of the voters support the Democratic nominee, 29 percent support the Republican, 14 percent support the third-party candidate, and 20 percent are undecided. Under the CPD's rules, the third-party candidate would be excluded. But if that third-party candidate could accomplish what Perot did as a result of the debates—increase his or her poll numbers by 285 percent—that third-party candidate would win the election. Or if that third-party candidate could accomplish what Ventura did as a result of the debates—increase his or her poll numbers by 270 percent—that third-party candidate would win the election.

Consequently, the CPD may be excluding would-be presidents from the debates. The *Portland Press Herald* editorialized that the 15 percent threshold meant:

> A third-party candidate could have the support of 28 million Americans of voting age, receive millions in public election financing and yet be denied the chance to debate his or her opponents. That would be an injustice, not only to the candidate, but to the independent-minded voters

who could be swayed by an articulate and persuasive third-nominee.[16]

Jesse Ventura called the CPD "just a clear case again of the two parties banding together to keep down the rise of a third party. It's a standard thing that has historically happened many, many times. I think the public should be outraged over this."[17]

Presidential debates are supposed to provide the public with information with which to choose a president. If the purpose of the debates is to inform the public, but the criterion for entry into the debates is a static measurement of predebate public opinion determined from little information, then the debates are not serving their purpose. The CPD's construction of the debates prevents the presentation of real debates, thereby institutionalizing the bipartisan status quo at the expense of voter education and participation. In 2000, Oliver North, former lieutenant colonel and talk show host, wrote:

> Given the appalling lack of engagement by Americans eligible to participate in our electoral process, the CPD should have paid more attention to their own mission, "to ensure that debates, as a permanent part of every general election, provide the best possible information to viewers and listeners." . . . Including Buchanan, Browne and Nader in the debates might or might not be in the best interest of the Republican and Democratic parties—and my advocating their inclusion won't endear me to most of my friends in the GOP. But if broadening participation in the debates increases public participation in our political process, that can only be good for America.[18]

Tax Dollars

The Constitution of the United States does not explicitly define a "legitimate" presidential candidate, other than that he or she must be a natural-born citizen, a resident for fourteen years, and at least thirty-five years of age. However, the federal government does distinguish between viable and nonviable *parties* by distributing matching funds. Once a party receives 5 percent of the popular vote, that party qualifies for millions of dollars in federal matching funds for the next election. This 5 percent threshold is the only figure written in legislation—and therefore the only figure established by elected representatives of the people—that sanctions the viability of nonmajor parties.

Consequently, setting the criterion at 15 percent in predebate polls raises the question: How is it that taxpayers can finance a candidate's campaign and yet not be able to see or hear him? Scott Reed, Dole's campaign manager, said, "Clearly the fact that you're getting federal matching funds and the fact that you're not allowed in the debates is a disconnect."[19] Indeed, in 1971, when debating the merits of what ultimately became the Federal Election Campaign Act, Senator Russell Long said that federal funds would allow voters to "help both parties as well as third parties. Then, *having heard the debates*, they can decide which candidate they think would be best for the nation's interest."[20] Mario Cuomo, former governor of New York, said, "Simple rule: If you're going to give them taxpayers' money on the theory that they're credible candidates, then you ought to let them participate."[21] Congressman John Lewis, a former CPD director, said, "I think it's pretty clear. If a candidate is receiving federal funds, then he should be invited to the debates. Why else are we giving him taxpayers' money?"[22]

Most scholars and activists who oppose the CPD's criterion have asked that the threshold be lowered to 5 percent. FEC Commissioner Scott Thomas said, "I think 5 percent might be the right threshold because it ties to the existing statute on public funding."[23] Mark Hertsgaard, host of *Spotlight*, asked, "Why should a rule devised by functionaries of the Democratic and Republican parties trump a standard endorsed by elected representatives of the people?"[24] Syndicated columnist Arianna Huffington criticized the 15 percent criterion:

> This is a particularly stringent test since it takes only 5 percent of the vote to qualify for public financing—and it all but ensures that the Democratic and Republican nominees won't have to share the national stage with any

pesky interlopers. Why not just skip the polling and hire armed guards to gun down any threat to the two-party domination of the debates instead?[25]

Taxpayers should have the opportunity to see the candidates they are financing in the presidential debates. In 2000, John McLaughlin, host of *The Mclaughlin Group*, said, "Our taxpayer money gives us a right to hear what Buchanan has to say." When asked whether the criterion should equal the 5 percent matching fund threshold, even CPD director Howard Buffett said, "You know what? I think that's a pretty valid argument."[26]

Will of the People

On *Larry King Live*, Larry King asked George W. Bush, "Nader and Buchanan, why aren't they in the debates? Should they be?" Bush replied, "I think the American people want to see Vice President Gore and me go toe-to-toe, that's what I think they want to see."[27]

On *Meet the Press*, Tim Russert asked Al Gore, "Would you want Mr. Nader and Pat Buchanan included in the presidential debates?" Gore replied, "I think that most people would like to see a set of one-on-one debates between Governor Bush and myself."[28] Bush and Gore were wrong.

On July 12, 2000, FOX News released a poll showing that 64 percent of registered voters wanted Ralph Nader and Pat Buchanan included in the presidential debates despite the CPD's criteria. Only 25 percent said that Nader and Buchanan should be excluded. The FOX News poll also found that 73 percent of registered voters believed the debates would be "more interesting" if Nader and Buchanan were allowed to participate.

These popular convictions were maintained even after the debates. A *Time*/CNN poll taken two days after the first 2000 presidential debate found that 54 percent of adults believed Nader should have been allowed to participate, and only 32 percent still opposed his inclusion.

In 1996, support for Perot's inclusion was overwhelming. An ABC News poll found that 65 percent of eligible voters wanted Perot in the 1996 debates, and a Harris poll found that 76 percent of adults wanted Perot in the debates.

The CPD is relying on polling data to reject third-party and independent candidates, but polling data show that a substantial majority of Americans want third-party and independent candidates in the debates. FEC Commissioner Scott Thomas said:

> I think it's very significant that a large segment of the population wants to see more candidates in the debates. I'm almost ashamed that our system has not opened arms to let these folks in and have an opportunity to present their views. If people in the Republican and Democratic parties have good ideas, they should be willing to state them and defend them.[29]

The CPD is simply posing the wrong polling question. If the CPD is going to rely on polling data, it could simply ask who the public wants in the debates. 2004 Democratic presidential candidate Al Sharpton wrote, "I support changing the question so that inclusion in the Presidential debates is determined by who the voters would like to see debate." Instead of trying to predict the "principal rivals" before having heard all the candidates' platforms, the American people would be determining which of the candidates on enough state ballots to win an electoral college majority possess sufficient appeal and leadership potential to present themselves to tens of millions of eligible voters. First Amendment attorney Harry Kresky explained:

> It's one thing to have a poll that says whom do you want in the debates. It really is manipulation to ask Americans who they want to become president and then use that to decide who's in the debate. It's kind of like asking people what you want for breakfast, and if a certain percentage say oatmeal, you're going to launch a first strike against Kosovo.[30]

CPD directors and major-party political operatives contemptuously reject determining candidate inclusion by asking the American people whom they want included in the presidential debates. "What does that question mean?" asked George Stephanopolous rhetorically. "I believe it means which television show do you want to watch. I don't think that's the best question to determine the participants of the most effective forum to decide the next president of the United States."[31] CPD spokesperson John Scardino said in all seriousness:

> That is a very different question. That question is, "What television program do you want to watch?" Sometimes democracy can be boring. Having a radical in the debates can be exciting. But sometimes the third-party candidate doesn't make sense. He talks about cold fusion or that aliens will land and destroy the world if you don't elect him. You have to have someone who is able to talk substantively and intelligently about the issues. That's why we don't ask that question.[32]

CPD director Alan Simpson said, "The issue is who do you want to be president. It's not who do you want to do a dress rehearsal and see who can be the cutest at the debate."[33] John Buckley, negotiator for the Dole campaign, said:

> If you ask that question, a majority of people might say, "Why not have fifty people in the debates?" But that would not be helpful for those who vote. It's not responsible to ask that question. . . . With that criteria you'll end up having talk show hosts and comedians getting equal rights as the major candidates, and someday, a mistake will be made and we'll end up like the Philippines, electing a matinee idol president.[34]

Paul Kirk said, "It's a matter of entertainment vs. the serious question of who would you prefer to be president of the United States. Otherwise you get into 'Wouldn't it be fun to have X,Y, Z?'"[35] Frank Fahrenkopf said, "We're not talking about putting on the most entertaining, funny debates."[36] Fred Malek, debate negotiator for Bush in 1992, said:

Debates are not entertainment. They are not soap operas. If we ask the American public, "Do you want to watch *Temptation Island* or would you rather watch the debates?" they may say *Temptation Island*. Does that mean we put on *Temptation Island* instead of the debates? It is fun to be entertained. But these are serious events for public discourse.[37]

Professor Diana Carlin, a member of the CPD's Advisory Committee, agreed, "People will say, 'I want this person in because they would make it more interesting, they would make it fun.'"[38] Professor Kenneth Thompson, a member of the Advisory Committee, said: "To simply ask who they want to have in the debate, they maybe haven't thought about it all. Where Nader's concerned, all they know is that they hate what he stood for recently or they love it, and they don't really know much about him."[39] Professor Richard Neustadt, chair of the Advisory Committee, said:

> By asking who would you like to see in a good television show is to change the intention of the debates. That does not sober people up. We may think they're both drags. Think about that. That's a very good television show. Good television is not appropriate. We need to sober voters up to the reality.[40]

CPD director Newton Minow irrationally lumped all third-party candidates together in a state of exclusion: "Well, let's say that happened. Let's include Nader. What would you do with the Libertarian candidate? I don't think that's fair. My basic point is that if you are going to have third parties, let's treat them equally. There are a hundred and six people who ran in 2000."[41] Scott Reed, Dole's campaign manager, said, "That's not, with all due respect, that's not a real polling question. Seventy-six percent want the sun to come out. Perot's crazy, everyone knows he's crazy. He would have been really disruptive. He was really disruptive to the campaign anyway."[42] Bob Teeter, President George H. Bush's campaign manager in 1992, said, "Americans will always say yes to this poll question. It's just an American value to include people. So what you get is a question that does not show the public has thought about the issues."[43]

These Republican and Democratic critics of the American people are not only remarkably condescending but also entirely wrong; voters can distinguish between presidential candidates, and they are intelligent enough to select credible debate participants. In 2000, a Zogby poll of 1,005 likely voters asked the following question: "I'm going to read you a list of presidential candidates. Please tell me if you believe each candidate should or should not be allowed to participate in the upcoming presidential debates with Democrat Al Gore and Republican George W. Bush":

> Green Party's Ralph Nader
> Reform Party's Pat Buchanan
> Natural Law Party's John Hagelin
> Libertarian Party's Harry Browne
> Constitution Party's Howard Phillips
> Socialist Party's David McReynolds

Sixty-one percent of likely voters said that Nader should be included in the presidential debates, and 29 percent said he should not. Fifty-nine percent said Buchanan should be included in the debates, and 34 percent said he should not. Forty-four percent said Harry Browne should be in the debates, and 40 percent said he should not. Thirty-eight percent said John Hagelin should be in the debates, and 42 percent said he should not. Thirty-eight percent said Howard Phillips should be in the debates, 42 percent said he should not. Thirty-five percent said David McReynolds should be in the debates, and 45 percent said he should not. Only two of the six third-party candidates in the poll—Nader and Buchanan—received support for inclusion from a majority of those polled. (Even a majority of Democrats and Republicans polled supported the inclusion of Nader and Buchanan.)

Moreover, support for including third-party candidates in the presidential debates doesn't merely stem from a desire to be entertained. It reflects a widespread demand for third-party candidates in general. A July 1999 Gallup poll found that 67 percent of adults nationwide support "having a third political party that would run candidates for president, Congress, and state offices against the Republican and Democratic candidates." Independents now constitute a plurality of eligible voters; about 40 percent of eligible voters are independent in preference, about 33 percent are Democratic, and about 27 percent are Republican.[44] Congressman John Lewis, a former CPD director who is now critical of the organization, said:

> I certainly wouldn't have a problem with having a criteria that asks the American people who they want in the debates. Because, in this country today, we have a huge block of independent voters who are not happy with the same two choices. They want new voices, and new candidates, and we should make sure they have the chance to hear from and see third-party and independent candidates. That's how a democracy works.[45]

American voters are increasingly disenchanted with the major parties. In 1960, 80 percent of the electorate considered themselves Democrats or Republicans, and over 62 percent of eligible voters cast a vote for Kennedy or Nixon. In 1996, however, only 60 percent of the electorate considered themselves Democrats or Republicans, and barely 44 percent of eligible voters cast a vote for Clinton or Dole. "I don't think it makes sense to even talk about the Republicans or the Democrats anymore," said Bill Kristol, former chief of staff to vice-president Quayle.[46] In fact, during every election for the past two decades, about half of the eligible voters chose not to vote at all. Anthony Mazzocchi, former legislative director of the Oil, Chemical, and Atomic Workers International Union and founder of the Labor Party, said, "You can't change a damn thing with the two major parties, and most people know that. So, most people don't vote. It's not because they're stupid. It's because they're smart."[47] Clarence Page, editorial writer for the *Chicago Tribune*, said:

> I think we've got to make some decisions in this country. Are we going to consecrate the two-party system, or are we truly going to give avenues for other parties to express themselves in a true national debate? . . . The

public has shown pretty lackadaisical support for both
the major-party candidates. I think it might reinvigorate
our elections in this country if we did let the Libertarians and Ralph Nader and Jesse Jackson and others get
on that stage.[48]

The public demand for third-party candidates is also evident in
television debate ratings. In 1992, when Perot was included, an average of 66.4 million Americans watched each of the three presidential debates. NBC News anchor Tom Brokaw said that Perot "made
everybody watch the debates."[49] In 1996, however, when Perot was
excluded, an average of only 41.2 million Americans watched the
presidential debates, a drop of 39 percent. In 2000, the *Washington
Post* editorialized that the inclusion of Nader and Buchanan would
likely "induce more people to tune in to the political process."[50]

The American people want third-party candidates included in
the presidential debates because they represent new choices, new
ideas, and new parties. They're tired of having to choose between two
increasingly similar and packaged candidates financed by the same
moneyed interests. Former congressman Tim Penny wrote, "Americans understand better than many elected and appointed officials
that campaigns for public office should serve to educate and expand
public dialogue, not to unnecessarily restrict debate among candidates."[51] Pat Buchanan summarized the conflict: "Should Frank Fahrenkopf and Paul Kirk tell the American people whom they may hear
in the critical presidential debates, or should the American people
decide that?"[52]

Third-Party Contributions

In 1826, the first national third-party sprang up in opposition to the
Masons, a powerful secret society devoted to "good works" and net-
working. Most of the Founding Fathers had been Masons, including
George Washington, and many members of the political establishment were part of the exclusive Masonic Order. Robert Remini, professor emeritus at the University of Illinois, said, "Unless you were

a Mason, you could not advance in law, you could not advance in business, you could not advance in anything."[53]

Americans resented this ultrapowerful rich man's club, and eventually something happened to fuel that resentment. William Morgan had a falling-out with his fellow Masons and threatened to reveal the secrets of the order. Morgan was arrested on trumped-up charges, and he disappeared the next day. Many believed he was taken from prison and drowned in the Niagara River. The presumed murder of Morgan enraged voters, and they immediately formed a political movement to get rid of all the Masons in public office.[54] The Anti-Mason Party held a nominating convention and selected William Wirth, a former Mason, as their presidential candidate. Although the Anti-Masons received only 8 percent of the vote and no longer existed by 1838, the party had a significant impact; membership in the Masonic Order plummeted from 100,000 to 40,000.[55]

Most third parties crumble. Only the Republican Party rose from a third party to become a major party. But fleeting third-party movements and losing third-party candidates have made remarkable social and political contributions. Popular third-party campaigns have raised critical issues first ignored and later co-opted by the major parties. Socialist Norman Thomas, a six-time presidential candidate, once said that he considered his "greatest accomplishment" to be the theft of his platform by the Democratic Party.[56] Central elements of Ross Perot's platform were also co-opted by the major parties. President Bill Clinton's economic policy largely rested on erasing the federal deficit, and the Republicans' Contract with America in 1994 echoed Perot's call for term limits, campaign finance reform, lobbying reform, and a balanced budget. In 2001, Russell Verney, senior advisor to Perot, said, "Today we have a balanced budget because of Ross Perot. Today we have campaign finance reform on the table because of Ross Perot. So, a third-party candidate doesn't have to win to win."[57] Historian John Hicks explained:

> Let a third party once demonstrate that votes are to be made by adopting a certain demand, then one or the other of the older parties can be trusted to absorb the new doctrine. Ultimately, if the demand has merit, it will

probably be translated into law or practice by the major party that has taken it up. . . . The chronic supporter of third-party tickets need not worry, therefore, when he is told, as he surely will be told, that he is "throwing away his vote." A glance through American history would seem to indicate that his kind of vote is after all probably the most powerful vote that has ever been cast.[58]

From the early labor parties of the 1830s, to the Free Soil Party of the 1850s, to the Prohibition Party of the 1890s, to the Bull Moose Party at the start of the twentieth century, to the Reform Party in the 1990s, third-party movements have forced policies and issues onto center stage and into mainstream political discourse. The result of these third-party campaigns has been the adoption of some of the most significant pieces of legislation in American history, such as the abolition of slavery, women's suffrage, the establishment of pensions, unemployment insurance, the minimum wage, Social Security, child labor laws, public schools, public power, the direct election of senators, the graduated income tax, paid vacation, the forty-hour workweek, higher civil service standards, the formation of labor unions, and democratic tools such as the initiative, the referendum, and the recall.

In many ways, however, the CPD nullifies the potential contributions of contemporary third parties; the 15 percent threshold excludes third-party candidates who promote cutting-edge policies supported by a public majority, and their platforms are more or less dismissed. Excluded third-party candidates can't break the bipartisan conspiracy of silence on issues where the major parties, possibly so as not to upset wealthy contributors, are at odds with most of the American people. In the modern era of mass media, televised debates set much of the boundaries of political discourse, and had there been exclusive televised presidential debates throughout American history, vital legislation—from Social Security to unemployment benefits—may have been permanently marginalized.

In 2000, opposition to "free trade" was virtually ignored as a consequence of third-party exclusion from the presidential debates. All five third-party candidates who were on enough state ballots to win an electoral college majority vigorously opposed the "free trade" agenda—NAFTA, the World Trade Organization, Permanent Normal Trade Relations with China, and other trade agreements. Although these five candidates—Ralph Nader, Pat Buchanan, Harry Browne, Howard Phillips, and John Hagelin— come from very different points on the political spectrum, they were unified in their conviction that "free trade" agreements transgress national sovereignty and hazardously subordinate health, environmental, and safety standards to the imperatives of commercial trade. "Let's have trade agreements that lift standards up toward our level," said Ralph Nader, "instead of allowing brutalized child labor to produce products with modern equipment and ship it to this country against our workers who are playing by the rules."[59] Pat Buchanan said:

> Ralph and I have been in this battle for almost six years since the great NAFTA fight. And we stand together firmly on one principle, that whatever the decisions about the economic destiny of Americans are, they will be made by the American people and not by the transnational corporations in collusion with this embryonic institution of world government.

A majority of the American people agreed with these third-party candidates. According to a November 1999 CNN/USA Today poll, 59 percent of adults nationwide believed free trade had mostly hurt American workers, and only 35 percent believed it had mostly helped American workers. Fifty-six percent believed it had mostly helped American companies. A February 2000 Pew Research Center poll found that 56 percent of adults opposed granting permanent trade status to China, and only 28 percent supported doing so.

However, because both Gore and Bush emphatically support "free trade" agreements and because third-party candidates were excluded from the 2000 presidential debates, the American public did not hear the issue discussed during the election. (See cartoon E.) In 2000, the *Washington Post* editorialized:

ADVOCATES FOR EXPANDING
FREE TRADE IN GOODS & SERVICES

ADVOCATES FOR EXPANDING
FREE TRADE IN IDEAS

CARTOON E

The best reason for inclusive debates is that minor candidates have a way of putting important issues on the table.
In 1992 Ross Perot advocated deficit reduction and trade
protectionism. The first idea was subsequently taken up
by both major parties; the second was attacked by both,
but Mr. Perot served the useful function of forcing Republicans and Democrats to sharpen their free-trade arguments. This year Mr. Buchanan and Mr. Nader would like
to give protectionist anti-globalization another airing,
and raise other issues too. Messrs. Bush and Gore should
take them on, not ignore them haughtily.[60]

The *San Jose Mercury News* concurred:

> Green Party candidate Ralph Nader deserves a place at the
> podium. . . . Nader expresses a loud and articulate voice
> of dissent from Republicans and Democrats on important
> issues that Texas Gov. George Bush and Vice President Al
> Gore are minimizing or ignoring, as they compete most
> feverishly for undecided moderate votes in mid-America.

Nader takes contrary positions on trade and the North American Free Trade Agreement, corporate "greed" and influence on politics, universal health care and the role of the Federal Reserve. (He'd sack Alan Greenspan if he could.) His stance on some of these issues is wrong, but he'd expand the political dialogue in expounding his views. And Nader's presence would guarantee that the debate would be lively, with more focus on substance than, for lack of disagreement, on style.[61]

Restricted debates leave Republicans and Democrats with an artificially skewed conception of voters' interests, which, ironically, undermines the major parties' appeal to the electorate. Without third-party voices, the major parties are less aware of public concerns and public opposition to some of their policies. Michael R. Beschloss, Annenberg Senior Fellow at Northwestern University, said, "Competition is healthy in all things. Third-party candidates in presidential debates will have the effect, ultimately, not of weakening the two-party system, but of strengthening it."[62]

Structural Barriers

Fahrenkopf and Kirk vigorously defend the 15 percent criterion by defining the presidential debates as the "finals" or the "Superbowl"— the concluding event after a series of accessible preliminary events designed to weed out unpopular candidates. On February 26, 2000, the CPD cochairs wrote an op-ed piece in the *Boston Herald*:

What schoolchild fails to understand that his or her team can't make the playoffs unless it wins enough games in season to be ranked a contender? Some teams make it. Others don't. It's that simple and that fair. It's why play-offs take place after competition narrows the field on the road to the championship. There is a parallel here to the general election debates sponsored by the nonpartisan and nonprofit Commission on Presidential Debates. A winnowing out process is one purpose of our long and expensive presidential campaigns. Well over a hundred candidates declare. Each has multiple opportunities to compete for popular support. . . . Toward the end of this process, voter opinion surveys reveal the principal contenders for the presidency. Some candidates make it. Others don't. It's that simple and that fair.[63]

Fahrenkopf and Kirk's perception of the electoral process preceding the presidential debates is inaccurate. Third-party candidates have no way of winning "enough games in season to be ranked a contender," and they don't have "multiple opportunities to compete for popular support." Throughout the predebate campaign trail, third-party candidates are systematically prevented from competing with major-party candidates on an even playing field. While the Democratic and Republican nominees are showered with money and media coverage, third-party candidates are kept off the screen and out of the minds of voters. James Pinkerton, former domestic policy advisor to President George H. Bush, wrote, "The structure of the U.S. electoral system is so stacked against third parties that the ideology that motivates them in the first place must take a back seat to process questions."[64]

Staggering structural barriers make it virtually impossible for an outsider to break 15 percent of the two-party grip over voting populations. Some of these structural barriers are a natural consequence of the electoral system:

1. HEREDITARY VOTERS

Because the major parties have dominated the political arena for so long, many families have developed deep emotional attachments to them, and these loyalties are passed on from generation to generation. Regardless of their platforms, third-party candidates confront millions of hereditary voters who will vote Democratic or Republican because their grandparents did.

2. WINNER-TAKE-ALL SYSTEM

The overwhelming majority of the world's democracies use a proportional representation system; if a party receives 5 percent of the vote, that party wins 5 percent of the seats in the legislative body. Every vote counts, every constituent has a voice in government, and victory can be defined in a number of ways. In contrast, the United States employs a winner-take-all system. Only one candidate can win a federal race, and all his or her opponents are officially losers. Theoretically, a party could win 49 percent of the vote in every House, Senate, and presidential election, yet end up without a single elected official in the entire federal government. Consequently, votes for candidates assured of defeat are routinely labeled "wasted votes," and on Election Day, many Americans choose the lesser of two evils rather than the candidate they would most like to see president. Only 57 percent of the voters who ranked John B. Anderson as their highest choice actually voted for him in 1980.[65] When a Harris poll asked eligible voters to "suppose Anderson had a real chance of winning" before soliciting their preference, the results gave Anderson 11 percentage points more than in the standard three-way question.[66]

Politicians and pundits criticize third-party challengers for "taking" votes away from one of the major-party candidates and for being "spoilers." In 2000, Nader's candidacy was severely attacked for its anticipated spoiler effect on Al Gore's campaign. Paul Begala, senior advisor to Gore, said on *Larry King Live*:

> There's a lot to admire in Ralph Nader. I admire him terrifically and the contributions he's made to our country. But if you vote for him, what you are voting for, be very clear, the reality will be that Jerry Falwell will be helping to pick the Supreme Court, that corporate polluters will be helping to run the Environmental Protection Agency, that the National Rifle Association will be writing our gun laws, that corporate lobbyists will be writing our campaign finance laws.[67]

The spoiler syndrome does have one benefit: it plainly reveals the hypocrisy of major-party campaign officials. During an online MSNBC forum held on March 15, 2000, a woman asked Paul Begala, "Should Buchanan debate despite the polls?" Begala answered, "Yes. Unless he's at zero or something. He brings a lot to the table. I disagree with Pat on nearly every issue, but he brings passion and eloquence and brainpower to his issues."[68] The same political operative who vociferously opposed Nader's inclusion in the presidential debates actually advocated Buchanan's inclusion. Begala knew that Buchanan would draw more votes from Bush than Gore.

OTHER MORE TANGIBLE structural barriers to third-party candidates were deliberately established by the major parties. "There are hurdles put into place by the state legislatures, which are dominated by Republicans and Democrats, that would make dictators in other countries blush," said Theresa D'Amato, Nader's campaign manager.[69]

3. BALLOT ACCESS

The United States has the most discriminatory ballot access laws of any democracy in the world. The number of signatures required for a party to get on the presidential ballot in California alone—about 150,000—exceeds the signature requirements a new party has to collect to get on the ballot in Canada, Australia, and all the European countries combined.

Before 1888, there were no ballot access requirements in the United States. You just signed up to run for office. After Teddy Roosevelt's Bull Moose Party captured 27 percent of the vote in 1912, Republicans made getting on the ballot more difficult for third-party candidates in a number of states. The relative success of Henry Wallace in 1948 and George Wallace in 1968 brought additional restrictions on third-party candidates. Now, new third-party candidates for president are required to obtain at least 701,089 petition signatures to be listed on the ballot in all fifty states and the District of Columbia. (Major-party candidates don't need to collect a single signature.) Dave Carney, National Field Director for the 1992 Bush/Quayle reelection campaign, said, "It's remarkable for a nonparty-structure person to get on 50 state ballots. Most people in the world don't understand how complicated it is."[70] During the last century, only ten non-major-party presidential candidates managed to get on all fifty state ballots.[71] Congressman Ron Paul (R-TX), who proposed legislation to establish fair ballot access standards, said:

Forty-two percent of the American people do not align themselves with a political party. Twenty-nine percent, approximately, align themselves with Republicans and Democrats. Yet, the rules and the laws are written by the major parties for the sole purpose of making it very expensive and very difficult, and sometimes impossible, to get on the ballot.[72]

4. FEDERAL FUNDS

In 1976, after the Watergate scandal, Congress amended the Federal Election Campaign Act to clean up the election process. The government began dispensing funds to presidential candidates to decrease their dependence on corporate, union, and special-interest contributions.

The presidential nominee of each major party—defined as a party that received at least 25 percent of the vote in the previous election—is eligible for a public grant of $20 million (in 1976 dollars) plus a cost-of-living adjustment. The presidential nominee of each minor party—defined as a party that received at least 5 percent of the vote in the previous election—is eligible for public funds based on the ratio of his party's vote in the preceding presidential election to the average vote for the major-party candidates. Since 1976, the program has provided nearly $1 billion to qualified presidential candidates and their nominating conventions.

Although somewhat fair and effective, this distribution of tax dollars undeniably helps institutionalize the two-party system. Nader didn't receive a penny from the government for the 2000 general election. Both Bush and Gore, however, accepted $67.5 million in federal funds.

5. CORPORATE SUPPORT

The business community supports the major parties, partly to influence lawmakers and partly to bolster candidates with pro-business policies. Multinational corporations and their executives express their support by contributing hundreds of millions of dollars to the major parties. According to the Center for Responsive Politics, when individual contributions, PAC contributions, and soft-money contributions are combined, the major parties collected over $1.2 billion from the business community for the 2000 election. This puts fledgling third parties, some of which spring up to counter major-party reliance on big business, at a clear disadvantage. Big business will not finance third-party candidates because they threaten a two-party system dependent on corporate cash, and many third-party candidates will not accept big business contributions in efforts to reform the system.

6. THE MEDIA

The overwhelming majority of third-party candidates are blacked out from mainstream media coverage. When was the last time you heard about Harry Browne or Howard Phillips on the nightly news? In 2000, only Ralph Nader and Pat Buchanan received noticeable coverage, and much of that coverage consisted of attacks on their candidacies.

The failure of the media to cover third-party candidates doesn't just stem from the candidates' lack of financial resources and low poll numbers. The commercial media provides pitiful coverage despite signs of grassroots enthusiasm. On July 30, 2000, the *Washington Post* ran a story titled "Gore, Family Taking It Easy in N.C.," but two and half months later, the paper chose not to run a story when fifteen thousand cheering New Yorkers filled Madison Square Garden to hear Ralph Nader. Gail Collins, one of the few columnists who has praised third-party challengers, wrote of a Nader rally, "The Republican and Democratic tickets probably could not get this kind of youthful turnout if they paid the audience."[73] Even David Broder of the *Washington Post* wrote, "Who's put on the best campaign? Who's made the most of his available resources and opportunities? I think the answer has to be Ralph Nader."[74] Nonetheless, Nader was largely ignored by the network news shows and the major newspapers. In the six months preceding the first 2000 presidential debate (April 2–October 2), the *New York Times*, the *Washington Post*, *USA Today*, and the *Wall Street Journal* published a total of 914 articles with Al Gore mentioned in the headline and a total of 852 articles with George W. Bush mentioned in the headline. The same four newspapers published only 45 articles with Nader in the headline and only 62 articles with Buchanan in the headline.[75] The lack of third-party coverage and a barrage of angry letters to the editor prompted the *Washington Post*'s ombudsman, E. R. Shipp, to write in September 2000:

> About a half-dozen articles might seriously be said to have looked at Nader as a candidate—and most of those were published around the time of the Green Party's nominating convention. Buchanan fared even less well, with four articles focusing on the candidate and his campaign, in addition to one column castigating him for his choice of running mate and another suggesting that his defection from the Republican Party had been "an unmitigated boon" to the Bush campaign. He also popped up in those television listings. By July 8, of course, regular readers of The Post, in print and online, knew a great deal more about Gore and Bush, as well as about Bill Bradley and John McCain, their unexpectedly strong but ultimately unsuccessful challengers. Those men had been the subject of hundreds of articles, editorials and columns, including lengthy biographical profiles that editors began assigning at the start of 1999.[76]

Pat Buchanan said, "I got more coverage when my latest book was published than I did when I was running for president."[77]

Moreover, the major newspapers, owned by political family dynasties ideologically committed to the major parties, print scathing editorial attacks on third-party candidates. In 2000, the *New York Times*, which endorsed Al Gore for president, ruthlessly assailed Ralph Nader. On June 30, the *Times* editorialized, "In running for president as the nominee of the Green Party, [Nader] is engaging in a self-indulgent exercise that will distract voters from the clear-cut choice represented by the major-party candidates.[78]

On October 26, the *Times* editorialized, "We would regard Mr. Nader's willful prankishness as a disservice to the electorate no matter whose campaign he was hurting. The country deserves a clear up-or-down vote between Mr. Bush and Mr. Gore, who have waged a hard, substantive and clean campaign." The editorial went on to call Nader's campaign "a wrecking-ball candidacy" and "an ego run amok."[79]

On November 3, the *Times* editorialized that Nader was spreading "a fallacious message" and that his campaign was "male chauvinism carried to a new extreme."[80]

On November 5, forty-eight hours before the election, the *Times* editorialized:

> Ralph Nader seems at this point to be beyond the reach of reason, but there is still time for his voters to consider whether they want to be enablers for a political narcissist. . . . It is an act of supreme arrogance for Mr. Nader to consign the country to bad policies for some imagined ideological payoff down the road. Our advice to Green Party voters confronted with Mr. Nader's effort to elect Mr. Bush is just say no.[81]

Russell Verney, campaign manager of Perot's 1996 campaign, said, "Editorial writers should be out blasting candidates who refuse to debate third-party candidates. We have, instead, editorial writers who are supportive of a particular partisan viewpoint."[82]

The television networks don't offer third-party candidates much hope either. The vast majority of television networks are owned by just a few multinational corporations, and this corporate ownership has sometimes led to the censoring of stories that decrease profit margins. According to a survey conducted by the Pew Research Center and the *Columbia Journalism Review*, 41 percent of reporters admit "that they have purposely avoided newsworthy stories or softened the tone of stories to benefit the interests of their news organizations."[83] One-half of all investigative journalists say "newsworthy stories are often or sometimes ignored because they conflict with a news organization's economic interests," and 61 percent of investigative journalists believe corporate owners "exert at least a fair amount of influence on decisions about which stories to cover."[84] Michael H. Jordan, then CEO of the CBS Corporation, said, "We are here to serve advertisers. That is our raison d'être."[85] Are AOL-TimeWarner (owner of CNN), Viacom (owner of CBS), Disney (owner of ABC), General

Electric (owner of NBC), or News Corporation (owner of FOX News) going to give third-party candidates, the most popular of which are vociferous critics of the corporate agenda, real media coverage? They don't want someone in the White House like Ralph Nader, who said, "What we own, the public airwaves, has been surrendered to myopic and avaricious corporations. It is time for a change."[86]

WHEN ACCUSED OF establishing overly restrictive criteria, Paul Kirk said, "Our role is not to jump-start your campaign and all of a sudden make you competitive."[87] Fahrenkopf put it another way, "The purpose of the general election presidential debates is not to provide a springboard for a relatively unknown candidate."[88] Newton Minow, vice-chairman of the CPD, said, "What third-party candidates and independent candidates usually want is an artificial boost."

Jump-start? Springboard? Artificial boost? Inviting popular third-party candidates to debate who have survived ballot access barriers, matching fund disparities, hereditary voting patterns, a winner-take-all system, and scant media coverage is not "jump-starting" a campaign. These qualified candidates deserve the opportunity to debate.

THE 15 PERCENT criterion is far higher than necessary, robs Americans of their voting prerogatives, may deprive would-be presidents of the chance to reach voters, disregards the allocation of tax dollars, nullifies potential legislative contributions from third parties, contravenes the wishes of the majority of Americans, and ignores structural barriers confronting third-party candidates. The 15 percent threshold undermines the democratic process, and it should be replaced with a screening mechanism designed to fulfill the aspirations of the electorate.

6

Issue Exclusion

CPD SPONSORSHIP HAS exacerbated the deterioration of presidential debate discourse. The range of disagreement in the debates is now minimal. When the CPD replaced the League of Women Voters in 1988, Bush and Dukakis agreed 11.50 percent of the time. In 1992, Perot's inclusion inspired a whole new world of rhetorical conflict, but in 1996, during the Clinton-Dole debates, the rate of agreement shot up to 27.50 percent. In 2000, Bush and Gore agreed a remarkable 37.30 percent of the time. "Where's the debate?" asked Michael Moore, author of *Dude, Where's My Country?*, "All that was missing—other than Ralph Nader—was, at the end, for Gore to go over there and plant one of those Tipper tongue-kisses on George Bush."[1]

During the second debate in 2000, the most agreeable presidential debate in history, Gore and Bush agreed: to spend more money on antiballistic missiles, on mandatory testing in schools, on training Colombian troops for the drug war, to make trigger locks available, that home owners have the right to own guns, to prevent gays from being allowed to marry, to sign a federal racial profiling law, to bail out Mexico with IMF loans, to maintain a "special" relationship with Israel, to not intervene in Rwanda . . .

At one point during the second debate, moderator Jim Lehrer asked, "Is there any difference?" Gore replied, "I haven't heard a big difference right in the last few exchanges."

"Well, I think it's hard to tell," said Bush. Later in the second debate, Bush remarked, "It seems like we're having a great love fest right now."

More important, fewer and less relevant issues are being addressed in the presidential debates. In 1976, the majority of debate discourse—defined as 50 percent or more of the words spoken by the debating candidates—focused on eight issues.[2] But in 2000, the majority of discourse focused on only five issues.

Issues discussed during presidential debates generally fall into four categories. There are *fundamental issues* confronted in almost every debate, issues such as tax plans, leadership experience, and health care. There are *transient issues* relevant only to particular time periods, such as Watergate in 1976, Reagan's age in 1984, the selection of Quayle as vice president in 1988, Saddam Hussein in 1992, and tobacco lawsuits in 1996. There are *systemic issues* that implicate the integrity of the democratic process itself, rather than a particular policy, such as the excessive influence of special interests over Congress in 1960, 1976, and 1992 and human rights in foreign policy in 1980 and 1984. There are *narrow issues* targeted toward very specific voting populations, issues such as farm subsidies in 1988 and prescription drugs in 2000.

With the exception of the 1992 debates, which included Perot, presidential debate content has increasingly consisted of *fundamental issues* and *narrow issues*, at the expense of *systemic issues* focused on the democratic process. Instead of speaking about topics that viscerally resonate with diverse voting populations, particularly issues dealing with the power structure in Washington and obstacles to democracy, major-party candidates delve deeper and deeper into the minutiae of tax cuts to find some degree of rhetorical difference.

In 1976, during the first and third presidential debates, the eight topics that constituted a majority of conversation were diverse in nature. About 13 percent of the two debates was devoted to unemployment and job growth; 7.1 percent to leadership experience; 6.6 percent to the size of government and federal bureaucracy; 6.5 percent to tax plans; 4.6 percent to corporate and special-interest tax breaks; 4.6 percent to the federal deficit and a balanced budget; 3.9 percent to the environment; and 3.9 percent to urban reconstruction. The unemployed, taxpayers, workers, critics of corporate influence over Washington,

CARTOON F

environmentalists, city dwellers, and poor minorities were all significantly addressed during the 1976 presidential debates.

In 1988, 9.3 percent of the two presidential debates was devoted to weapons spending, the military budget, and military readiness; 8.3 percent to illegal drug use and the drug war; 8.1 percent to poverty and homelessness; 7.4 percent to the federal deficit; 5.6 percent to abortion; 5.3 percent to health insurance, Medicare, and Medicaid; 4.7 percent to Social Security; and 4.7 percent to tax plans. These eight diverse issues primarily addressed voters concerned with military spending, drug users and parents, the poor and homeless, taxpayers, pro- and antiabortion advocates, Americans worried about health insurance, and senior citizens.

In 2000, during the first and third presidential debates, 14.5 percent of the discourse was devoted to education; 12.1 percent to tax cuts; 11.0 percent to leadership experience; 10.4 percent to prescription drugs under Medicare; and 9.0 percent to Social Security reform. These presidential debates only substantially addressed taxpayers, senior citizens, and voters concerned about education. Almost 20 percent of the two debates was devoted to prescription drugs and

Social Security—topics that resonate primarily with senior citizens. Ten percent of the debates was spent describing, in excruciating detail, exactly how each candidate would provide cheaper prescription drugs to senior citizens. In previous debates, broad, pioneering health care issues were discussed—from universal coverage to drug research—but in 2000, prescription drug coverage under Medicare ruled the health care "debate." With less to argue over, the candidates spoke to senior citizens in Florida who could make an electoral difference. Russell Verney, senior advisor to Perot in 1996, said:

> Because Ralph Nader and Pat Buchanan weren't allowed in, we essentially had a vigorous debate over pills. An incredible debate over pills. If you put another candidate in there that says, "Wait a minute, I need a pill just to listen to you pills," you're going to start discussing something other than what is aimed at a specific target voter in a specific state, and you're going to have to talk about the future of this country.[3] (See cartoon F.)

What about government waste? What about civil liberties? What about corporate crime? What about immigration? What about the trade deficit? What about the environment? What about the drug war? What about innovative industry? What about campaign finance reform? What about child poverty? What about unemployment? What about family farms? What about globalization? What about military spending? What about media concentration? What about urban renewal? These topics were either ignored or discussed less frequently than in the past, subordinated to battles over five issues. In 2000, the *San Francisco Chronicle* editorialized, "The presidential debates have allowed only perfunctory discussion of vital questions that face the United States, now the only superpower and major architect of globalization."[4]

That these other topics were largely ignored is not reflective of their being less significant to the electorate. On the contrary, about one in five American children is living in poverty, military spending is rapidly growing despite the end of the cold war, global warming is of international concern, the annual trade deficit has reached

$500 billion, affirmative action programs have been curtailed in a number of states, and as a consequence of crime, sprawl, and the underfunding of housing and education programs, many cities are in the worst shape since the 1970s. After the first presidential debate in 2000, the *Washington Post* editorialized:

> The first presidential debate laid out the terrain on which the main candidates will fight: taxes, health care, Social Security, abortion, humanitarian intervention. There are other issues that don't get mentioned because the two candidates sensibly agree: Both favor free trade, the independence of the Federal Reserve and engagement with allies. But there is a third category that is ignored for lack of courage to confront hard issues, such as gun control or capital punishment. The problem of poverty, along with the sometime related question of drugs, incarceration and race, also deserves more attention than it draws from any of the candidates, with the exception of Ralph Nader. America's poverty rate is roughly twice as high as that of other industrialized nations, and in many respects the government's response is inadequate or counterproductive.[5]

The spectrum of debate discourse has actually shifted in the opposite direction of real-life trends. Despite growing poverty over the last two decades, discussion of poverty and/or unemployment made up 13 percent of debate discourse in 1976, 3.2 percent in 1984, 8.1 percent in 1988, 0 percent in 1992, 0 percent in 1996, 0 percent in 2000. Despite the deterioration of many cities over the last two decades, discussion of urban revitalization plans constituted 3.9 percent of debate conversation in 1976, 0.7 percent in 1984, 3.5 percent in 1988, 1.3 percent in 1992, 0 percent in 1996, 0 percent in 2000.

Even discussion of the five dominant issues in 2000 occurred in a larger context of agreement. The candidates passionately agreed on the need to distribute prescription drugs to seniors under Medicare. The candidates agreed on increasing federal education spending as well as establishing testing standards. They agreed that Social Security needs serious reform. They agreed that taxpayers deserved a significant tax cut. Instead of a real debate over a wide range of issues, the candidates engaged in a vigorous conversation over how they would achieve four shared policy goals.

Major Party Convergence

The CPD cannot be held principally responsible for the narrowing of debate discourse. Two broad political shifts have taken place within the two-party system over the last twenty-five years—a convergence toward the ideological "center" and a convergence toward money. The Republican and Democratic parties have increasingly focused on winning over centrist voters, particularly in swing states, who are undecided at the onset of the election season. As a result, the major parties have taken their base constituencies—liberals and conservatives, traditional minorities and devout Christians—for granted. This has also produced a lackluster, redundant focus on "centrist" issues—taxes, education, Social Security, and so on. To many voters, the major parties have shed their ideological distinctions. Karl Rove, chief political advisor to President George W. Bush, said, "There are differences between the two American parties, but the differences are increasingly seen by the American people about issues that are no longer relevant to them."[6] Henry McMaster, South Carolina Republican state chair, told eight hundred high school seniors in the city of Charleston, "Democrats are for beer and girls. Republicans are for cold beer and hot girls."[7]

The two parties are also becoming less distinguishable as their funding sources increasingly overlap. The explosion of television in the latter half of the twentieth century convinced candidates to propagate their message through paid television commercials. This phenomenon made the major parties dependent on networks of fundraisers, rather than grassroots organizers. When Congressman Lee Hamilton announced his intention not to seek reelection in 1997 after serving thirty-four years in Congress, he said, "My colleagues talk about money constantly. The conversation today among members of Congress is so frequently on the topic of money: money, money, money and the money chase. Gosh, I don't think I ever heard it when I first came here." The money has primarily come from the bastions

of wealth and capital—multinational corporations and their executives. In 2000, the *Christian Science Monitor* editorialized:

> The media are covering politics less, forcing candidates
> to rely on TV ads more. And the cost of buying more
> ads has pushed the two major parties to become more
> beholden to well-heeled donors, be they corporations
> or rich individuals. A pre-election debate that brings in
> a wider range of views can only strengthen the vibrant
> dialogue that's needed to inform voters.[8]

According to the Center for Responsive Politics, when individual
contributions, PAC contributions, and soft-money contributions
are combined, $514,492,491 of the $722,256,129 donated to Democrats for the 2000 election came from businesses—a whopping 71.23
percent. (Labor donations to the Democrats—$84,836,563—made
up only 11.75 percent of the financial contributions.) Republicans
were only slightly more dependent on corporate cash; $705,918,973
of the $896,519,634 raised by Republicans came from businesses—
78.74 percent. In sum, 75.28 percent of the $1,634,288,415 donated
to the major parties for the 2000 election came from businesses.
"We have devolved from a representative democracy to a corporate
democracy in this country," said Democratic Senator Russ Feingold.[9] George Stephanopolous, former senior advisor to President
Clinton, lamented, "I think one of the sad developments of the
last twenty years has been the Democratic Party becoming part of
the system to compete more for money to stay competitive, and it
made them more beholden, I think, on the whole than they used to
be to big-time corporate interests."[10]

As a result, the Republican and Democratic parties have shifted
so heavily in favor of multinational corporations that the political
spectrum has been partially redefined so as not to seriously threaten
corporate profits. Today, where one stands on the political spectrum,
from left to right, has less to do with one's position on corporate power
issues than one's position on gay marriage. Pat Caddell, former Democratic pollster for President Jimmy Carter, said, "We have a pro-life
corporate party and a pro-choice corporate party, and therefore we

will debate over this issue that really is not on the table, while every other crime is committed in our names."

The CPD's Role

The CPD, of course, is not directly responsible for the convergence of the major parties, which has helped produce shallow debates. However, the CPD is directly responsible for two debate-numbing procedures: (1) excluding third-party candidates and (2) awarding major-party candidates absolute control over format.

The CPD's exclusion of third-party candidates furthers convergence within the two-party system. In shifting toward the ideological center and ignoring some of their traditional supporters, the major parties have created ripe constituencies for third parties to tap into. And by welcoming corporate contributions, the Republican and Democratic Parties have alienated many voters, both liberal and conservative, who believe that money has corrupted the federal government and that corporations have too much power. A September 2000 *Business-Week* poll found that 72 percent of Americans believe business has "too much power over too many aspects of their lives," and 74 percent believe big companies have "too much political influence."

Diverse third-party candidates have emerged to attract steadfast liberals and conservatives and to draw on the widespread frustration with corporate malfeasance. The *Washington Post* editorialized that Nader and Buchanan's "candidacies respond to a widely shared sense that established politics is oddly narrow. Both Republicans and Democrats have united behind sons of political families who rely on overlapping cliques of wealthy donors: It would be amazing if anti-establishment sentiment failed to rear its head somewhere." Buchanan said on CNN:

> We have two establishments in Washington, very powerful. Mr. Bush's establishment raised $67 million for him in his first four months. What they do, these two powerful establishments, both funded by the same corporations and the same lobbyists, they pick two individuals. We've got one from St. Albans and one from Phillips Andover,

one from Harvard and one from Yale, one who's dad's a president, the other's dad's a senator. And they say, these are the choices the American people have.[11]

The CPD, however, makes sure that third-party candidates never have a chance to reach disaffected voters. By silencing third-party challengers, the CPD allows the major-party candidates to ignore their respective left- and right-wing bases and to raise corporate contributions without paying a substantial political price. Disaffected voters have nowhere else to go. They can only vote for the better of the two major-party candidates, if they insist on voting for a candidate with a chance of victory. The existence of the CPD permits the major parties to *freely* shift away from their liberal and conservative voters and to freely embrace corporate contributions. Had third-party candidates been allowed to participate in the 2000 presidential debates, they would have made chasing after both corporate cash and the ideological center less attractive to the major parties.

More important, the CPD prevents third-party candidates from contributing viewpoints and policies to the debates themselves. In 2000, third-party candidates fervently disagreed with Gore and Bush, even concerning the selection of debate topics. Before the presidential debates, Nader listed critical subject matters he correctly predicted Gore and Bush would entirely avoid:

> Corporate welfare giveaways that could be better used to provide for human needs; weak enforcement against corporate crime, fraud and abuse; restrictive labor laws that are keeping tens of millions of low-wage workers from forming trade unions; media concentration; racism; renewable energy; full public funding of election campaigns; universal, accessible health insurance for all Americans; and the renegotiation of global trade treaties with labor, environmental and consumer rights standards that pull communities up rather than pushing them down.[12]

David Broder of the *Washington Post* called Libertarian presidential candidate Harry Browne "articulate and quick-witted" and wrote that "there'd be some value in having 100 million Americans hear him ask what he says is the key question: 'Would you be willing to give up your favorite government program if you didn't have to pay any income tax the rest of your life?'"[13]

Assuming that effective presidential debates should highlight the candidates' differences on a variety of salient issues, third-party candidates let onstage have significantly enhanced debate quality. In 1992, Perot created disagreement over almost every topic by providing different answers than Bush and Clinton. From controversial assertions that Bush green-lighted Saddam Hussein's invasion of Kuwait to criticisms of government inefficiency to somewhat innovative education reform ideas, Perot communicated a unique third voice in the presidential debates that appealed to disaffected voters. During the first 1992 debate, when Bush and Clinton suggested that he lacked political experience, Perot said:

> Well, they've got a point. I don't have any experience in running up a $4 trillion debt. I don't have any experience in gridlocking government, where nobody takes responsibility for anything and everybody blames everybody else. I don't have any experience in creating the worst public school system in the industrialized world; the most violent, crime-ridden society in the industrialized world. But I do have a lot of experience in getting things done.

The majority of debate discourse in 1992 consisted of nine issues, exceeding the presidential debate average of 7.4 issues.[14] These issues received virtually equivalent amounts of time, suggesting that Perot's inclusion prevented the dominance of a few benign issues. Seven percent of the first and third 1992 presidential debates was devoted to discussion of leadership experience; 6.8 percent to the loss of manufacturing jobs as a result of trade agreements; 6.4 percent to the federal deficit; 6.1 percent to the influence of special interests, through lobbyists and PAC contributions, over the federal government; 5.9 percent to tax plans; 5.6 percent to health care coverage and Medicaid; 5.4 percent to stimulating the economy and job growth;

5.4 percent to education; and 4.0 percent to the invasion of Iraq and Saddam Hussein. Perot pushed discussion of the federal deficit, the hazardous influence of special interests, and the loss of manufacturing jobs due to trade agreements onto center stage. He addressed two systemic issues that only Jimmy Carter had the courage to discuss in a presidential debate sixteen years earlier: the failure of the democratic process itself and the negative impact of growing corporate influence over Washington.

Perot also introduced new issues in the 1992 presidential debates: the gas tax, American support for criminal dictators such as Manuel Noriega, the conversion of defense industries into civilian industries, the Savings and Loan scandal, urban revitalization plans for deteriorating cities, and the destruction of the airline industry through megamergers.

Because of Perot's inclusion, a total of forty-two issues were discussed, substantially more than the thirty-issue average.[15] These issues reverberated with the American electorate, and Perot's poll numbers jumped from 7 to 19 percent in one week. He was not targeting Florida's retirement homes; he was speaking to every potential American voter, particularly the plurality of independent voters, nonvoters, and alienated voters. As a result, according to Andrew Kohut, director of the Times Mirror Center, the 1992 debates "spurred more interest among voting groups who usually don't participate at very high rates: young adults, minorities, members of lower socioeconomic groups."[16]

In 1980, John B. Anderson also introduced new issues in the only general election presidential debate in which he participated. Anderson advocated pumping several billion dollars, which would come from excise taxes on alcohol and tobacco, into rundown cities in order to provide jobs, affordable housing, and essential services. He ridiculed the mobile missile program, which was supported by both Carter and Reagan, as a "costly boondoggle." He advocated a fifty-cent-a-gallon tax on gasoline to promote conservation, finance mass transit systems, increase usage of renewable energy sources, and decrease the dependence on oil imports. (Although separated by twelve years, both Anderson and Perot introduced the gas tax and made bloated military spending and urban revitalization plans debate priorities.) All three issues were ignored or superficially mentioned in the ensuing 1980 Reagan-Carter debate.

An NBC News poll found that 38 percent of likely voters named Anderson the winner of the debate, compared with 35 percent who judged Reagan the winner.[17] The day after the Reagan-Anderson debate, the *New York Times* editorialized:

> To protect taxpayers against "bracket creep," Mr. Anderson would index tax rates. He would help rebuild the military by encouraging "lateral entry"—hiring experts from civilian life. He calls for a form of two-tier minimum wage, to help ghetto youth find jobs. And he proposes relief for crumbling cities in the form of an urban reinvestment trust fund, to rebuild streets, bridges, sewers and water mains. . . . Right or wrong, issues like that is what Presidential debates are supposed to be about.[18]

Two weeks later, the *Times* editorialized in support of Anderson's inclusion in the second presidential debate, "It seemed important to include Mr. Anderson in the first debate for reasons of fairness; now it seems important to include him to enhance the quality of the argument."[19]

Had the CPD invited Perot to the 1996 presidential debates or Nader and Buchanan to the 2000 presidential debates, it would have improved the quality and relevancy of debate discourse. In 1996, Philip Gailey, columnist for the *St. Petersburg Times*, wrote, "Without Perot and Choate in the ring, the voters wouldn't hear much about big-money lobbyists and Washington's money-driven political culture, which both Clinton and Dole are reluctant to disturb."[20] In 2000, Lance Morrow of *Time* magazine wrote that Nader and Buchanan "would bring authenticity, a depth and passion of thought, to what will otherwise be dimensionless debates."[21]

The CPD also undermines debate quality by allowing the candidates to dictate the format. The major-party campaigns select middle-of-the-road panelists and moderators who rarely question the status quo. They ask about "increasing the GDP" rather than unemployment or the distribution of wealth. They ask about prescription drugs under

Medicare, not about universal health care or medical malpractice lawsuits. They ask about the entertainment industry, not about the lack of airtime for candidates or the giveaway of the $70 billion digital spectrum. They ask about tax cuts, not about tax loopholes for special interests or tax credits for poor families. They ask about drilling for oil in Alaska, not about mass-transit systems or solar energy. They ask about social welfare, not corporate welfare. According to focus group studies conducted by Professor Diana Carlin during the 1992 and 1996 presidential debates, most viewers were "disappointed in the questions asked" and "annoyed with the redundancy" of the candidates' responses.[22] During CPD-sponsored debates, not a single question has ever been posed concerning the viability of the two-party system or excessive corporate power. Jeff Milchen, executive director of ReclaimDemocracy,org, described the 2000 presidential debates:

> In a country where corporations are the dominant political and economic force, why did three debates pass without the word "corporation" being spoken? The World Trade Organization, "free trade," and labor also were omitted. How can so many issues of vital interest to Americans freely be ignored while Slobodan Milosevic is cited 17 times? Answer: because the two dominant parties own and operate the debates.[23]

The following six questions that should have been asked during the 2000 presidential debates were selected from a list written by Morton Mintz, a former *Washington Post* reporter, former chairman of the Fund for Investigative Journalism, and author of four books, including *America Inc.: Who Owns and Operates the United States*. CBS News anchor Dan Rather called the first 2000 presidential debate "pedantic, dull, unimaginative, lackluster, humdrum, you pick the word"—which is why the audience was smaller for the second debate and even smaller for the third. These questions would have made it far more interesting:

1. We maintain an arsenal of 7,500 strategic nuclear warheads. Each has twenty times the destructive power of the atom bomb that

leveled Hiroshima. If we had just 1,000—at a savings of billions of dollars, would you say we would no longer have an adequate deterrent for any nation contemplating use of weapons of mass destruction?

2. After a decade of unparalleled prosperity, 13.5 million children— one in every five—are hungry; and three out of four of the hungry children have parents who work. What would you do about this?

3. Do you support capital punishment for corporate executives who knowingly and willfully market tires, motor vehicles, medical devices, and other products with defects that they know will kill people?

4. Some people earning $30,000 a year pay a bigger share of their income in taxes—federal, state, and local income taxes, plus Social Security—than do some people who earn $30 million, or one thousand times as much. What would you do about this?

5. The *American Heritage Dictionary of the English Language* defines a bribe as "something, such as money or a favor, offered to or given to a person in a position of trust to influence that person's views or conduct." Special interests give tens of millions of dollars to people who hold or seek "a position of trust," including the presidency and vice presidency, whose "views or conduct" they seek to influence. Have the campaign-finance laws effectively legalized bribery?

6. Forty-three million Americans have no health insurance and millions more have policies with big holes in coverage. Every industrialized country except the United States has had universal health care for decades. Should we?

In recent presidential debate history, the only stretches of spontaneous discourse materialized during the 1992 town hall debates, which took place *before* the candidates required the screening of audience questions and banned follow-up questions from similar events. Absent these restrictions in 1992, town hall questioners introduced several issues that were never really discussed in the two single moderator debates: term limits, public works, negative campaigning, minorities in politics, and pension funds. The 1992 town hall format also revealed the extent of Perot's substantive appeal; in that debate, his three central issues—the influence of special interests over government, the loss of manufacturing jobs due to trade agreements, and the federal deficit—were discussed more often than in the two single moderator debates. Through privately drafted Memoranda of Understanding, however, major party candidates have made sure that such deviation from "traditional" subject matters hasn't happened again.

SOME APOLOGISTS FOR the CPD argue that broad political discourse is of little interest to the American electorate—that is to say, low viewership can be attributed to an indifferent citizenry rather than superficial debates. But polls and examples prove otherwise. In 1994, a Boston television station (WBC-TV), a Boston radio station (WBUR), and the *Boston Globe* sponsored debates between Senator Edward Kennedy and Republican challenger Mitt Romney during a midterm election. The three media sponsors surveyed citizens to discern their key concerns and recruited an intelligent citizens' panel to set the agenda for the debate. Although Senator Kennedy was leading the race by eighteen points, the debates attracted higher ratings than the O. J. Simpson car chase or the Superbowl.[24] Columnist Mary McGrory wrote, "The first debate between Sen. Edward M. Kennedy and Mitt Romney was more like a prize fight, with a million people tuning in. Opinions differ as to who won, but there is no question that the white-hot hour in Faneuil Hall was terrific theater worthy of the most political city in the Republic."[25] If three local media outlets can use citizen participation to shape a congressional debate that attracts a massive audience during an uncompetitive midterm election, a presidential debate sponsor absent the shackles of the two major parties could electrify the country.

7

Failed Restitution

I T'S TIME TO fix the presidential debate process. The CPD
deprives voters of full choice and robust debate. However, the
channels through which the presidential debate process must be
reformed are almost as compromised and biased in favor of the two-
party system as the presidential debate process itself.

Internal Revenue Service

The CPD is a 501(c)3 tax-exempt organization, and contributions to
the CPD are tax-deductible. To maintain its tax-exempt status, the
CPD must comply with Internal Revenue Service (IRS) regulations,
which prohibit "political activity" that "consists of participating in, or
intervening in, any political campaign on behalf of (or in opposition
to) any candidate for public office."[1] The IRS broadly defines prohibited
political activity to include "certain expenditures by organizations
that are formed primarily to promote the candidacy (or prospective
candidacy) of an individual for public office and by organizations
that are effectively controlled by a candidate and are used primarily
to promote that candidate."[2] With respect to candidate debates, the
IRS stipulates: "Organizations may sponsor debates or forums to
educate voters. But if the forum or debate shows a preference for or
against a certain candidate, it becomes a prohibited activity."

The CPD violates the spirit, if not the letter, of these IRS restrictions. The CPD "shows a preference for" Republican and Democratic

candidates and "a preference against" all third-party candidates. The CPD is "effectively controlled by" the Republican and Democratic candidates, who dictate the terms of debate. Congressman Tim Penny called the CPD "an outgrowth of the two parties."[3]

The CPD ostensibly operates for the purpose of "voter education," although IRS regulations provide that "*nonpartisan* voter education and participation activities must show no preference for or against a candidate or party." The CPD, however, is *bipartisan,* not nonpartisan, and its "voter education" activities overtly favor major-party candidates at the expense of third-party candidacies.

The IRS is responsible for investigating violators of IRS regulations. But rather than investigate the CPD, the IRS seems to have internalized the CPD's propaganda and logic. In an IRS training manual published annually for auditors, IRS attorneys Judith E. Kindell and John Francis Reilly wrote:

> Many times, the number of legally qualified candidates for a particular office is so large that an IRC 501(c)3 organization may determine that holding a debate to which all legally qualified candidates were invited would be impractical and would not further the educational purposes of the organization. For example, in 1996, more than 280 people declared themselves to be candidates for the office of President, while for the 2000 election, over 250 people declared themselves to be candidates for the Presidency.

(In 1996 only six candidates, and in 2000 only seven candidates were on enough state ballots to win an electoral college majority.)

Federal Election Commission

FEC regulations prohibit corporations from contributing to debate sponsors unless the sponsors "use preestablished objective criteria" and can "show that their objective criteria were used to pick the participants, and that the criteria were not designed to result in the selection of certain pre-chosen participants." The FEC also provides that it is unlawful for any candidate to "knowingly . . . accept or receive" corporate contributions.

In 1988, 1992, and 1996, the CPD did not use "preestablished objective criteria," but merely a laundry list of subjective indicators.[4] Mickey Kantor, Clinton's campaign manager, said, "You should only use objective criteria, of course, which the commission didn't do. They used subjective criteria."[5] Even Professor Neustadt, chair of the Advisory Committee, admitted that a "realistic chance of election" is a "a standard for the future, and to that extent it is by nature subjective."[6]

Moreover, at times, the CPD didn't rely on criteria to select the debate participants. In 1992, Bush and Clinton agreed to include Ross Perot and exclude all other third-party challengers. In 1996, Dole and Clinton agreed to exclude all third-party challengers, including Perot. The major-party candidates knew that they would be determining, through secret debate negotiations, exactly who would and wouldn't be participating in the debates. And they issued those instructions to the CPD in the form of Memoranda of Understanding.

In 1996, immediately after the CPD announced his exclusion from the debates, Perot filed a complaint with the FEC. Eighteen months later, the general counsel of the FEC, Lawrence Noble, responded with a powerful thirty-seven-page report claiming that there was "reason to believe" that corporate contributions to the CPD were illegal.[7] Noble contended that the CPD's criteria for third-party inclusion were subjective, rather than "preestablished objective." He wrote, "Some of the factors appear to be subjective on their face and other factors are so vague as to be imprecise in their definition."[8]

Furthermore, Noble expressed suspicion that the criteria were not applied at all: "The role played by Clinton/Gore and Dole/Kemp in CPD's debate participant selection process and the role played by the DNC and the RNC in the creation of CPD suggest that CPD's major purpose may be to facilitate the election of either of the major party's candidates for president."[9] Noble accused the Clinton and Dole campaigns of "violating 2 U.S.C section 441b(a) by knowingly accepting a prohibited corporate contribution from CPD."[10] During an interview, Noble explained, "The bottom line for me was that this looked like it was a negotiation between the two major parties and their campaigns, and they really weren't using the criteria."[11]

Noble proposed a thorough investigation to determine exactly what took place between Clinton, Dole, and the CPD that resulted in Perot's exclusion. However, when Noble submitted his report, the FEC commissioners voted unanimously to override his recommendation, stating, "The pool of experts used by CPD consisted of top-level academics and other professionals experienced in evaluating and assessing political candidates. By basing its evaluation of candidates upon the judgment of these experts, CPD took an objective approach in determining candidate viability."[12]

In response to Noble's contention that major-party candidates were issued automatic invitations to the debates, the FEC commissioners wrote, "The CPD flatly denies it based its decision on this factor alone." The FEC commissioners also hurriedly dismissed Noble's central accusation—that the criteria are irrelevant because the major-party candidates decide everything: "There certainly is no credible evidence to suggest the CPD acted upon the instructions of the two campaigns to exclude Mr. Perot. To the contrary, it appears one of the campaigns wanted *to include* Mr. Perot in the debates."[13]

The FEC commissioners rejected a request to investigate whether the CPD was connected to the Republican and Democratic parties on the specious ground that there was not sufficient evidence of a connection. A thorough FEC investigation would have confirmed all of Noble's accusations.

Why did the FEC so readily discard the general counsel's report? The FEC is governed by six commissioners, who are appointed for six-year terms by the president and confirmed by the Senate. *U.S. News and World Report* reported, "That means the commissioners owe their $115,700-a-year jobs to party machinery."[14] One Senate staffer said, "You get political payoffs, and so you get lower-quality people. Some of [the commissioners] don't believe in the law they're supposed to be enforcing."[15]

No more than three FEC commissioners can belong to one party, so three seats are given to Democrats and three to Republicans. Because a majority of four votes are necessary to accomplish anything, very little happens. When Democratic commissioners want to investigate a Republican campaign committee, the Republican commissioners vote against it and vice versa. Lawrence Noble explained:

> Partisan politics clearly plays into what they do. There
> are decisions that are made there that are very hard to
> define or very hard to remove from partisan politics, and
> I will tell you that they see themselves as representing
> the commission and law, but also representing the par-
> ties. They're very concerned about fairness *between* the
> Republicans and Democrats.[16]

This bipartisan balance perfectly suits a political duopoly but fails to ensure an inclusive democratic process. Russell Verney, campaign manager for Perot in 1996, said, "What we have is an appointed band of Republicans and Democrats deciding that the Republicans and Democrats are innocent of rigging the debates, despite overwhelming evidence to the contrary presented to them by their own lawyers. What kind of system is it that allows them to serve as their own judge and jury?"[17]

To make matters worse, when the FEC angers the major parties, Congress strikes back by withholding funds. For example, when the FEC wrote rules outlawing the use of campaign funds to purchase personal items such as country club memberships, outraged members of Congress rescinded nearly $3 million in already appropriated funds from the FEC. Tony Coelho, former congressman and former campaign manager of the Gore campaign, said, "Over the years, there's basically been an attempt on the part of people to try to make the FEC noneffective by withholding money. And they succeeded to a great extent."[18] The FEC employs only two investigators in its enforcement division to cover thousands of cases.

FEC commissioners have ideological, political, and budgetary incentives to protect the two-party system. Their commitment to equality is restricted to eliminating comparative advantages between the major parties—not protecting the rights of third-party candidates—which is why they unanimously overruled their general counsel's recommendation for an investigation of the CPD. Lawrence Noble explained:

> The FEC does recognize the existence of third parties,
> but when you get down to a real push-comes-to-shove

type of situation, partisan politics is going to come into play. I have no doubt about that. Frankly, on the debate one, I think that they just didn't see any way that they wanted to seriously challenge what the debate commission was doing. I think one of the problems the FEC has, and a lot of people fall into this in Congress, is they view themselves as bipartisan, and in fact, it's supposed to be nonpartisan. . . . Their main focus was making sure that the Republican candidate and the Democratic candidate were treated equally and could negotiate what they wanted out of the debate regulations.[19]

Noble's report wasn't the first time FEC commissioners had opposed the conclusions of their own staff to protect the major parties from inclusive debates. On February 8, 1994, after years of research, FEC staff proposed new debate regulations that would clarify acceptable "preestablished objective criteria." The staff listed ballot access, receipt of federal matching funds, and diverse contributors as examples of acceptable criteria. The staff explicitly disqualified "polls or other assessments of a candidate's chances of winning," "subjective evaluations of whether an individual is significant," and "nomination by a major party." But their recommendations were rejected by the FEC commissioners.

In 1999, Reform Party officials filed a "rule-making petition" with the FEC, urging the agency to require all presidential debate sponsors to include any candidate who has spent at least $500,000 on the campaign and is on enough state ballots to win an electoral college majority. The FEC accepted public comments on the petition for a period of two months. Of the 1,258 comments received, 1,256 advocated criteria that would broaden participation to include more third-party and independent candidates. Only the CPD and the Republican Party submitted letters of opposition. (Reaching new levels of hypocrisy, the CPD accused petitioners of "co-opting federal law to place the partisan interests of minor candidates above the public's interest.") It is unlikely, however, that the FEC will seriously address the concerns raised in the petition. Scott E. Thomas, the lone FEC commissioner who supports lowering presidential debate barriers to third-party candidates, said, "It's not easy convincing three of my colleagues to open up the debate process. . . . We just don't have the staff available now and my colleagues haven't expressed the slightest enthusiasm to discuss the issue."[20]

The Courts

Most significant third-party candidates, including Ross Perot, Pat Buchanan, and Ralph Nader, have filed lawsuits against the CPD for violating FEC regulations. The lawsuits accuse the CPD of functioning as "bipartisan" rather than "nonpartisan," setting subjective rather than "preestablished objective" criteria, and channeling illegal corporate contributions to the major parties. Arthur Block, an attorney for Lenora Fulani, explained, "The parties can go off and spend their own money and do their own candidate debates. Fine. We don't think it is fair, but they can do it. It is not illegal. But to have tax-exempt organizations using a Federal Election Commission regulation to conduct debates like this is unconstitutional and it is an abuse of power."[21]

Although often sympathetic with third-party complaints, judges have consistently ruled in favor of the CPD, primarily because the courts tend to defer to the FEC on election matters. Challenges to the FEC must first be heard by the FEC. In 1996, Perot's motion for injunctive relief was denied, even though he argued that the FEC would not act in time to prevent the CPD from causing him irreparable damage. "The decision is regrettable with respect to democracy—certainly it does not reflect the opinion of the American people," said District Judge Thomas Hogan of his own ruling. "It is my hope that there is a different arrangement for these debates in the future."[22] Nothing was heard from the FEC for another two years. Lawrence Noble said, "It's one of those situations in which the courts say, 'I would have done it differently, but there's nothing I can do about it.'"[23] The courts must yield to the FEC and then the FEC dismisses complaints about the CPD. "To cut to the chase, the fix is in," said Greta Van Susteren, host of CNN's *Burden of Proof.*[24]

After the FEC has responded to an election complaint, a third-party candidate can challenge the FEC's ruling in court. However, courts give agency decisions great deference. Rather than taking a fresh look at the question of whether the CPD violated federal debate regulations, judicial review is limited to assessing whether the FEC committed an "arbitrary or capricious" action or "abused its discretion." In other words, third-party candidates can file suit after exhausting FEC channels, but they will lose as long as the FEC can provide a plausible rationale for its ruling.

In 2000, Pat Buchanan filed suit against the FEC after it dismissed a complaint from his campaign. In his ruling on the case, Federal District Court Judge Richard Roberts wrote:

> An ordinary citizen might easily view the circumstances surrounding the creation of the CPD along with the evidence of major-party influence over the past three debates as giving some "reason to believe": that the CPD always has supported, and still does support, the two major parties to the detriment of all others. But, for better or worse, that is not the standard I must apply here. ... As long as the FEC presents a coherent and reasonable explanation of that decision, it must be upheld. ... While reasonable people could certainly disagree about whether the CPD's credibility determination was correct, under the extremely deferential standard of review that I must apply, the FEC is entitled to the benefit of the doubt even if the unfortunate by-product of the FEC's decision is increased public cynicism about the integrity of our electoral system.[25]

In 1998, a Supreme Court decision, *Forbes v. Arkansas Education Television Commission*, delivered a serious blow to excluded third-party candidates seeking restitution through the FEC or the courts. The Supreme Court case concerned Ralph Forbes, a religious conservative who launched an independent campaign for Arkansas's Third Congressional District in 1992, after winning the Republican nomination for lieutenant governor two years earlier. The Arkansas Educational Television Network (AETN), a state agency, sponsored televised congressional debates but invited only the Republican and Democratic candidates to participate, although Forbes met the statutory criteria for eligibility and ballot access. AETN simply argued that Forbes was "not perceived as a viable candidate."[26]

Forbes filed suit, claiming that his First Amendment rights had been violated. He achieved a victory in the Eighth Circuit Court of Appeals, where Chief Judge Richard Arnold concluded that government-sponsored congressional debates were limited public forums, that Forbes naturally fit into the class of speakers invited to such public forums, and that the government cannot exclude such a speaker solely on the basis of party affiliation.[27] Judge Arnold found that Forbes's viability as a candidate was a "judgment to be made by the people of the Third Congressional District, not by officials of the government in charge of channels of communication."[28]

AETN appealed, and the Supreme Court reversed the decision by a vote of six-to-three. The Court rejected Forbes's claim that state-sponsored debates should be treated as "public forums" in which all qualified candidates have a right to participate. Instead, the Court held that excluding balloted candidates is permissible if not "based on the speaker's viewpoint." Justice Anthony Kennedy, author of the opinion, argued that AETN had made "candidate-by-candidate determinations" to select qualified candidates. Referring to Susan Howarth, the executive director of AETN, Justice Kennedy wrote:

> She further testified Forbes was excluded because (1) "the Arkansas voters did not consider him a serious candidate"; (2) "the news organizations also did not consider him a serious candidate"; (3) "the Associated Press and a national election result reporting service did not plan to run his name in results on election night"; (4) Forbes "apparently had little, if any financial support, failing to report campaign finances to the Secretary of State's office or to the Federal Election Commission"; and (5) "there was no 'Forbes for Congress' campaign headquarters other than his house." . . . It is, in short, beyond dispute that Forbes was excluded not because of his viewpoint but because he had generated no appreciable public interest.

But AETN didn't even use a formal screening process. It merely restricted invitations to the major-party candidates and justified Forbes's exclusion after the fact. And how did Ms. Susan Howarth know if Arkansas voters considered Forbes a serious candidate? How did she know if the news organizations considered Forbes a serious candidate? Who cares if the Associated Press did not plan on running his name on election night? Why did Forbes's financial support have anything to do with his seriousness as a candidate? Is there anything wrong with running a campaign from one's house? What about real objective criteria, such as the six thousand signatures Forbes collected to get on the ballot? Didn't his ability to win the Republican nomination for lieutenant governor say more about his viability than the location of his headquarters? Professor Jamin Raskin contemptuously summarized Justice Kennedy's "perfectly tautological" argument: "The government can open its facilities to speech by a specific class of citizens without creating a designated public forum simply by excluding members of the speaking class who would normally be expected to be included."[29]

What matters in the Forbes case is not so much that the Supreme Court defended the right of government to exclude third-party candidates, but rather the degree to which the Supreme Court defended arbitrary criteria. Unlike AETN, the CPD is not a government body, and thus is not bound by First Amendment prohibitions on viewpoint discrimination. But the CPD must comply with FEC regulations—that the candidate screening mechanism use "preestablished objective criteria." The Supreme Court's interpretation of AETN's criteria suggests how broadly the court might define "preestablished objective."

Justice Kennedy's opinion sets a dangerous precedent in which irrelevant criteria established *after* the exclusion process can be utilized to artificially distinguish one class of speakers from another. If the location of campaign headquarters can be deemed a sufficient criterion to help justify the predetermined exclusion of third-party candidates, then the Supreme Court would likely find the CPD's irrelevant criteria sufficiently "preestablished objective," despite evidence of major-party manipulation. Newton Minow, vice-chairman of the CPD, said, "The Forbes case did not get any attention in the media, but it's a very, very important decision."[30]

Congress

In 1980, hoping to force President Jimmy Carter to debate Ronald Reagan, Senator Bob Dole proposed legislation requiring recipients of public funds to participate in presidential debates. "No debate, no dollars," said Dole.[31] (Ironically, sixteen years later, Dole excluded Perot from the presidential debates, despite Perot's receipt of public funds.) Several other members of Congress have since proposed various forms of legislation to rectify the flaws in the presidential debate process.

Congressman Ed Markey (D-MA) and Senator Bob Graham (D-FL) proposed a National Presidential Debates Act in 1989, 1990, 1991, 1992, and 1993. The bill required recipients of public funds to participate in three presidential debates and one vice-presidential debate. "Four debates is the least the voters can expect in return for their $110 million investment in public financing," said Rep. Markey. Linking debate participation to the receipt of federal matching funds would prevent major-party candidates from forcing demands upon debate sponsors by threatening not to debate. It would allow candidates of any party that won 5 percent of the popular vote in the previous election to debate. And it would deprive the CPD of the primary justification for its existence by statutorily institutionalizing presidential debates.

Critics of tying debate participation to public funds argue that such legislation would violate free speech rights. "Candidates have a First Amendment right not to debate," said Fahrenkopf.[32] But Fahrenkopf is muddying the issue. Under Markey's bill, candidates do not have to participate—they would simply lose their federal funding if they chose not to. This is nothing new. Accepting federal funds currently imposes a whole set of restrictions—to not accept contributions, to maintain certain record-keeping requirements, to not incur qualified campaign expenses in excess of the funds received, and so forth. Former presidential candidates Jimmy Carter, Michael Dukakis, and Walter Mondale support making the receipt of federal matching funds conditional on debate participation.

The 1989 version of the Markey bill included protections for third-party candidates as well as demands for confrontational formats, including required candidate-to-candidate questioning. But in 1991, to increase congressional support for their legislation, Rep. Markey and Senator Graham modified their bill to broaden the definition of acceptable sponsor. Markey explained on the floor of the House of Representatives:

> The bill we introduce today requires that the debates be sponsored by "a nonpartisan or bipartisan organization." The initial version of the legislation allowed sponsorship only by a nonpartisan organization. This change was made in order to include the possibility of sponsorship by the Commission on Presidential Debates, which skillfully staged the 1988 general election debates and which has continued to play an active and positive role in calling for institutionalized debates.[33]

Although the late Senator Paul Wellstone (D-MN) strongly supported the bill, he had specific reservations about the nature of the sponsor: "I would like the commission to be a nonpartisan commission sponsoring it and make sure that eligibility is defined in such a way that, indeed, we make sure we do not block out any serious independent candidate."[34] Regardless, Rep. Markey's bill did not pass. It never even made it past the House Subcommittee on Elections. Professor Sidney Kraus described the loss as "the most devastating blow to televised presidential debates since their hiatus between 1960 and 1976."[35]

On February 4, 1991, Rep. Tim Penny (D-MN) introduced the Democracy in Presidential Debates Act, which required debate sponsors to invite any candidate who is on at least forty state ballots and has raised $500,000 or received public financing. Rep. Penny said on the House floor:

> The narrowness of the presidential debates, their scripted nature, is the source of their lack of vitality and credibility. Including significant independent and minor-party candidates is a critical aspect of democratizing the debates and broadening our national dialogue. The American public has made it clear they want broadness and inclusion.[36]

However, Rep. Penny's bill didn't make it past the House Committee on House Administration.

On September 28, 1996, Rep. Bill McCollum (R-FL) proposed replacing the CPD with a federally funded Presidential Debate Commission. No more than six of the ten members of the Presidential Debate Commission could be affiliated with the Democratic or Republican Party. No later than sixty days before the election, the Presidential Debate Commission would host a preliminary debate that included all candidates who were either on all fifty state ballots or the choice of at least 5 percent of likely voters. After the preliminary debate, the rest of the presidential debates would be restricted to candidates polling at least 10 percent nationally. "We need to have an established framework with defined ground rules to ensure fairness in the system," said Rep. McCollum. His bill never made it past the House Committee on Oversight.

On September 16, 1997, Rep. Ron Paul (R-TX) proposed legislation prohibiting recipients of federal matching funds from participating in presidential debates that excluded candidates who were on forty or more state ballots. On the House floor, Rep. Paul explained:

> This amendment does not dictate to those who hold debates, but it would require that those major-party candidates who take the taxpayers' money, they take it with the agreement that anybody else who qualifies for taxpayers' funding, campaign funds, or gets on 40 ballots, would be allowed in the debate. I cannot think of anything that could boost the interest in the debates more.[37]

Rep. Paul's bill never made it past the House Committee on Oversight.

On July 22, 1998, Rep. James Traficant (D-OH) proposed forcing sponsoring organizations to invite all presidential candidates who qualify for federal matching funds. Introducing his bill in the House, Rep. Traficant said:

> Staging organizations should not be given the subjective authority to bar a qualified candidate from participation

in a presidential debate simply because a subjective judgment has been made that the candidate does not have a reasonable chance of winning the election. The American people should be given the opportunity to decide for themselves whether or not a candidate has a chance to be elected president.[38]

Rep. Traficant's bill never made it past the House Committee on Oversight.

On July 18, 2000, Rep. Jesse Jackson Jr. (D-IL) proposed lowering the criterion for third-party inclusion from 15 to 5 percent in the polls. He explained, "A 5 percent requirement makes more sense and has legal precedent, as it mirrors the 5 percent level of support mandated for eligibility for federal campaign funding. It allows independents and nominees of minor or new parties to spread their message to the American people." However, Rep. Jackson Jr.'s bill never made it past the House Committee on House Administration.

A clear pattern emerges regarding the viability of federal legislation that attempts to regulate the presidential debate process. To the delight of the CPD, none of these pieces of legislation attained even marginal congressional support, and according to Bobby Burchfield, debate negotiator for Bush in 1992, "they'll never pass."[39]

The CPD fiercely opposes government regulation of the presidential debate process. Fahrenkopf said, "It horrifies me to believe that the Congress of the United States is going to get into the business of setting up a criteria or structure by which we are going to tell our presidential candidates how, where, how many, and who is going to run the debate process."[40] Barbara Vucanovich, a former CPD director and congresswoman, said, "Congress ought to mind its own business."[41]

Political opposition to statutory reform of the debate process is substantial. All but a handful of the 535 members of Congress are Republicans and Democrats. The major parties want to protect their duopoly, and members of Congress don't want to undermine their presidential candidates. Rep. Bob Livingston (R-LA) said, "It seems an individual candidate is better prepared to address his own needs, his own best advantage better in an open negotiating process than is the government to set one. I, frankly, shrink at the thought of saying we are just automatically going to get a nonpartisan group to put it on."[42] But what about the needs of the voters? Rep. John Lewis, a former CPD director, said:

> I think Congress should take a look at the debate process, and the way all the decisions are made. Congress has a role in making sure our democracy functions properly. The American people should never be led to feel that there are only two meaningful parties. That's not true and it creates cynicism and apathy. Congress should change that. And it will probably happen sometime down the road, when people get more upset. But now, Congress is not moving in that direction.[43]

THE IRS HAS not seriously addressed the CPD's bipartisan activities; FEC commissioners rejected a request by their own general counsel to investigate the CPD; third-party candidates cannot file effective lawsuits because the courts defer to the FEC; and Congress has failed to pass transformative debate regulations. There is no way to reform the presidential debate process through traditional political and legal channels.

8

Citizens' Debate Commission

THE CPD'S EXCLUSIONARY practices and the candidates' inability to stop them through legal and political channels generated protest during the 1996 and 2000 elections, and activists launched dozens of creative efforts to open up the 2000 presidential debates. Four online petitions demanding the inclusion of third-party candidates collected hundreds of thousands of signatures. Working Assets, a progressive long-distance telephone company, told all its customers that the CPD "had set up rules that unfairly restrict the public's right to be informed."[1] The Reform Party initiated a nationwide boycott of Anheuser-Busch, a major sponsor of the CPD. The Open Debate Society, the DC Statehood Party, the Alliance for Democracy, Reform America, and the Washington Action group held weekly demonstrations with former presidential candidate John B. Anderson at the CPD's Washington office. Hundreds of people dumped television sets into the Boston harbor from the Boston Tea Party ship to protest candidate exclusion.[2] Thousands more protested at the actual presidential debates. "Their sheer numbers are disrupting traffic," said Massachusetts Police Captain Robert Bird during the first 2000 presidential debate.

University professors, civic leaders, journalists, politicians, scientists, and artists came together to criticize the CPD. The hosts of FOX *News Watch—Newsday* columnist James Pinkerton, communications professor Jane Hall, syndicated columnist Cal Thomas, FOX News media analyst Eric Burns, and Jeff Cohen, president of Fairness and Accuracy In Reporting—issued a joint statement:

> We are media critics and commentators who are rarely unanimous in our opinions. Yet we are united in our belief that voters would be better served by broader debates than those sponsored by the Commission on Presidential Debates. . . . As believers in free speech and in the marketplace of ideas, we five think a better approach would be to invite—at least to the first debate—any candidate on the ballot in enough states to have a mathematical chance of winning an Electoral College majority (which means they've overcome often difficult ballot-access hurdles). . . . In an era of decline in major-party affiliation and a rise in independent voters, presidential debates should not be controlled by the two major parties and the debate commission they jointly established.[3]

A larger group of forty civic leaders, professors, journalists, actors, musicians, and elected officials (including Randall Hayes, president of the Rainforest Action Network; Gene Nichol, dean of the University of North Carolina Law School; David Brower, chairman of Earth Island Institute; John Cavanagh, director of the Institute for Policy Studies; Noam Chomsky, professor at the Massachusetts Institute of Technology; Donella H. Meadows, director of the Sustainability Institute; Edward Norton, actor; Bonnie Raitt, musician; and Anita Roddick, founder and cochair of the Body Shop) wrote a letter to the CPD demanding the inclusion of Nader and Buchanan:

> The American people are ready to move beyond the current two-party system. This is because many of the issues we care most about—the expanding prison/industrial complex, the failed drug war, and corporate globalization—continue to be ignored by the two major parties. To a growing number of Americans, it does not appear coincidental that many of the larger campaign contributors benefit from ignoring such issues. Candidates for

the Office of President of the United States should be
confident, if not eager, to debate other candidates. We
ask that the CPD not only open the debates to Mr. Nader
and Mr. Buchanan, but open up its own decision-making
process to major third-party representatives as well.

Even major-party primary candidates criticized the CPD. During a Republican primary debate in 2000, presidential candidate
Gary Bauer said, "This process ought to be as open as possible. The
American people deserve that. And they certainly deserve not to
have elites, whether it's some organization or pollster somewhere,
deciding who they're going to get a chance to hear from and who
they're not going to have a chance to hear from." Former Republican presidential candidate Steve Forbes called the CPD a "corrupt duopoly."[4] Former Republican presidential candidate Alan
Keyes said:

> I want to see my party achieve victory based on what we
> have to offer this country and our ability to offer it with
> integrity. I don't want to see us achieve victory based
> on the fact that we are better at rigging the game than
> other people, that we can put our hands together in col-
> lusion with corrupt Democrats and keep others from
> being heard. Why should we be afraid to have people
> whose views we can with integrity oppose be heard by
> the American people?[5]

Internal Reform?

All this protest helped publicly discredit the CPD, and broadly exposing its failings is the first step in reforming the presidential debate
process. George Stephanopolous said that the major-party candidates
"can set up any debate they want" because Americans "don't really
know anything about the commission."[6] If more Americans were
aware of the composition and intent of the CPD, existing resentment
might grow into majoritarian outrage, and public protest could facilitate the *replacement* of the CPD.

The CPD itself, though, is unlikely to internally reform, regardless of public pressure. Its raison d'être is to secretly award control of the presidential debates to the Republican and Democratic candidates, and it shields those candidates by diverting public criticism onto itself. The CPD expects public opposition to its sanitized debates, and it dismisses such opposition to the extent possible. The CPD was designed to defy the electorate's wishes, not surrender to them.

In 1995, for example, the Twentieth Century Fund, a former sponsor of the CPD, assembled a task force to study the presidential debate process. The task force consisted of prominent political figures and media executives, including Michael Dukakis, former Democratic presidential candidate; Wyche Fowler Jr., former Democratic senator from Georgia; Lowell Weicker, former independent governor of Connecticut; Ted Turner, vice-chairman of AOL Time Warner; Lawrence K. Grossman, president of Horizons Cable Network; Dotty Lynch, political editor of CBS News; Carole Simpson, senior general correspondent for ABC News; Ernest Tollerson, national correspondent for the *New York Times*; and Thomas Winship, chairman of the Center for Foreign Journalists. The task force produced five commendable recommendations, including:

1. The Presidential Debates Commission should broaden its criteria beyond its current threshold of whether a candidate has a "realistic chance" of being elected to consider whether he or she has "a real likelihood of having a substantial impact on the outcome of the election."

2. There should be at least four presidential and one vice presidential debates, with the first presidential debate taking place in early September to provide a benchmark for the campaign. The rest of the debates should continue to be concentrated in the "mini-series" format used in 1992, during the final weeks of October.

3. Debates should take place at a time likely to attract the widest television audience, and, to allow maximum exposure, they should be rebroadcast at other times and on networks other than those airing them originally.

4. Citizen participation, begun in the 1992 Richmond debate, should be continued; bolder, more innovative formats should be employed that stimulate interaction and actual debate between candidates.

5. The Commission on Presidential Debates should develop a more broadly based membership by including two members who are not identified with the Democratic or Republican parties; institute a specific procedure for appointing members and staggering their terms of service; expand its public presence and educational activities.

If implemented, these recommendations would have substantially improved the presidential debate process. But the CPD did not adopt a single one of them. Other scholarly panels made similar proposals to no avail. In 1998, The Task Force on Campaign Reform, which was commissioned by the Pew Charitable Trusts and included several leading political scientists, recommended that the CPD "be significantly revamped" in order to be "capable not only of maintaining the cooperation of both major parties, but also of representing the interests of the broader public." In 2002, the Vanishing Voter Project of the Joan Shorenstein Center on the Press, Politics and Public Policy at Harvard University concluded that the "CPD should expand its criteria for judging the significance of third-party candidates. Any such candidate who can 'win' should be included in the debates. But so should any candidate who has captured the public's attention with a message it clearly wants to hear and consider."[7] The CPD predictably ignored these recommendations, demonstrating a complete unwillingness to end Republican-Democrat control over the presidential debates.

Federal Government?

An alternative, nonpartisan debate sponsor must be created. "We need to break the monopoly the CPD has over the debates," said Bob Teeter, chairman of the 1992 Bush campaign. "They do not serve the electoral process well."[8]

Few nonpartisan institutions could secure the participation of the major-party candidates, let alone challenge their demands. Syndicated talk show host Neal Boortz said, "Sure, third-party candidates were meticulously excluded from many of the debate processes, but there were other debate processes that were open to them that they agreed to go to, but Gore and Bush stayed away."[9] Only three nonpartisan structures likely carry enough weight to defy the demands of major-party candidates and survive as national debate sponsor: the federal government, the television networks, and a conglomerate of civic leaders and civic organizations.

In 2000, during Mexico's first democratic elections in decades, the Federal Election Institute hosted a presidential debate. Financed by the Mexican government, the Federal Election Institute is comprised of "noteworthy academics and respected community leaders," and the first presidential debate they sponsored involved six Mexican candidates. (When three candidates later emerged as the clear front-runners, another debate was held exclusively between them.) Pat Buchanan said, "We ought to call the president of Mexico and see if he can send observers to the United States to show Americans how to conduct free and fair and open elections."[10]

After the voting debacle in Florida during the 2000 election, a bipartisan group of lawmakers took the first step toward the construction of something similar to the Mexican Federal Election Institute. They proposed the creation of an independent Federal Elections Review Commission to "study the nature and consequences of the Federal electoral process and make recommendations to ensure the integrity of, and public confidence in, Federal elections." The bill stipulated that the directors of the Federal Election Review Commission should "represent a broad cross section of regional and political perspectives in the United States." Along with ballot access barriers, voter registration methods, and other electoral issues, the Review Commission would specifically address the flaws of the presidential debate process. However, the bill did not pass.

Instead, the University of Virginia's Miller Center and the Century Foundation privately organized a National Commission on Federal Election Reform (NCFER). This commission delivered a much-anticipated report to Congress outlining specific recommendations for improving the election process, including simplified absentee voting, a national election holiday, and advanced voting machinery. But the reforms did not mention presidential debates. Considering the composition of the NCFER, this is not surprising. Jimmy Carter and Gerald Ford, honorary cochairs of the CPD, were honorary cochairs of the NCFER. Lloyd Cutler, who served as White House counsel for President Bill Clinton, cochaired the NCFER. Robert H. Michel, a former Republican congressman who lobbies for Hogan & Hartson, the law firm of which Frank Fahrenkopf is a partner, also cochaired the NCFER. CPD director John Danforth served on the board of the NCFER. Professor Kenneth Thompson, who served on the CPD's Advisory Committee, is a director emeritus of the Miller Center, which organized the NCFER. Scott McLarty, media coordinator for the Green Party, said, "Like the debate commission, the Commission on Federal Election Reform is run by and for Democrats and Republicans. I fear that the new commission's real purpose is to strengthen the two-party system, which is not the same as strengthening democracy."[11]

The federal government will not create a nonpartisan presidential debate sponsor in the foreseeable future.

Television Networks?

In Canada, leaders' debates are models of democratic discourse. (This is to be expected from a country that automatically registers every citizen to vote, limits the amount of money candidates can spend on their campaigns, sets up a polling booth for every 350 voters on Election Day, and routinely boasts a voter turnout near 70 percent.) What make Canadian debates so distinctly successful are the efforts of the sponsoring organization: a broadcast consortium of five television networks. These Canadian networks have participated in grueling debate negotiations, up against seasoned politicians, that devolved into partisan shouting matches. They have disrupted their programming schedules and lost millions of dollars in advertising revenue. Broadcasters have even been sued by political parties for differences over negotiating proposals. Why, then, do the Canadian networks do this? To put it simply, their news divisions possess civic integrity. "In

Canada, both in the public and private broadcast sector, there exists strong news divisions which act differently from the entertainment, drama, sports and financial divisions of their corporations," wrote Arnold Amber, an executive producer with the Canadian Broadcasting Corporation. "For television news the debates are about journalism, public service and a responsibility under the broadcasting licenses they hold."[12]

As a united force, the Canadian networks have successfully countered the demands of the major parties. In 1993, the networks realized that Canada's three-party system was disintegrating; a new populist movement named the Reform Party elected their first members to the House, and nine Quebec parliamentarians quit their parties to form Bloc Quebecois. The networks decided that the two new parties would participate in the debates, even if securing their inclusion proved to be unusually tumultuous. Arnold Amber wrote, "Things got so bad and tension so high during the negotiations that a two-hour heated yelling match on whether or not there should be an audience and, if so, how it should be recruited and what its role would be was considered a welcome respite from the circular argument over who was going to be allowed to debate and in what languages."[13] The networks eventually triumphed and sponsored two debates among all five candidates.

NBC News anchor Tom Brokaw supports a similar form of network sponsorship for American presidential debates. Brokaw said that the networks "won't be pushed around by the candidates or their campaign managers. If a candidate cannot agree to the common terms of the debate, then the network should choose to broadcast a discussion with his or her opponent."[14] In 2000, Ralph Nader wrote letters appealing to the executives of NBC, CBS, ABC, PBS, and CNN: "Debates sponsored by the major networks would highlight popular issues ignored by the two major parties. . . . [There is] a public interest duty to save the American people from massive amounts of No-Doz as they try to deal with a series of soporific debates between the drab and the dreary. . . . So do the nation and your shareholders a favor—set up a series of debates that include all four major candidates."[15]

The television networks refused to set up inclusive debates. In fact, NBC and FOX didn't even broadcast the 2000 presidential debates.

"It is deplorable, really, that networks that use the public airwaves and have some responsibility here with respect to the public good and public interest, have decided that presidential debates are not important enough to preempt other programming," said Senator Byron Dorgan (D-ND).[16] American television networks simply do not possess a Canadian-like commitment to the public interest, and Congress will not change that in the foreseeable future. As a consequence, since 1991, the networks have been perfectly happy letting the CPD run the show. "The networks have, for all intents and purposes, reached the conclusion that they like us to do it," said Fahrenkopf. "Then they don't get into problems."[17] Walter Cronkite angrily accused the networks of "acquiescing" to "phony debates."

Citizens' Debate Commission

The most viable option for fixing the corrupt presidential debate process is to replace the Republican-Democratic-controlled CPD with a genuinely nonpartisan debate commission. Marvin Kalb, former moderator of *Meet the Press,* said, "A bipartisan commission is inadequate when a Ross Perot is running. It is not a bi- or tripartisan commission that is needed, but a neutral commission."[18] Congressman John Lewis, a former CPD director, said, "The debate commission should be broadened to include third-party members and independents and others, or it should be replaced. The two major parties are becoming so much alike, and the American people know it. They want more choices. Maybe, if we let other people participate in the debates, people will start believing that politics matter."[19] 2004 Democratic presidential candidate Dennis Kucinich wrote, "While I think it is always a challenge to find a truly nonpartisan entity, I believe the attempt should be made. The presidential political debates do not belong to the two major parties. They belong to the American people and arbitrary exclusion of other viewpoints is repugnant to a true democracy."[20]

Rising to the challenge, national civic leaders from the left, center, and right of the political spectrum have joined forces to form a nonpartisan Citizens' Debate Commission (www.citizensdebate.org). The Citizens' Debate Commission, which aspires to sponsor the 2004 presidential debates, consists of seventeen civic leaders committed to maximizing voter education:

JOHN B. ANDERSON: Former U.S. Congressman, former presidential candidate, and current chair of the Center for Voting and Democracy

ANGELA BAY BUCHANAN: President of The American Cause and former U.S Treasurer

VERONICA DE LA GARZA: Executive director of the Youth Vote Coalition

NORMAN DEAN: Executive director of Friends of the Earth and chair of CERES

GEORGE FARAH: Executive director of Open Debates

TOM FITTON: President of Judicial Watch

TOM GERETY: Executive director and Brennan Center Professor of the Brennan Center for Justice at NYU School of Law and former President of Amherst College

JEHMU GREEN: Executive director of Rock the Vote

ALAN KEYES: Former GOP presidential candidate, former Ambassador to the United Nations, and chairman of the Declaration Foundation

JEFF MILCHEN: Founder and Executive Director of ReclaimDemocracy.org

LARRY NOBLE: Executive director of the Center for Responsive Politics and former general counsel of the Federal Election Commission

TONY PERKINS: President of the Family Research Council and a former Louisiana state representative

CHELLIE PINGREE: President and CEO of Common Cause and former Maine Senate Majority leader

RANDALL ROBINSON: Author and founder of TransAfrica Forum

DAN STEIN: Executive director of the Federation for American Immigration Reform

MARK WEISBROT: Codirector of the Center for Economic and Policy Research

PAUL WEYRICH: Chair and CEO of the Free Congress Foundation and founding president of the Heritage Foundation

The Citizens' Debate Commission also has an Advisory Board consisting of more than fifty civic organizations, including Accuracy In Media, Alliance for Better Campaigns, Center for Food Safety, Center for Voting and Democracy, Democracy Matters, Earth Island Institute, Ella Baker Center for Human Rights, Fairness and Accuracy In Reporting, Free Press, Fund for Constitutional Government, Greenpeace, Institute for Agriculture and Trade Policy, League of Rural Voters, National Voting Rights Institute, National Youth Advocacy Coalition, Public Campaign, and the Voting Rights Project of the Institute for Southern Studies.

The general purpose of the Citizens' Debate Commission is to host presidential debates free of excessive candidate control that maximize voter education and reverse the decline in debate viewership. The specific purpose of the Citizens' Debate Commission is to set fair criteria for candidate inclusion, employ engaging formats and operate with full transparency. The Citizens' Debate Commission advocates employing the following basic schedule, candidate selection criteria, and format requirements in future presidential debates:

SCHEDULE

Candidates would participate in five ninety-minute presidential debates and one ninety-minute vice-presidential debate.

CRITERIA

The Citizens' Debate Commission would utilize criteria developed by the Appleseed Citizens' Task Force on Fair Debates, a project of the Appleseed Electoral Reform Project at American University Washington College of Law. The Appleseed Task Force on Fair Debates consisted of numerous civic leaders, professors, and elected officials, including John C. Brittain, dean of the Thurgood Marshall School of Law; John Bonifaz, executive director of the National Voting Rights Institute; Steve Cobble, former political director of the National Rainbow Coalition; Edward Still, director of the Voting Rights Project of the Lawyers' Committee for Civil Rights Under Law; John C. Berg, director of graduate studies in the Department of Government at Suffolk University; and Rob Ritchie, executive director of The Center for Voting and Democracy.

The Appleseed criteria invite all candidates on enough state ballots to win an electoral college majority who either (1) register at 5 percent in national polls or (2) register a majority in national polls asking eligible voters which candidates they would like to see included in the presidential debates.

The Appleseed criteria are the most effective and justifiable. The criteria ensure that popular third-party challengers are allowed to participate without drowning out the voices of the leading contenders for the presidency. In 1988, only the major-party candidates fulfilled the Appleseed criteria; in 1992 and 1996, only Ross Perot and the major-party candidates managed to meet the Appleseed threshold; and in 2000, only Ralph Nader, Pat Buchanan, and the major-party candidates satisfied the criteria.

The two prongs of the Appleseed criteria that trigger inclusion— 5 percent and majority support—are rooted in democratic principles and federal law. The 5 percent threshold matches the public financing threshold for minor parties, which is the only legislative standard for measuring the viability of non-major parties. Elected officials accountable to the public codified 5 percent in the Federal Election Campaign Act, and taxpayers finance candidates whose parties attract 5 percent of the popular vote. The second prong of the Appleseed criteria—support for inclusion from a majority of eligible voters—is inherently democratic. After formulating its criteria, the Appleseed Task Force issued the following statement: "Particularly in this era where access to money drives access to voters and media coverage, the debates should be an opportunity for voters to see debates among the candidates from whom they wish to hear."

FORMAT

The Citizens' Debate Commission advocates the following format stipulations for future presidential debates:

1. Follow-up questions must be permitted in every debate.
2. At least one debate must include candidate-to-candidate questioning.
3. At least two debates must include rebuttals and surrebuttals.

4. Response times must not be overly restrictive.

5. Candidates may exercise only a limited number of vetoes concerning the selection of moderators and panelists.

The Citizens' Debate Commission also proposes the following four basic formats for future presidential debates:

1. **TWO SINGLE-MODERATOR DEBATES:** The single-moderator format focuses attention on the candidates rather than on the questioners. At least one of the single-moderator debates would include direct candidate-to-candidate questioning, loose time restrictions, and minimal interference from the moderator.

2. **AUTHENTIC TOWN-HALL DEBATE:** An authentic town-hall debate would be organized that prohibits the screening of questions and includes a representative sampling of Americans in the audience.

3. **YOUTH DEBATE:** The first-ever youth-run and youth-oriented presidential debate would be established. Young people are increasingly dismayed by and detached from electoral politics. A youth debate could inspire millions of young adults to tune into the presidential debates, raise atypical subject matters for national discourse, and prevent the candidates from anticipating many debate questions.

4. **PANEL DEBATE:** Historically, panel debates have allowed educated reporters to question the candidates' policy plans and backgrounds. But rather than the panel consisting exclusively of reporters, the Citizens' Debate Commission would assemble a diverse panel of academic, civic, artistic, religious, media, labor, and business leaders to pose questions.

Transparency

Only one ingredient is needed to replace the CPD with the Citizens' Debate Commission: an unwavering commitment from the

Republicans and Democrats to participate in presidential debates sponsored by the Citizens' Debate Commission. Obtaining that commitment, however, is no easy task; the candidates use the CPD to control the debate process without revealing that control to the public, and they will not relinquish this power unless doing so serves their political interests. Consequently, a successful campaign to displace the CPD must create overwhelming public pressure on the major-party candidates to refuse participation in CPD-sponsored debates. The political cost of rejecting the Citizens' Debate Commission must trump the political benefit.

It is possible, though, that the Republican and Democratic parties will ignore the demands of an organized public. John Buckley, communications director of the Dole campaign, said, "The campaigns can make decisions on what they're going to do and that's the way it's going to be because they have the two most important ingredients: the candidates. The debate commission, or any other sponsor for that matter, can't do anything about it. Everyone can try to force the ideal onto the campaigns, but it will fail. The candidates will do what they want."[21]

Even if the CPD crumbled, the Republicans and Democrats could set up their own debates, exclude popular third-party candidates, employ stilted formats, and ignore pressing national issues. Nobody could stop them from exercising that First Amendment right, and television networks would surely broadcast their debates. So, argue Buckley and other major-party strategists, the CPD is merely improving upon inevitable structures imposed by the major-party candidates. The CPD lays out a worthy debate schedule, pressures the candidates to participate, hires professional producers, finances education and research projects, and generally institutionalizes the process. That, claim many supporters of the CPD, is really the best any debate sponsor can hope for, which is far better than direct party sponsorship.

But this analysis ignores a critical component of CPD sponsorship: deception. There is a significant benefit to party-sponsored debates that should not be overlooked—they make the major-party candidates accountable for the debates. Under the auspices of party sponsorship, the public would realize that third-party challengers, revealing formats, and important national issues were excluded for political reasons, and major-party candidates would likely pay a price on Election Day. Before joining the CPD, Newton Minow advocated transparent party sponsorship, partly to ensure accountability. In 1984, he wrote:

> Placing responsibility in the hands of the political parties is really a truth-in-advertising measure, with the added benefit of accountability. If the debates do not take place, then it will be the fault of the political parties. If severe problems develop with the debates, then that too will be the responsibility of the parties. And if the debates are established and institutionalized, as they should be, then that should be the parties' accomplishment.[22]

This degree of transparency would force the major-party candidates to reconcile the benefits of third-party exclusion and format manipulation with the desire to appear democratic, which, in and of itself, would increase the likelihood of third-party inclusion and revealing formats. Bob Dole wondered during an interview, "Do you do yourself harm by being the party or the candidate saying they shouldn't be in the debates?"[23] Frank Donatelli, debate negotiator for Dole, said, "Believe me, politicians are risk-averse, the parties are risk-averse. The last thing they're gonna want to do is to alienate a substantial segment of the public by being perceived as the person that kept out a legitimate candidate who could be president."[24] Under direct party sponsorship, the voters' demands—currently made irrelevant by the CPD—would directly impact the candidates' strategic decisions. And the debate over debates would become a unique voter education tool; we would learn to what extent major-party candidates value their personal political ambitions over the democratic process. In 2002, Newt Gingrich, former Speaker of the House, advocated a transparent debate process:

> I'd put the burden on the candidates. If the last two presidential candidates for the two major parties had to say publicly, "No, I won't debate you," then they would have borne whatever political cost came. . . . The point is the

diversity and the debate ought to be up to the candidates you are going to hold accountable by giving them your vote, and not by some kind of screening mechanism, however it's rigged, because that screening mechanism then becomes an excuse for the political leaders to not have to be accountable. I'm for more open debates. I think we have nothing to fear by allowing people to be seen and to argue and to talk with each other and I think the very concept of an elite commission deciding for the American people who deserves to be heard is profoundly wrong.[25]

The CPD is an excuse for the Republican and Democratic nominees to avoid accountability. The Dole campaign, for example, excluded Perot in 1996 without suffering a severe public backlash. "We were able to hide behind the commission," said Scott Reed, Dole's campaign manager. "The commission went out and did their own study, and we were able to use them as the excuse."[26] A September 23, 1996, Hotline poll found that only 5 percent of eligible voters held the Clinton campaign responsible for Perot's exclusion; only 13 percent blamed the Dole campaign; and over 50 percent blamed the CPD. The *New York Times* editorialized, "The commission should not be in the business of shielding the two major parties from spirited independent challenges."[27]

Under the auspices of the CPD, the reputations of Republican and Democratic candidates are unfairly preserved, and the reputations of third-party candidates are unfairly damaged, their exclusion perceived solely as a reflection of their viability rather than as a by-product of major-party collusion. Alan Keyes, former Republican presidential candidate, said:

What's happening in these debates is that, they are standing up and saying, "Here are the nonpartisan debates, at which we are presenting the serious candidates for president on a nonpartisan basis so that we can educate the people of this country in a fair fashion." If you are going to present a partisan brawl, in which you have excluded anybody but your chosen few, I would say just do it. You have the right to do it. It's a free country. Don't pretend, however, to do it under a rubric of nonpartisanship. Don't pretend to do it in a fashion that then uses monies that are supposed only to be used for nonpartisan purposes. That's cheating. That's corruption. That's lying. That's an effort to manipulate the perception of the voters in order to favor your power.[28]

THE EMERGENCE OF the Citizens' Debate Commission is a promising sign that the American public is attempting to regain control of its presidential debates. Two possible outcomes are likely to result from the efforts of the Citizens' Debate Commission. The Citizens' Debate Commission may succeed in hosting presidential debates that showcase popular candidates discussing important issues in an unscripted manner. Such debates would energize voters, broaden the presentation of issues, and truly educate Americans about the candidates for the most important job in the world.

The other possible outcome is that the Republican and Democratic candidates reject the public entreaties of the Citizens' Debate Commission. But that rejection, along with continued exposition of the CPD's operations, would help generate widespread recognition of Republican-Democratic collusion and control of the presidential debates. The mere existence of the Citizens' Debate Commission—as a representation of what could be, of what the CPD isn't, and of what the major-party candidates fear—would educate the public about the Republican and Democratic nominees' antidemocratic practices. Sponsorship can only become more transparent, and candidates can only become more accountable.

How to democratize the presidential debates:

- The Citizens' Debate Commission—composed of national civic leaders from the left, center, and right of the political spectrum—gains national prominence.

- Civic groups successfully organize a massive public education campaign to expose the antidemocratic practices of the CPD, making the organization unsuitable for debate sponsorship.

- The major-party candidates, pressured by public opinion, agree to participate in debates sponsored by the Citizens' Debate Commission.

- The Citizens' Debate Commission adopts the Appleseed criteria, allowing for the inclusion of candidates whom the American people want to see.

- The Citizens' Debate Commission employs revealing and diverse formats that elicit unscripted debate, instead of memorized sound bites, and address a variety of important issues.

- The Citizens' Debate Commission participates in all debate negotiations and makes public the collectively drafted Memoranda of Understanding.

- Congress passes legislation requiring recipients of public funds to participate in presidential debates sponsored by the Citizens' Debate Commission.

Conclusion

W HEN A PRESIDENTIAL debate commences, an unnerving sense of vulnerability materializes onstage. The candidates cannot access their advisors, hide behind their reputations, or buy their way out with their tens of millions of dollars. The candidates are presented unaided for direct public scrutiny. Anything, it seems, is possible. And this seeming unpredictability excites voters, who have tuned in to see the candidates face off for the first time in the competition for the White House.

But most viewers are soon disappointed. The appearance of vulnerability and spontaneity is just a mirage. Weeks earlier, the Republican and Democratic candidates secretly determined every element of the presidential debates, from selecting compliant moderators to excluding other candidates to prohibiting candidate-to-candidate dialogue. And having eliminated the factors that engender real and unrehearsed debate, the two candidates now safely deliver their prepared speeches and prepackaged sound bites. The two candidates safely spout the focus group–tested rhetoric of their increasingly unpopular parties, rather than actually debate each other or debate articulate third-party challengers. The two candidates focus on language that resonates with senior citizens in Florida, rather than raise new and refreshing ideas.

Americans are getting tired of these manufactured bipartisan press conferences, and they are turning off their television sets. In 1980, 60 percent of American households tuned in to the presidential debates; in 2000, less than 30 percent of American households tuned in to the sanitized debates. Twenty-five million *fewer* people watched the 2000 presidential debates than watched the 1992 presidential debates.

174 CONCLUSION

Most voters don't know why debate discourse has eroded, or why many intriguing candidates are excluded, or why Jim Lehrer moderates all the debates, or why participating candidates can't ask each other questions. The reason is the Commission on Presidential Debates—and it avoids public censure by deceiving the American people. The CPD claims to be nonpartisan, but it is bipartisan. It claims to serve voters' interests, but it really serves the colluded interests of the Democratic and Republican parties. The CPD claims to maximize voter education, but it really excludes popular third-party candidates with new ideas. The CPD claims to establish revealing debate formats, but it really permits the candidates to put on orchestrated news conferences. The CPD claims to raise civic donations, but it really funnels bipartisan corporate contributions. The CPD claims to strengthen democracy, but it does the opposite: it undermines voter choice, voter confidence, and voter participation.

The CPD's determination to ensure that Republican-Democratic interests trump the wider democratic process stems from breathtaking political arrogance. Most CPD officials and their supporters have deep-seated contempt for third-party candidates. At a hearing on presidential debates, Senator Pat Roberts, an avid CPD supporter, described third-party challengers as "candidates who stand for green leafy vegetables of some kind."[1] Theo Lippman Jr., a retired editorial writer for the *Baltimore Sun* and a CPD supporter, wrote that Nader and Buchanan "aren't really candidates in the traditional sense" but rather "extremist pamphleteers 'running' for personal aggrandizement only" and therefore "the political equivalent of a circus sideshow's bearded lady or alligator man."[2]

Republican-Democatic contempt for third-party candidates is, in some respects, a natural consequence of an illegitimate duopoly; it comes as no surprise that many elected officials denigrate third-party threats to justify arbitrary exclusion. But CPD officials and their supporters are not just contemptuous of third-party candidates. They're also contemptuous of *you*.

Most CPD directors and debate negotiators come from opposing political parties and various occupations, but they share a certain disdain for us, the American voter. These leaders of the political establishment believe that Americans cannot handle a real democracy—it would be hazardous for the country. They don't think you should be presented with all the candidates you want to see because you might vote for the "wrong" one. They don't think you should ask unfiltered questions of the participating candidates because you might ask a "silly" question. Instead, to help us navigate the democratic process, these Republican and Democratic operatives have erected a bounded democracy that allows vying forces to collude in order to eliminate all other competition and unpredictable questions.

In doing so, the CPD contradicts two fundamental principles of the democratic process—that the marketplace of ideas should not be censored and that the power to choose public servants belongs to the people. "Whenever the people are well-informed, they can be trusted with their own government," said Thomas Jefferson. Whether the two-party system should be strengthened or permanent multiple parties should be established, allowing voters to see the candidates they want to see discussing issues they want to hear about is a precondition to an authentic representative democracy.

It's time to take back our democracy from calculating political parties. It's time to let voters regain influence over the election process, not just the election. It's time to have a debate sponsor—a Citizens' Debate Commission—that expands, rather than diminishes, the role of the voting public. It's time to demand unscripted and open presidential debates, with the range of debate reflecting the composition of the electorate.

The current undemocratic setup will change when the American people discover who is force-feeding them narrow subjects of discourse. When the CPD no longer can deceive, it becomes inoperative. Fahrenkopf said, "We can only do it because people believe we have integrity and there is stature to us." Janet Brown said, "It is very important that the debate sponsor can be trusted, and as soon as that sponsor's credibility is ruined, they can no longer sponsor the debates."[3] Let's hope so.

Appendix A

1996 Memorandum of Understanding

THIS MEMORANDUM OF understanding ("the Agreement") constitutes the agreement between the Dole/Kemp '96 and Clinton/Dole '96 General Committee, Inc. ("the Committees") regarding the rules that will govern any Presidential and Vice Presidential debates in 1996 ("debates"). This Agreement will be binding upon the Committees, and, if it agrees to sponsor the debates, on the Commission on Presidential Debates ("Commission'), and on any other entity that may sponsor these Presidential and Vice Presidential debates.

1. Number

There will be two (2) Presidential debates and one (1) Vice Presidential debate before live audiences. The parties agree that they will not (1) issue any challenges for additional debates, (2) appear at any other debates or adversarial forum with any other presidential or vice presidential candidate, or (3) accept any network air time offers that involve a debate format or otherwise involve the simultaneous appearance of more than one candidate.

2. Dates

The parties agree that the Presidential debates will be held on October 6, 1996 and October 16, 1996. The parties agree that the Vice

Presidential debate will be held on October 9, 1996.

3. Participants

The participants in the two Presidential debates will be Bill Clinton and Bob Dole. The participants in the Vice Presidential debate will be Al Gore and Jack Kemp.

4. Sponsorship

The debate will be sponsored by the Commission, provided that the Commission agrees to all provisions of this Agreement. In the event that the Commission does not accept the provisions of this Agreement or is unable to fulfill the provisions of this Agreement, representatives of the two (2) candidates who are signatories to the Agreement will immediately use their best efforts to obtain a mutually agreeable alternate sponsor or sponsors for the debates on the dates set forth and only on the same terms and conditions agreed upon herein.

5. Location

The cities of Hartford, Connecticut; St. Petersburg, Florida; and San Diego, California will be the sites of the First Presidential debate, the Vice Presidential debate, and the Second Presidential debate, respectively.

6. Time

Each debate will last for a total of ninety (90) minutes, including all introductory proceedings, opening statements, questions, answers, and closing statements. All debates will start at 9:00 P.M. Eastern Daylight Time.

7. Process for selection of moderators

Representatives of each of the campaigns signatory to this Agreement will promptly submit a list of one (1) or two (2) possible moderators to the other in accordance with the dates and times set forth below, Eastern Daylight Time:

Dates and times by when lists of moderators are to be submitted:

First Presidential debate by 5:00 P.M. on Saturday, September 28, 1996

Vice Presidential debate by 3:00 P.M. on Sunday, September 29, 1996

Second Presidential debate by 3:00 P.M. on Monday, September 30, 1996

Each side will then have the opportunity to approve or delete names from the other's proposed list. In the event a party fails to select any moderators from the list of the other party, the rejecting party will immediately notify the submitting party, and the submitting party will promptly submit additional names to the rejecting party. When each side agrees upon at least one (1) possible moderator from the other side's list, then these two (2) or more names will be submitted to the Commission which will then select at random one (1) of these individuals to be the moderator for the respective debate. If necessary, the process set forth in this paragraph will be repeated until the agreed upon number of names are submitted to the Commission. The same process will be followed for the second Presidential debate and for the Vice Presidential debate. There will be a different moderator for each of the three (3) debates.

8. Format

The First Presidential debate and the Vice Presidential debate will be a moderator-only format ("moderator debates"). The Second Presidential debate will be a moderator and audience participation format ("town hall debate"). Each debate will have a single moderator responsible for enforcing the rules set forth in this Agreement.

A. MODERATOR DEBATE FORMAT

This format applies to both moderator debates:

(i) The moderator will ask questions of candidates as provided in this section 8(A). In the First Presidential debate, each candidate will be entitled to an opening statement of not more than two (2) minutes in length. In the Vice Presidential debate, no opening statements will be permitted. The first question will be to the candidate who, as determined by the provisions of this Agreement, will give the first closing statement in this debate ("Candidate A"). The moderator will limit the question to not more than thirty (30) seconds. The moderator will not state the topic of the question prior to asking the question. The candidate will limit his response to ninety (90) seconds. The other candidate ("Candidate B") will have sixty (60) seconds to comment on the question or on Candidate A's answer. Candidate A may then respond for up to thirty (30) seconds. No follow-up questions by the moderator will be permitted, and no cross-questions by candidates or cross-conversation between the candidates will be allowed under these rules.

(ii) The moderator will then ask a question of Candidate B, with rebuttal and surrebuttal to be conducted pursuant to section 8(A)(i) of this agreement.

(iii) The moderator will then ask a question of Candidate A with all questioning thereafter to rotate between the two candidates. No questions will be asked of a candidate by the moderator if less than six minutes remain in the First and Second Presidential debates or if less than eight minutes remain in the Vice Presidential debate.

(iv) In the First Presidential debate, each candidate will be entitled to make a closing statement of not more than two (2) minutes in length. In the Vice Presidential debate, each candidate will be entitled to make a closing statement of not more than three (3) minutes in length.

(v) The moderator will open and close the debate and will use his or her best effort to enforce all time limits. The moderator will

ensure that the questions asked of the candidates are on a broad
range of topics, including questions on foreign, domestic, and
economic policy. There will be no limitations on topics. The
moderator will vary the topics on which he or she questions
the candidates, and will ensure that the topics of the questions
are fairly apportioned between the candidates. The moderators
may use any reasonable method to ensure that the agreed-upon
format is followed by the candidates and the audience.

(vi) The positions for (a) opening statements, (b) answering the
questions for each topic, and (c) closing statements, will be
determined by the flip of a coin conducted by the Commission in the presence of representatives of the Committees. The
winner of the coin flip will choose either the A position or the
B position below.

Opening statement	Answer first question	Closing statement
A (first)	A (first)	A (first)
B (second)	B (second)	B (second)

The positions of the Presidential candidates for the town hall
debate will be reversed from their positions for the First Presidential debate. The Commission will conduct a separate coin
toss for the Vice Presidential debate, and the winner of that toss
will choose either the A position, in which case the candidate
will answer the first question and make the first closing statement, or the B position, in which case the candidate will answer
the second question and make the second closing statement.

B. MODERATOR AND AUDIENCE PARTICIPATION
FORMAT

(i) The Second Presidential debate will be a format featuring a
single moderator with audience members asking questions
("the town hall") and will be governed by this section 8(B).
The moderator will be selected according to the procedure
described in section 7 above.

(ii) The moderator in the town hall debate will introduce the candidates, open and close the debate, and facilitate audience members in asking questions to each of the candidates. The moderator will be permitted to ask brief follow-up questions to clarify or restate ambiguous questions. The moderator will ensure that the questions asked alternate between the two candidates and that the subject matter of questions encompass a broad range of topics, including foreign, domestic and economic policy. There will be no limitations on topics. The moderator will attempt to limit excessively long questions and move the debate along. The moderator will exercise full authority and responsibility to select the questioners from the audience.

(iii) The moderator may move about the audience with a wireless microphone. The Commission will endeavor to seat the audience in a horseshoe configuration around the stage. In the event that this is not possible, the Commission will endeavor to seat the audience in an informal and intimate style that is conducive to the audience asking questions.

(iv) The town hall debate will take place in an appropriately small facility before a live audience of approximately 250 people who shall be seated and who describe themselves as likely voters who are "uncommitted" as to their 1996 Presidential vote. These participants will be selected by an independent research firm agreed upon by the Committees. The research firm will have sole responsibility for selecting the nationally demographically representative group of voters. There will be no advance submissions of questions to the candidates. There will be no stools used during the debate. The candidates will stand in a structure that will allow each candidate to move easily and directly to the front opening and which will accommodate the physical needs of the candidate. The structures shall be recommended by the Commission's executive producer and/or stage designer and mutually agreed upon by the representatives of both campaigns. The precise staging arrangement will be recommended by the

Commission's executive producer and/or stage designer and mutually agreed upon by representatives of both campaigns.

(v) Each candidate will have the option to make an opening statement that will not exceed two (2) minutes in duration and a closing statement that will not exceed two (2) minutes in duration. The order of statements will be determined by the procedure set forth in section 8(A)(vi) above. Additionally, the provision in section 8(D) below, concerning the candidates' entitlement to closing statements irrespective of whether the debate runs beyond the planned ending time shall apply to the town hall format.

(vi) The candidate who is asked the question from the audience will have ninety (90) seconds to respond. The other candidate will have sixty (60) seconds to rebut the answer, and the candidate who initially answered the question will have thirty (30) seconds for surrebuttal. No cross questioning or cross conversation between the candidates will be permitted.

(vii) Each candidate will be entitled to make a closing statement not to exceed two (2) minutes in duration.

(viii) Each candidate will have either a type of wireless, hand-held microphone or a wireless lapel microphone to allow them to move about, as otherwise provided for in this paragraph, and to face different directions while responding to questions from the audience. Each candidate may choose his own microphone within the terms set forth in this paragraph, and the Commission will have at each debate at least one back-up microphone for each candidate. Each candidate may move about in a pre-designated area to be mutually determined at the site by the parties. The pre-designated areas of the candidates may not overlap.

(ix) All members of the audience will be requested by the moderator before the debate goes on the air and by the moderator after the debate goes on the air not to applaud or respond by any means other than silent observation, other than for persons selected by the moderator to ask questions of the candidates. The moderator will advise the audience prior to the debate that no audience responses will be permitted and that any member of the audience who violates this rule will be asked to leave the building.

C. FILM FOOTAGE

It is agreed that neither film footage nor video footage from a debate may be used publicly by any candidates or candidates' campaign.

D. CLOSING STATEMENT

Irrespective of whether a debate runs beyond the planned ending time, each candidate in the two Presidential debates will be entitled to make a closing statement not to exceed two (2) minutes in duration and each candidate in the Vice Presidential debate will be entitled to make a closing statement not to exceed three (3) minutes in duration. The Commission will use its best efforts to ensure that the TV networks carry the entire debate even if it runs past the specified ending time.

E. MANNER OF ADDRESS

Each candidate will determine the manner by which he prefers to be addressed by the moderators and will communicate this to the Commission.

9. Staging and production

A. When the debate programs go on the air, the candidates will be standing in place on the stage.

B. Other than as may be permitted by section 8(B) (town hall format) of this Agreement, the candidates will stand at separate podiums for each debate.

C. Other than as may be provided in section 8(B) (town hall format), the Commission will construct the podiums, and each shall be identical to view from the audience side. These podiums will be constructed in a style mutually agreed upon by representatives of the signatories to this Agreement. Each podium shall measure fifty-two (52) inches from the stage floor to the outside top of the podium facing the audience, unless otherwise mutually agreed to by the representatives of both candidates participating in the debate. Other requirements for these podiums will be verbally transmitted to the Commission by representatives of the candidates. There will be no writings, markings or emblems of any kind on the fronts of the podiums. No candidate will be permitted to use risers or any other device to create an appearance of elevated height, and no candidate shall be permitted to use chairs, stools or other seating devices during the debates. Within these rules, the Commission will make every effort to accommodate any special requirements requested by the candidates.

D. The microphone for each candidate will be attached to the podium, and in no case will any microphone be physically attached to a candidate except during the town hall debate, as is otherwise provided in this Agreement.

E. For both Presidential debates, Bob Dole will occupy the stage-right position, and Bill Clinton will occupy the stage-left position. For the Vice Presidential debate, Al Gore will occupy the stage-left position, and Jack Kemp will occupy the stage-right position.

F. The podiums will be equally canted toward the center of the stage at a degree to be determined by the Commission's producer. The podiums will not be more than ten (10) feet apart from each other; nor will they be closer than eight (8) feet to each other; such distances will be measured from the left-right center of a podium to the left-right center of the podium immediately next to it.

G. All members of the audience will be instructed by the moderator before the debate goes on the air and by the moderator after the debate goes on the air not to applaud or otherwise participate in the debate by any means other than by silent observation. The moderator will use his or her best efforts to enforce this provision.

H. In the moderator debate, the moderator will be seated so as to be positioned between the candidates and the cameras to which the candidates may direct their answers.

I. Time cues will be given to a candidate when he has thirty (30) seconds remaining in his answer, and a separate and distinct time cue will be given to a candidate when he has fifteen (15) seconds remaining in his answer. The form of the time cues will be mutually agreed upon by the signatories to this Agreement. There will be a separate set of cues (one (1) for each candidate), and these cues will be large and in each candidate's direct line of sight to the camera to which he is giving his answer. The candidates will not be required to look up, down or sideways to see these cues.

J. Each candidate will be permitted to have a complete, private, production and technical briefing and walk-through ("Briefing") at the location of the debate on the day of the debate. Each candidate will have a maximum of one (1) hour for this Briefing. Production lock-down will not occur for any candidate until that candidate has had his Briefing.

K. There will be no filming or taping allowed during the candidates' Briefing.

L. All persons, including but not limited to the press; other candidates and their representatives; and the employees or other agents of the Commission other than those necessary to conduct the Briefing, shall vacate the debate site while a candidate has his Briefing. The Commission will provide to each candidate's representatives a written statement and plan which describes the measures to be taken by the Commission to ensure complete privacy of all Briefings.

M. No press will be allowed into the auditorium where the debate
will take place during the candidates' Briefing.

N. The candidates may take notes during the debate on the size, color,
and type of paper each prefers. Each candidate must submit to the
staff of the Commission prior to the debate all such paper and any
pens or pencils with which a candidate may wish to take notes
during the debate, and the staff of the Commission will place
such paper, pens, and pencils on the podium of each candidate.
No candidate will be permitted to take or use any notes, other
written materials, props, or other material into the debate.

O. In addition to Secret Service personnel, the President's military
aide, and the President's physician, each candidate will be permitted to have at least one (1) pre-designated staff member in
the wings or in the immediate backstage area during the debate.
The number of staff permitted and their precise location will be
mutually agreed upon by representatives of the Committees at
each site. All other staff must vacate the wings or immediate
backstage areas no later than five (5) minutes after the debate
has begun and may not return sooner than five (5) minutes
before the debate concludes. In addition, each candidate will
be permitted to have one (1) pre-designated staff member in the
production facility prior to and during the debate. A PL phone
line will be provided between each candidate's staff member in
the production facility and that candidate's staff work area. No
other staff member may enter the production facility at any time
during the debate.

P. Other than security personnel, not more than two (2) aides will
accompany each candidate on the stage before the program
begins.

Q. Each candidate shall be allowed to have one (1) still photogra-
pher present on the stage before the debate begins and in the
wings during the debate, as desired, and on the stage immedi-

ately upon the conclusion of the debate. Photos taken by these photographers may be distributed to the press as determined by each candidate.

R.   The color and style of the backdrop will be recommended by the Commission and mutually determined by the representatives of the Committees.

S.   The set will be completed and lit no later than 3 P.M. at the debate site on the day before the debate will occur.

10. Cameras

A.   Camera placement will be recommended by the Commission's producer and mutually agreed upon by the Committees.

B.   Except for the town hall debate, TV cameras will be locked into place during all debates. They may, however, tilt or rotate as needed.

C.   TV coverage shall be limited to shots of the candidates and questioners. During the moderator debates, the shots will be limited to the moderator when he or she is asking the question or to the candidates when each candidate is answering the questions. Except for the town hall debate, in no case shall any television shots be taken of any member of the audience (including candidates' family members) from the time the first question is asked until the conclusion of the closing statements. During the town hall debate, one roving camera will be permitted, provided that such camera may be used only to take shots of the audience members asking the questions during the time that he or she is asking the question.

D.   There will be no tally lights lit on any of the cameras during the broadcast of the debate.

E. Each camera to which a candidate will direct his answers shall be distinctively marked so that each candidate can clearly determine where he should direct his remarks if desiring to do so into a camera.

F. There will be no TV cut-aways to any candidate who is not responding to a question while another candidate is answering a question nor to a candidate who is not giving an opening or closing statement while another candidate is doing so.

11. Ticket distribution and seating arrangements

A. Each candidate will directly receive one-third of the tickets for each moderator debate with the remaining one-third going to the Commission. Other than tickets for audience participants, there will be no tickets distributed in connection with the town hall debate, except the Commission will ensure that the immediate families of the respective candidates will be admitted to the town hall debate, as well as to the other debates.

B. It is the intent of the parties that the supporters of each candidate attending the debates be interspersed among supporters of the other candidate. The Commission will make every effort to ensure that supporters are properly interspersed. The immediate family members of each candidate will, however, be seated as described in paragraph (D) immediately below.

C. The Commission will invite from their allotment (two (2) tickets each) an agreed upon list of officeholders such as the U.S. Senate and House Majority and Minority Leaders, the Governor and Lieutenant Governor of the state holding the debate, that state's congressional delegation, appropriate state legislative representatives and the Mayor and City Council members of the city holding the debate.

D. In the event supporters of the candidates attending the debates cannot be seated as described in paragraph (B) immediately above then the following shall apply. Each candidate's family and supporters shall be given seats on the side of the auditorium from which their candidate is speaking. Each candidate shall have the first four (4) rows of his half of the auditorium for his personal use, and succeeding rows on his half of the auditorium will be made available for supporters of that particular candidate.

E. Any press seated in the auditorium can only be accommodated in the two (2) rows of the auditorium farthest from the podiums. Two (2) still-photo pool stands may be positioned near either side of the TV camera stands located in the audience. (A press center with all necessary feeds will be otherwise available.)

F. Tickets will be delivered by the Commission to the campaign manager of each candidate's campaign or his representative by 12:00 noon on the day preceding the debate.

12. Dressing Rooms/Holding Rooms

A. Each candidate will have a dressing room available of adequate space for the staff the candidate desires to have in this area. An equal number of other backstage rooms will be available for other staff members of each candidate. All of these rooms may be furnished as deemed necessary by the candidates' representatives. Each candidate's rooms will be reasonably segregated from those designated for the other candidate. If sufficient space is not available, the Commission will rent a trailer of adequate size for each candidate and his staff to use. The number of individuals allowed in these rooms or trailers shall be determined by each candidate. Backstage passes (if needed) will be issued to the candidates' representatives as requested. The Commission will not restrict the issuance of these passes. The rooms mentioned in the preceding paragraph will be available at least seventy-two (72) hours in advance of the beginning of each debate.

B. The Commission will provide each candidate with a direct television feed from the production truck to two (2) monitors placed in the candidate's dressing room and staff holding rooms as requested by the candidate's representatives. In addition, the Commission will provide four (4) additional functioning TV sets for each candidate. These sets will be located as desired by representatives of each candidate.

C. Each candidate may use his own make-up person, and adequate facilities will be provided at the debate site for make-up.

13. Press

A. Each candidate will receive not less than thirty (30) press passes for the Press Center and more if mutually agreed upon by the Committees.

B. Each candidate will be allowed to have an unlimited number of people in the Press Center upon the conclusion of the debate.

C. The Commission will be responsible for all press credentialing.

14. Amendments

This Agreement will not be changed or amended except in writing signed by both persons who signed this Agreement or their designees.

Clinton/Gore '96   Dole/Kemp '96

_____   _____

by: by:
date: date:

Appendix B

News from the . . .
DEMOCRATIC AND REPUBLICAN
NATIONAL COMMITTEES

Release: Wednesday, February 18, 1987

Contact: Robert P. Schmermund, RNC   Terry Michael, DNC
          202/863-8550   202/863-8020

RNC AND DNC ESTABLISH COMMISSION ON PRESIDENTIAL DEBATES

Washington, D.C.—Republican National Committee Chairman Frank J. Fahrenkopf, Jr. and Democratic National Committee Chairman Paul G. Kirk, Jr. announced the creation of the Commission on Presidential Debates at a joint press conference today at the Capitol.

The 10-member commission is a bipartisan, non-profit, tax-exempt organization formed to implement joint sponsorship of general election presidential and vice presidential debates, starting in 1988, by the national Republican and Democratic committees between their respective nominees.

In launching this new initiative, the two party chairmen said, "A major responsibility of both the Democratic and Republican parties is to inform the electorate on their philosophies and policies as well as those of their respective candidates. One of the most effective ways of accomplishing this is through debates between their nominees. By jointly sponsoring these debates, we will better fulfill our party responsibilities to inform and educate the electorate, strengthen the role of political parties in the electoral process and, most important of all, we can institutionalize the debates, making them an integral and permanent part of the presidential debate process."

In emphasizing the bipartisan nature of the commission, both chairmen noted the contributions to the debate process by the League of Women Voters: "We applaud the League for laying a foundation from which we can assume our own responsibilities. While the two party committees will be sponsors for all future presidential general election debates between our party nominees, we would expect and encourage the League's participation in sponsoring other debates, particularly in the presidential primary process."

Kirk and Fahrenkopf, in stressing the need to institutionalize the debates, said it will be the Commission's goal to recommend the number of presidential and vice presidential debates, as well as the dates and locations of these debates, before the 1988 nominating conventions. Potential candidates for the parties' respective nominations have committed to support party-sponsored debates. The Commission's recommendations will be forwarded to all potential candidates for concurrence as soon as they are completed.

"This degree of certainty about the debates going into the general election," the chairmen said, "is an historic breakthrough in institutionalizing them. It means that we won't spend most of the general election campaign debating about debates, as we have too often in the past. The American people have an expectation that debates will occur every four years; this process is designed to assure that that expectation will be realized."

Fahrenkopf and Kirk will serve as co-chairs of the new Commission. They appointed as vice-chairs:

• Richard Moe, Washington lawyer and partner in the firm of Davis, Polk & Wardell;

• David Norcross, Washington lawyer and partner in the firm of Myers, Matteo, Rabil, Pluese & Norcross.

Others named on the Commission are:

- U.S. Rep. Barbara Vucanovich (R-NV);

- former U.S. Senator John Culver (D-IA), now a partner in the Washington law firm of Arent, Fox, Kintner, Plotkin & Kahn;

- Republican Gov. Kay Orr of Nebraska;

- Vernon Jordan, a Democrat, former president of the Urban League, now a partner in the firm of Akin, Gump, Strauss, Hauer & Feld;

- Pamela Harriman, chairman of Democrats for the '80's;

- U.S. Senator Pete Wilson (R-CA).

The two chairmen said the Commission will hire staff and open a Washington office shortly. They said articles of incorporation for the Commission have been filed in the District of Columbia as well as an application for tax exemption with the Internal Revenue Service.

Kirk and Fahrenkopf concluded by saying, "We have no doubt that with the help of the Commission we can forge a permanent framework on which all future presidential debates between the nominees of the two political parties will be based. It is our responsibility as Party chairmen to have an informative and fair presidential debate process. The establishment of the Commission on Presidential Debates will go a long way toward achieving that goal."

Today's announcement stems from a recommendation of the Commission on National Elections, which during 1985 studied the presidential election system. On Nov. 26, 1985, Kirk and Fahrenkopf signed a joint memorandum agreeing in principle to pursue the party sponsorship concept.

Notes

1: DEBATE CARTEL

1   Alan Schroeder, *Presidential Debates: Forty Years of High Risk TV* (New York: Columbia University Press, 2001), 202–203.

2   Frank Fahrenkopf, interview by the author, 27 March 2001.

3   *Arkansas Education Television Commission v. Forbes*, 118 Sup. Ct. 1633, 1640 (1998).

4   House Committee on House Administration, *Presidential Debates: Hearing Before the Subcommittee on Elections of the House Committee on House Administration*, 103d Cong., first session, 17 June 1993, Washington, 173.

5   John B. Anderson, interview by Jim Lehrer, *Debating Our Destiny*, Public Broadcasting System, 13 September 1999.

6   House Committee on House Administration, *Presidential Debates: Hearing Before the Subcommittee on Elections of the House Committee on House Administration*, 196.

7   Jamin Raskin, "The Debate Gerrymander," *Texas Law Review* 77 (1999): 1988–89.

8   John B. Anderson, interview by Jim Lehrer, *Debating Our Destiny*, Public Broadcasting System, 13 September 1999.

9   Sidney Kraus, *Televised Presidential Debates and Public Policy* (Hillsdale, NJ: Lawrence Erlbaum Associates, 2000).

10 Lawrence Noble, interview by the author, 3 November 2001.

11 "The Debate Debate," *Washington Post*, 28 August 1980.

12 David Greenberg, "Presidential Debates: Politics as Entertainment," TomPaine.com, 2 October 2000.

13 Martin Plissner, *The Control Room: How Television Calls the Shots in Presidential Elections* (New York: The Free Press, 1999), 129.

14 Hedrick Smith, "Carter Clouds the Issue, So Who's on First?," *New York Times*, 14 September 1980.

15 Plissner, *The Control Room*, 136.

16 House Committee on House Administration, *Presidential Debates: Hearing Before the Subcommittee on Elections of the House Committee on House Administration*, 40.

17 House Committee on House Administration, *Presidential Debates: Hearing Before the Subcommittee on Elections of the House Committee on House Administration*, 40.

18 J. Y. Smith, "Ambassador, Socialite Pamela Harriman Dies," *Washington Post*, 6 February 1997.

19 Karen Branch-Brioso, "'Nonpartisan' Board Has Failed to Tame Debates," *St. Louis Post-Dispatch*, 17 September 2000.

20 "Newsweek Cover: The Secret Vote That Made Bush President," press release, 9 September 2001.
21 Dorothy Ridings, interview by the author, 19 March 2001.
22 Newton Minow, interview by the author, 14 July 2001.
23 Alan Simpson, interview by the author, 18 March 2002.
24 Congressman John Lewis, interview by the author, 17 September 2002.
25 Chris Black, "Candidates May Meet at Kennedy Library," *Boston Globe*, 3 December 1991.
26 Barbara Vucanovich, interview by the author, 23 July 2001.
27 David Norcross, interview by the author, 26 March 2001.
28 Scott Reed, interview by the author, 2 April 2001.
29 Michael Rezendes, "Debate Panel Widely Faulted for Asking Perot's Exclusion," *Boston Globe*, 19 September 1996.
30 "Commission on Presidential Debates Co-Chairmen Discuss Gore-Bush Agreement," *Early Edition*, CNN, 15 September 2000.
31 Ibid.
32 Doug Ireland, "Eating Ross," www.citypages.com, 25 September 1996.
33 "Easy Money!: A Report on the Gambling Industry and Its Economic and Political Clout," *Frontline*, Public Broadcasting System, 1997.
34 Reverend Tom Grey, interview by the author, 12 October 2001.
35 www.opensecrets.org
36 Oren Weinrib, "Heads or Tails: You Lose," www.TomPaine.com, 26 October 2000.
37 Ron Crickenberger, interview by the author, 23 September 2001.
38 Jonathan Groner and Sheila Kaplan, "Buying Smoke and Mirrors at the Debates," *Legal Times*, 2 November 1992.
39 Joe Battenfeld, "Company Sponsors' Funds 'Ad' Up," *Boston Herald*, 2 October 2000.
40 Dana Milbank, *Smashmouth: Two Years in the Gutter with Al Gore and George W. Bush* (New York: Basic Books, 2001), 334.
41 Frank Donatelli, interview by the author, 12 October 2001.
42 Antonia Hernandez, interview by the author, 18 January 2002.
43 Nancy Neuman, interview by the author, 24 August 2001.
44 Jo Mannies, "Agreement to Sponsor Debates Reflects Anheuser-Busch Growing Political Profile," *St. Louis Post-Dispatch*, 7 January 2000.
45 Nathan Johnson, "Presidential Debates Betray Democracy," *Press and Dakotan*, 17 October 2000.
46 "Election 2000: Debating Debate Exclusion," *Burden of Proof*, CNN, 3 October 2000.
47 Frank Fahrenkopf, interview by the author, 27 March 2001.
48 Ibid.
49 Scott Reed, interview by the author, 2 April 2001.
50 Frank Donatelli, interview by the author, 12 October 2001.

51 David Von Drehle, "The Debates: Defining Moments," *Washington Post*, 22 October 2000.

52 Alan Schroeder, *Presidential Debates: Forty Years of High Risk TV* (New York: Columbia University Press, 2001), 24.

53 Frank Fahrenkopf, interview by the author, 27 March 2001.

54 Bob Teeter, interview by the author, 31 July 2001.

55 David Norcross, interview by the author, 26 March 2001.

56 Sidney Kraus, *Televised Presidential Debates and Public Policy*, 45.

57 House Committee on House Administration, *Presidential Debates: Hearing Before the Subcommittee on Elections of the House Committee on House Administration*, 128.

58 Janet Brown, interview by the author, 1 August 2001.

59 John Culver, interview by the author, 23 March 2001.

2: HOSTILE TAKEOVER

1 Michael Blumfield, "League Selects L.A. as Site of One Presidential Debate," *Los Angeles Times*, 29 July 1987.

2 Kathleen Hendrix, "The League Turns Seventy: Where to Now?" *Los Angeles Times*, 16 March 1990.

3 Arthur Unger, "Staging the TV Debates," *Christian Science Monitor*, 27 October 1980.

4 David Norcross, interview by the author, 26 March 2001.

5 Public Papers of the Presidents of the United States: Carter (Washington, DC: GPO, 1980), 2272–73.

6 Jacqueline Tescott, "First Lady of the League," *Washington Post*, 10 September 1980.

7 "Why Not Three Times Two?" *Christian Science Monitor*, 11 September 1980.

8 Ben Franklin, "For Baltimore, Debate Means Getting Down to Business," *New York Times*, 21 September 1980.

9 "The Next Debate," *New York Times*, 23 September 1980.

10 Newton Minow, interview by the author, 14 July 2001.

11 Nancy Neuman, interview by the author, 10 September 2001.

12 Bernard Weinraub, "League May Rearrange Panel Selection Method," *New York Times*, 8 October1984.

13 Rushworth M. Kidder, "Why the Press Was the Loser in This Year's Presidential Debates," *Christian Science Monitor*, 22 October 1984.

14 Phil Gaily, "Voters' League Names Four to Ask the Questions Sunday," *New York Times*, 19 October 1984.

15 Nancy Neuman and Victoria Harian, "The League of Women Voters Should Sponsor Debates," in *Presidential Debates: 1988 and Beyond*, 10.

16 David Norcross, interview by the author, 26 March 2001.

17 John Buckley, interview by the author, 2 February 2002.

18 Janet Brown, interview by the author, 1 August 2001.

19 Howell Raines, "Two Party Chairmen Weigh Plan to Assume Debates' Sponsorship," *New York Times*, 16 May 1984.

20 House Committee on House Administration, *Presidential Debates: Hearing Before the Subcommittee on Elections of the House Committee on House Administration*, 103d Cong., first session, 17 June 1993, Washington, 90. Paul Kirk said, "When Frank and I and our fellow directors created the commission, we were acting as agents of those individuals who served on those prior study commissions."

21 Phil Gailey, "Two Parties to Run Political Debates," *New York Times*, 27 November 1985.

22 Frank Fahrenkopf and Paul Kirk, *Memorandum of Agreement on Presidential Candidate Joint Appearances*, 26 November 1985.

23 "G.O.P Seeks a City for '88," *New York Times*, 26 January 1986.

24 "News from the Democratic and Republican National Committees," 18 February 1987.

25 Ibid.

26 Phil Gailey, "Democrats and Republicans Form Panel to Hold Presidential Debates," *New York Times*, 19 February 1987.

27 Frank Fahrenkopf, interview by the author, 27 March 2001.

28 Commission on Presidential Debates Web page, www.debates.org

29 Tom Brokaw, "Networks Should Sponsor Debates," in *Presidential Debates: 1988 And Beyond*, 74.

30 Mary McGrory, "Presidential Debates: Not Broken," *Washington Post*, 1 December 1985.

31 Nancy Neuman and Victoria Harian, "The League of Women Voters Should Sponsor Debates," in *Presidential Debates: 1988 and Beyond*, 10.

32 James Baker, interview by the author, 13 September 2001.

33 Jack Nelson, "Bipartisan Group to Sponsor L.A. Debate After League of Women Voters Drops Out," *Los Angeles Times*, 4 October 1988.

34 Nancy Neuman, interview by the author, 10 September 2001.

35 League of Women Voters, press release, 3 October 1988.

36 "Score One for the Truth," *Chicago Tribune*, 5 October 1988.

37 Sidney Kraus, *Televised Presidential Debates and Public Policy*, 78.

38 Scott Reed, interview by the author, 2 April 2001.

39 Bobby Burchfield, interview by the author, 5 April 2001.

40 John Buckley, interview by the author, 2 February 2002.

41 George Stephanopolous, interview by the author, 20 March 2001.

42 Bob Neuman, interview by the author, 10 September 2001.

43 Scott Reed, interview by the author, 2 April 2001.

44 James Baker, interview by the author, 13 September 2001.

45 Martin Plissner, interview by the author, 3 April 2001.

46 Richard Neustadt, interview by the author, 24 August 2001.

47 Frank Fahrenkopf, interview by the author, 27 March 2001.
48 Dorothy Ridings, interview by the author, 19 March 2001.
49 Richard Moe, interview by the author, 16 April 2001.
50 Martin Plissner, interview by the author, 3 April 2001.
51 James B. Lemert, William R. Elliott, James M. Bernstein, William L. Rosenberg, and Karl J. Nestvold, *News Verdicts, the Debates, and Presidential Campaigns* (New York: Praeger Publishers, 1991).
52 Paul Taylor, interview by the author, 19 March 2002.
53 Kay Maxwell, interview by the author, 17 January 2002.
54 Committee for a Unified Independent Party, press conference, Washington, DC, 8 May 2000.

3: CANDIDATE EXCLUSION

1 Ben Wattenberg, *A Third Choice: The Story of Third Party Candidates in America*, Public Broadcasting System, 1996.
2 *Public Papers of the Presidents of the United States: Carter* (Washington, DC: GPO, 1980), 2272–73.
3 David Norcross, interview by the author, 26 March 2001.
4 Ibid.
5 Richard Moe, interview by the author, 16 April 2001.
6 Newton Minow and Lee Mitchell, "Formalize Debates," *New York Times*, 30 May 1984.
7 Alan Simpson, interview by the author, 18 March 2002.
8 Mickey Kantor, interview by the author, 16 September 2001.
9 Lawrence Noble, interview by the author 3 November 2001.
10 "The Debate Debate," *NewsHour*, Public Broadcasting System, 17 September 1996.
11 Richard Neustadt, interview by the author, 24 August 2001.
12 Diana Carlin, "Constructing the 1996 Debates: Determining the Setting, Formats, and Participants," in *Presidential Debates: 1988 and Beyond*, 143.
13 Marc Fisher, "Vernon Jordan Is a Man Comfortable with Power," *Washington Post*, 27 January 1998.
14 Richard Neustadt, interview by the author, 24 August 2001.
15 House Committee on House Administration, *Presidential Debates: Hearing Before the Subcommittee on Elections of the House Committee on House Administration*, 150.
16 Jamin Raskin, "The Debate Gerrymander," *Texas Law. Review* 77 (1999): 1967.
17 Ibid., 1981.
18 Ira Glasser, "Ending Democracy As We Knew It: A Radical Proposal from Clinton and Dole," *Visions of Liberty*, 13 October 1996.
19 Richard Neustadt, interview by the author, 24 August 2001.
20 Scott Reed, interview by the author, 2 April 2001.

21 Kenneth Thompson, interview by the author, 20 April 2001.

22 John B. Anderson, conversation with the author, 18 March 2003.

23 Charles T. Royer, *Campaign for President: The Managers Look at 1992* (Hollis, NH: Puritan Press, 1994), 164–65.

24 During an interview by the author, Professor Kenneth Thompson said, "First time I ever visited Paris, doing a survey of studies in politics and so on, we went by the General Assembly, and the cab driver said that's our insane asylum. You know, the multiparty thing can drive you in that direction, and the two-party system forces disparate groups to come together and meld some of their interests and go with those of others. Unless the parties become so unrepresentative that they don't really stand for any group in society, why, I'd be in favor of the continuation of two parties."

25 House Committee on House Administration, *Presidential Debates: Hearing Before the Subcommittee on Elections of the House Committee on House Administration*, 45–46.

26 Ibid., 47.

27 Ann Devroy, "Bush Makes 4-Debate Offer," *Washington Post*, 30 September 1992.

28 Mickey Kantor, interview by the author, 16 September 2001.

29 Michael K. Frisby, "Clinton Assails Foe's 'Debate Day' Absence," *Boston Globe*, 23 September 1992.

30 House Comittee on House Administration, *Presidential Debates: Hearing Before the Subcommittee on Elections of the House Committee on House Administration*, 50–51.

31 Mickey Kantor, interview by the author, 16 September 2001.

32 Charles T. Royer, *Campaign for President: The Managers Look at 1992*, 238.

33 House Committee on House Administration, *Presidential Debates: Hearing Before the Subcommittee on Elections of the House Committee on House Administration*, 137.

34 Mickey Kantor, interview by the author, 16 September 2001.

35 Diana Carlin, "Constructing the 1996 Debates: Determining the Setting, Formats, and Participants," in *Presidential Debates: 1988 and Beyond*, 142.

36 David Broder, *Campaign for President: The Managers Look at '96* (Hollis, NH: Hollis Publishing Company, 1997), 165.

37 Frank Fahrenkopf, interview by the author, 27 March 2001.

38 Stephen Bates, *The Future of Presidential Debates* (Washington, DC: The Annenberg Washington Program in Communications Policy Studies of Northwestern University, 1993).

39 Bobby Burchfield, interview by the author, 5 April 2001.

40 "The Debate Debate," *NewsHour*, Public Broadcasting System, 17 September 1996.

41 Frank Fahrenkopf, interview by the author, 27 March 2001.

42 Janet Brown, interview by the author, 1 August 2001.

43 Bob Teeter, interview by the author, 31 July 2001.

44 Mickey Kantor, interview by the author, 16 September 2001.

45 Charles T. Royer, *Campaign for President: The Managers Look at 1992*, 239.

46 Martin Plissner, *The Control Room: How Television Calls the Shots in Presidential Elections* (New York: The Free Press, 1999), 151.

47 "Perot Says He'll Be at Debate Site," *USA Today*, 20 September 1996.

48 Martin Plissner, *The Control Room: How Television Calls the Shots in Presidential Elections*, 155.

49 Barbara Vobejda, "Dole 'Rude and Arrogant'; Reform Nominee Says Debate Snub May Harm Others in GOP," *Washington Post*, 23 September 1996.

50 Bennett Roth, "Committee to Rule on Debate with Perot; Dole, Clinton Split on His Participation," *Houston Chronicle*, 11 September 1996.

51 George Will, "Buchanan Has Right to Be in the Debate," *Washington Post*, 21 September 1999.

52 Scott Reed, interview by the author, 2 April 2001.

53 Frank Donatelli, interview by the author, 12 October 2001.

54 "Debate Negotiators Detail Their Format Proposals," CNN, 18 September 1996.

55 George Stephanopolous, interview by the author, 20 March 2001.

56 Ernest Tollerson, "Perot Shifts Focus from the Presidency to Dole and Politics," *New York Times*, 26 September 1996.

57 David Broder, *Campaign for President: The Managers Look at '96*, 162.

58 E-mail from Scott Reed to the author.

59 Scott Reed, interview by the author, 2 April 2001.

60 Mickey Kantor, interview by the author, 16 September 2001.

61 During an interview by the author, Advisory Committee member Dorothy Ridings confessed to having "no idea" what the criteria for inclusion in the 1996 presidential debates were. She wasn't even sure whether the polling threshold for inclusion in the 2000 presidential debates was 15 percent or 20 percent.

62 Neil Leis, "How Debates Panel Decided to Exclude Perot," *New York Times*, 19 September 1996.

63 "Clinton and Dole Campaigns Far Apart in Debate Talks," CNN, 18 September 1996.

64 David Broder, *Campaign for President: The Managers Look at '96*, 162.

65 David Norcross, interview by the author, 26 March 2001.

66 Mickey Kantor, interview by the author, 16 September 2001.

67 David Broder, "Stop Playing Games with Presidential Debates," *Washington Post*, 25 September 1996.

68 Ibid., 170.

69 Ibid., 178.

70 Mickey Kantor, interview by the author, 16 September 2001.

71 Professor Diana Carlin, Advisory Committee member, wrote:

Perot argued that his numbers were identical in the two election years. Examination of the polls supplied for our deliberations disproves this claim. The Advisory Committee held a conference call on October 5, 1992, to review Perot and the other candidates. The polls we were given showed Perot with a low of 9% (*Newsweek*) and a high of 20% (Gannet/Harris). A *Washington Post* poll from October 2, 1992, had him at 14%. Given that Perot reentered the 1992 race on October 1, 1992, those numbers were significant. In contrast, the polling data received in 1996 showed Perot in single digits in all but one poll taken in September. The exception was the *Los Angeles Times*, which had him at 10%. Most polls showed him in the 4% to 6% range.

72 George Stephanopolous, interview by the author, 20 March 2001.

73 A *USA Today*/CNN poll put Perot at 8 percent on October 4. An ABC News/*Washington Post* poll put Perot at 8 percent on October 5. A CBS News/*New York Times* poll put Perot at 7 percent on October 5. A Harris Poll put Perot's support at 9 percent on October 5. NBC/*Wall Street Journal* and the *Los Angeles Times* did not publish polls that asked who the polltaker would vote for during that time period.

74 The *Los Angeles Times* put Perot at 10 percent on September 10. A Harris poll put Perot's support at 7 percent on September 10. ABC News/*Washington Post* measured Perot's support at 7 percent on September 15. *USA Today*/CNN, which conducted polls almost daily, put Perot at 7 percent on September 13, 7 percent on September 14, 8 percent on September 15, 6 percent on September 16, and 6 percent on September 17. CBS/*New York Times* and NBC/*Wall Street Journal* did not publish polls that asked who the polltaker would vote for during that time period.

75 "Stacked Against Perot," *Boston Globe*, 19 September 1996.

76 "The Debate Debate," *NewsHour*, Public Broadcasting System, 17 September 1996.

77 Toni Locy, "Jackson Says Excluding Perot 'Stinks,'" *Washington Post*, 26 September 1996.

78 Nancy Neuman, interview by the author, 10 September 2001.

79 David Broder, "Stop Playing Games with Presidential Debates," *Washington Post*, 25 September 1996.

80 "Fixing the Presidential Debates," *New York Times*, 18 September 1996.

81 Barbara Vobejda, "Dole 'Rude and Arrogant'; Reform Nominee Says
    Debate Snub May Harm Others in GOP," *Washington Post*, 23 September 1996.

82 Nancy Othen, "Judge Denies Perot Spot in Presidential Debates," www.
    Alligator.org, 2 October 1996.

83 Scott E. Thomas, interview by the author, 12 November 2001.

84 Lawrence Noble, interview by the author, 3 November 2001.

85 Nancy Neuman, interview by the author, 10 September 2001.

86 David Broder, "Presidential Debate Panel Reviewing Entry Rules," *Washington Post*, 26 October 1999.

87 Benjamin Parke, "New Reform Party Candidate John Anderson Added
    to Ballot," *Daily Bruin Online*, 3 February 2000.

88 Antonia Hernandez, interview by the author, 18 January 2002.

89 Bob Neuman, interview by the author, 10 September 2001.

90 Scott Reed, interview by the author, 2 April 2001.

91 Editorial, *Fort Lauderdale Sun-Sentinel*, 9 January 2000.

92 Scott Reed, interview by the author, 2 April 2001.

93 *Late Edition*, CNN, 6 August 6, 2000.

94 "Include Four Candidates in Presidential Debate," *Seattle Times*, 4 June 2000.

95 Peter Marks, "Bush, Facing Criticism, Abandons Debate Stance," *New York Times*, 19 September 2000.

96 Elaine Kamarck, interview by the author, 2 August 2001.

97 Glen Johnson, "Debate Panel Takes Control," *Boston Globe*, 15 September 2000.

98 Martin Plissner, interview by the author, 3 April 2001.

99 B. Drummond Ayres, "Campaign Briefing," *New York Times*, 29 June 2000.

100 George Stephanopolous, interview by the author, 20 March 2001.

101 E-mail from William Daley to the author, 7 August 2001.

102 Peter Knight, interview by the author, 4 February 2002.

103 John Buckley, interview by the author, 2 February 2002.

104 Mickey Kantor, interview by the author, 16 September 2001.

105 Congressman John Lewis, interview by the author, 17 September 2002.

106 Ralph Nader, interview by the author, 5 January 2003.

4: STILTED FORMATS

1 Network Proposal to Sponsor Debates, 1991

2 Leslie Phillips, "The Great Debate: The Debates," *USA Today*, 26 September 1991.

3 A. Corrado, ed., *Let America Decide: The Report of the Twentieth Century Fund Task Forces on Presidential Debates* (New York: Twentieth Century Fund, 1995), 77.

4   Network Proposal to Sponsor Debates, 1991.

5   Ibid.

6   Leslie Phillips, "The Great Debate: The Debates," *USA Today*, 26 September 1991.

7   Frank Fahrenkopf and Paul Kirk, "Debates and the Networks' Role," *Washington Post*, 27 October 1991.

8   Martin Plissner, "Debates: You Can Trust the Networks," *Washington Post*, 5 November 1991.

9   Martin Plissner, interview by the author, 3 April 2001.

10 Frank Fahrenkopf, 27 March 2001.

11 E-mail from David Norcross to the author, 2 August 2001.

12 Sidney Kraus, *Televised Presidential Debates and Public Policy*, 128.

13 Frank Fahrenkopf, interview by the author, 27 March 2001.

14 Howard Kurtz, "The Game Must Go On," *Washington Post*, 12 October 1992.

15 Roger Simon, "So, Let the Debates Begin Already," *U.S. News and World Report*, 2 October 2000.

16 D. Birdsell, "What Should Debates Be? Standards of Public Discourse," in *Presidential Campaigning and America's Self Images*, A. H. Miller and B. E. Gronbeck, eds. (Boulder, CO: Westview Press, 1994), 128–42.

17 Martin Plissner, *The Control Room: How Television Calls the Shots in Presidential Elections*, 131.

18 Sidney Kraus, *Televised Presidential Debates and Public Policy*, 147.

19 Mary McGrory, "Politics Without Punditry," *Washington Post*, 20 September 1992.

20 Nancy Neuman, interview by the author, 10 September 2001.

21 Carole Simpson, interview by Donita Moorhus in Washington, DC, 17 June 1994 (Washington Press Club Foundation, interview 9), 160–88.

22 Charles T. Royer, *Campaign for President: The Managers Look at 1992*, 254.

23 Scott Reed, interview by the author, 2 April 2001.

24 Arthur Unger, "Staging the TV Debates," *Christian Science Monitor*, 27 October 1980.

25 Arthur Unger, "Bill Moyers—'Conscience of American TV'?" *Christian Science Monitor*, 31 October 1980.

26 David Norcross, interview by the author, 26 March 2001.

27 Howard Kurtz, "Posing Debate Questions to Be Chosen by Bush, Clinton Camps," *Washington Post*, 4 October 1992.

28 Richard Berke, "Debate on Debates Over, Debate on Panel Begins," *New York Times*, 6 October 1992.

29 Kay Maxwell, interview by the author, 17 January 2002.

30 Jon Margolis, conversation with the author, 1 May 2000.

31 Richard Berke, "Critics Accuse Moderator of Letting Debate Wander," *New York Times*, 17 October 2000.

32 Ibid.
33 Howard Buffett, interview by the author, 18 October 2001.
34 Alan Schroeder, *Presidential Debates: Forty Years of High Risk TV,* 137.
35 Ibid.
36 Stephen Coleman, *Televised Election Debates: International Perspectives* (New York: St. Martin's Press, 2000), 14.
37 Roger Simon, *Divided We Stand: How Al Gore Beat George Bush and Lost the Presidency* (New York: Crown Publishers, 2001), 243.
38 Janet Brown, interview by the author, 1 August 2001.
39 William Daley, e-mail interview by the author, 7 August 2001.
40 George H. W. Bush, interview by Jim Lehrer, *Debating Our Destiny,* Public Broadcasting System, 10 April 1999.
41 Diana Carlin, "A Defense of the 'Debate' in Presidential Debates," *Argumentation and Advocacy: The Journal of the American Forensic Association* 25 (1980): 208–13.
42 Howard Buffett, interview by the author, 18 October 2001.
43 Tim Haley, interview by the author, 13 March 2002.
44 Walter Cronkite, "Reporting Presidential Campaigns," in *The Politics of News: The News of Politics,* Doris Graber, ed. (New York: CQ Press 1998).
45 "A Naked Look at the Debate," *New York Times,* 17 October 1980.
46 Sidney Kraus, *Televised Presidential Debates and Public Policy,* 50–51.
47 Bobby Burchfield, interview by the author, 5 April 2001.
48 James Baker, interview by the author, 13 September 2001.
49 George H. W. Bush, interview by Jim Lehrer, *Debating Our Destiny,* Public Broadcasting System, 10 April 1999.
50 Roger Simon, "So, Let the Debates Begin Already," *U.S. News and World Report,* 2 October 2000.
51 "Democrats Called Audience Shots at Bentsen-Quayle Debate," *San Diego-Union Tribune,* 10 May 1990.
52 House Committee on House Administration, *Presidential Debates: Hearing Before the Subcommittee on Elections of the House Committee on House Administration,* 104.
53 Nancy Neuman, interview by the author, 10 September 2001.
54 Felicity Barringer and Dale Russakoff, "Baltimore's Two Faces: A Stage for the Great Debate, Rubble, and Renovation," *Washington Post,* 22 September 1980.
55 Ed Fouhy, interview by the author, 19 September, 2001.
56 Geraldine Ferraro, interview by Jim Lehrer, *Debating Our Destiny,* Public Broadcasting System, 13 June 1990.
57 John F. Harris, "Perot's Status in Debates Won't Be Easily Resolved," *Washington Post,* 17 September 1996.
58 Roger Simon, *Divided We Stand: How Al Gore Beat George Bush and Lost the Presidency* (New York: Crown Publishers, 2001), 235.

59 Scott Reed, interview by the author, 2 April 2001.
60 George H. W. Bush, interview by Jim Lehrer, *Debating Our Destiny*, Public Broadcasting System, 10 April 1999.
61 Alan Schroeder, *Presidential Debates: Forty Years of High Risk TV*, 39.
62 House Committee on House Administration, *Presidential Debates*, 22.
63 Geraldine Ferraro, interview by Jim Lehrer, *Debating Our Destiny*, Public Broadcasting System, 13 June 1990.
64 Charles T. Royer, *Campaign for President: The Managers Look at 1992*, 253.
65 Alan Schroeder, *Presidential Debates: Forty Years of High Risk TV*, 120.

5: THE 15 PERCENT FICTION

1   Janet Brown, interview by the author, 1 August 2001.
2   Paul Kirk, interview by the author, 5 December 2001.
3   *The Early Show*, CBS, 12 October 2000.
4   Deborah Mathis, "Third Parties Find Invitation Debatable," *USA Today*, 6 October 1999.
5   "A Transparent Farce," *Las Vegas Review-Journal*, 10 January 2000.
6   George Will, "Buchanan Has Right to Be in the Debate," *Washington Post*, 21 September 1999.
7   Frank Fahrenkopf, interview by the author, 27 March 2001.
8   Ibid.
9   Richard Marin, "Are Presidential Debates Too Exclusive?" *Washington Post*, 1 May 2000.
10 *Nightline*, ABC, 31 October 2000.
11 "Making the Rules for Presidential Debates: Who Plays and Who Wins," press conference at the National Press Club sponsored by the Century Foundation, Washington, DC, 26 October 1999.
12 www.jessjacksonjr.org.
13 Committee for a Unified Independent Party, press conference, Washington, DC, 8 May 2000.
14 *Nightline*, ABC, 31 October 2000.
15 "Should Perot Debate?" *NewsHour*, Public Broadcasting System, 11 September 1996.
16 "Commission Should Lower the Bar for Next Fall's TV Debates," *Portland Press Herald*, 13 January 2000.
17 Jesse Ventura, *Face the Nation*, CBS, 9 January 2001.
18 Bruce Cain and Todd Lochner, "Crime, Punishment, and Campaign Finance," *Institute of Governmental Studies Public Affairs Report* 40, no. 4 (September 1999).
19 Scott Reed, interview by the author, 2 April 2001.
20 *Congressional Record*, 117 (22 November 1971).
21 Mario Cuomo, *The Early Show*, 1 October 2000.

22 Congressman John Lewis, interview by the author, 17 September 2002.

23 Scott E. Thomas, interview by the author, 12 November 2001.

24 "Monopoly of the U.S. Democratic Process Will Not Shift Until Control Over the Presidential Debates Is Taken Away from the Republicans and Democrats," *All Things Considered*, National Public Radio, 3 October 2000.

25 Arianna Huffington, "The Debates Debate," Arianna Online http://www.ariannaonline.com/columns/files/021700.html, 17 February 2000.

26 Howard Buffett, interview by the author, 18 October 2001.

27 George W. Bush, *Larry King Live*, CNN, 19 September 2000.

28 "Vice President Al Gore Discusses the Presidential Race," *Meet the Press*, NBC, 16 July 2000.

29 Scott E. Thomas, interview by the author, 12 November 2001.

30 Committee for a Unified Independent Party, press conference, Washington, DC, 8 May 2000.

31 George Stephanopolous, interview by the author, 20 March 2001.

32 John Scardino, interview by the author, 15 April 2001.

33 Alan Simpson, interview by the author, 18 March 2002.

34 John Buckley, interview by the author, 2 February 2002.

35 Don Hazen, "The Nader Wildcard," *Christian Science Monitor*, 9 July 2000.

36 Frank Fahrenkopf, interview by the author, 27 March 2001.

37 Fred Malek, interview by the author, 30 August 2001.

38 Diana Carlin, interview by the author, 17 November 2001.

39 Kenneth Thompson, interview by the author, 20 April 2001.

40 Richard Neustadt, interview by the author, 24 August 2001.

41 Newton Minow, interview by the author, 14 July 2001.

42 Scott Reed, interview by the author, 2 April 2001.

43 Bob Teeter, interview by the author, 31 July 2001.

44 Gordon Lack, "The End of the Two-Party Era," *Polling Report*, 18 September 1995.

45 John Lewis, interview by the author, 17 September 2002.

46 Charles T. Royer, *Campaign for President: The Managers Look at 1992*, 295.

47 Anthony Mazzocchi, acceptance speech for the Joe A. Callaway Award for Civic Courage, Washington, DC, 3 December 2001.

48 "Should Perot Debate?" *NewsHour*, Public Broadcasting System, 11 September 1996.

49 Alan Schroeder, *Presidential Debates: Forty Years of High Risk TV*, 120.

50 "Extra Debates—With Other Faces," *Washington Post*, 19 September 2000.

51 House Committee on House Administration, *Presidential Debates: Hearing Before the Subcommittee on Elections of the House Committee on House Administration*, 13.

52 *Late Edition*, CNN, 2 July 2000.

53 *A Third Choice: The Story of Third-Party Candidates in America*, Public Broadcasting System. 1996

54 Ibid.

55 Ibid.

56 Ralph Nader, interview by the author, 5 January 2003.

57 Russell Verney, interview by the author, 12 March 2001.

58 Bernard Barmann, "Third-Party Candidates and Presidential Debates: A Proposal to Increase Voter Participation in National Elections," *Columbia Journal of Law and Social Problems* 23 (1990): 444–45.

59 "Buchanan and Nader Discuss Their Political Agendas," *Larry King Live*, CNN, 2 October 2000.

60 "Extra Debates—With Other Faces," *Washington Post*, 19 September 2000.

61 "Nader Is an Articulate Voice of Dissent; Put Him in the Debates," *San Jose Mercury News*, 1 September 2000.

62 Stephen Bates, *The Future of Presidential Debates* (Washington, DC: The Annenberg Washington Program in Communications Policy Studies of Northwestern University, 1993).

63 Paul G. Kirk Jr. and Frank J. Fahrenkopf Jr., "Yes, Presidential Debate Rules Are Fair," *Boston Herald*, 26 February 2000.

64 James Pinkerton, "System Stacked against Nader, Buchanan," *Newsday*, 1 July 2000.

65 John F. Bibby, "Political Parties in the United States," www.usinfo.state.gov.

66 Albert Cantril, "The Polls Shouldn't Govern the Debate," *New York Times*, 7 September 1980.

67 *Larry King Live*, CNN, 30 October 2000.

68 MSNBC's Paul Begala, hosted by Chris Donohue, 15 March 2000.

69 Institute of Politics at Harvard University, *Campaign for President: The Managers Look at 2000* (Hollis, NH: Hollis Publishing, 2003).

70 Charles T. Royer, *Campaign for President: The Managers Look at 1992*, 177.

71 Theodore Roosevelt of the Bull Moose Party in 1912, Eugene Debs of the Socialist Party in 1912, Allan Benson of the Socialist Party in 1916, Robert La Follette of the Progressive Party in 1924, Independent candidate John Anderson in 1980, Ed Clark of the Libertarian Party in 1980, Lenora Fulani of the New Alliance Party in 1988, Andre Marrou of the Libertarian Party in 1992, Ross Perot of the Reform Party in 1992 and 1996, and Harry Browne of the Libertarian Party in 1996.

72 Amendment Offered by Mr. Paul to the Amendment in the Nature of a Substitute No. 13 Offered by Mr. Shays, *Congressional Record*.

73 Gail Collins, "The Last Angry Man," *New York Times*, 22 September 2000.

74 David S. Broder, "The Best Campaign," *Washington Post*, 5 November 2000.

75 Figures exclude letters to the editor, editorial, and op-ed pieces.

76 E. R. Shipp, "All Candidates Are Not Created Equal," *Washington Post*, 3 September 2000.

77 Pat Buchanan, interview by the author, 12 February 2003.

78 Editorial, "Mr. Nader's Misguided Crusade," *New York Times*, 30 June 2000.

79 Editorial, "Mr. Nader's Electoral Mischief," *New York Times*, 26 October 2000.

80 Editorial, "Al Gore in the Home Stretch," *New York Times*, 3 November 2000.

81 Editorial, "The Power of the Undecideds," *New York Times*, 5 November 2000.

82 Russell Verney, interview by the author, 12 March 2001.

83 "Self-Censorship: How Often and Why," *Pew Research Center* and *Columbia Journalism Review* (30 April 2000): 1–2.

84 "Self-Censorship: How Often and Why," 1–2.

85 Robert W. McChesney, "The Global Media Giants," *Extra!*, November/December 1997.

86 Ralph Nader, interview by the author, 5 January 2003.

87 Jake Tapper, "No Thirds Allowed," www.salonmag.com, 22 June 2000.

88 House Committee on House Administration, *Presidential Debates: Hearing Before the Subcommittee on Elections of the House Committee on House Administration*, 83.

6: ISSUE EXCLUSION

1 Michael Moore, speaking at a Ralph Nader for President Rally, New York City, 14 October 2000.

2 An issue is defined here as a topic discussed for greater than 0.5 percent of the debate.

3 Russell Verney, interview by the author, 12 March 2001.

4 "Message of the Debates," *San Francisco Chronicle*, 19 October 2000.

5 "The Campaign's Missing Issues," *Washington Post*, 11 October 2000.

6 Institute of Politics at Harvard University, *Campaign for President: The Managers Look at 2000*.

7 Valerie Bauerlein, "Beer and Girls' Debate at Boys' State Criticized," *The State*, 23 June 2001.

8 "Room at the Debate Table," *Christian Science Monitor*, 15 June 2001.

9   Senator Russell Feingold addressing the Shadow Convention, Los Angeles, 13 August 2000.
10 George Stephanopolous, interview by the author, 20 March 2001.
11 "Should Third-Party Candidates Get Seats at the Debates," *Newsstand*, CNN, 18 September 2000.
12 Ralph Nader, "Why Voters Will Lose Out in Tuesday's Debate," *Boston Globe*, 30 September 2000.
13 David Broder, "Online, and Off Center, You'll Find Libertarians on the Rise," *Washington Post*, 11 July 1996.
14 Calculated for all presidential debates *since 1976*.
15 Ibid.
16 House Committe on House Administration, *Presidential Debates: Hearing Before the Subcommittee on Elections of the House Committee on House Administration*, 67.
17 "Poll Finds No Clear Winner in Anderson-Reagan Debate," *New York Times*, 27 September 1980.
18 "Between the Platforms," *New York Times*, 3 September 1980.
19 "The Next Debate," *New York Times*, 23 September 1980.
20 Philip Gailey, "Perot Has a Place at the Debates," *St. Petersbug Times*, 15 September 1996.
21 Lance Morrow, "Why Ralph and Pat Should Be in the Debates," Time.com, 23 June 2000.
22 Stephen Coleman, *Televised Election Debates: International Perspectives* (New York: St. Martin's Press, 2000), 162.
23 Jeff Milchen, "The Poverty of Debates," reclaimdemocracy.org, October 2000.
24 Stephen Coleman, *Televised Election Debates: International Perspectives*, 182.
25 Mary McGrory, "Kennedy Scores in Boston Brawl," *St. Louis Post-Dispatch*, 31 October 1999.

7: FAILED RESTITUTION

1   Department of Treasury, Internal Revenue Service, Publication 557, *Tax-Exempt Status for Your Organization*, Rev. November 1999, 14.
2   Ibid., 40.
3   House Committee on House Administration, *Presidential Debates: Hearing Before the Subcommittee on Elections of the House Committee on House Administration*, 20.
4   Diana Carlin testified, "I know from having been a member of the Neustadt Committee in 1988 and 1992, it would have been very easy to apply objective criteria. The subjective criteria, however, puts one in a position of being similar to a Supreme Court Justice and interpreting some things, and that is what I felt like during that process."

5   "Debate Negotiators Detail Their Format Proposals," CNN, 18 September 1996.
6   David Broder, *Campaign for President: The Managers Look at '96*, 165.
7   First General Counsel's Report on MURs 4451 and 4473, FEC 29 (1998).
8   Ibid., 17.
9   Ibid., 29.
10 Ibid., 23.
11 Lawrence Noble, interview by the author, 3 November 2001.
12 Statement of Reasons on MURs 4451 and 4473, FEC 1 (1998).
13 Ibid., 11.
14 "Designed for Impotence," *U.S. News and World Report*, 20 January 1997.
15 Ibid.
16 Lawrence Noble, interview by the author, 3 November 2001.
17 Reform Party of Oklahoma, "FEC General Counsel: Evidence of Violations in Perot Exclusion from '96 Debates," press release, 23 March 1998.
18 "Designed for Impotence," *U.S. News and World Report*, 20 January 1997.
19 Lawrence Noble, interview by the author, 3 November 2001.
20 Scott E. Thomas, interview by the author, 12 November 2001.
21 House Committee on House Administration, *Presidential Debates*, 132.
22 Nancy Othen, "Judge Denies Perot Spot in Presidential Debates," www.Alligator.org, 2 October 1996.
23 Lawrence Noble, interview by the author, 3 November 2001.
24 "Election 2000: Debating Debate Exclusion," *Burden of Proof,* CNN, 3 October 2000.
25 *Patrick J. Buchanan v. Federal Election Commission,* no. 00-1775.
26 *Forbes v. Arkansas Education Television Commission Network Found.*, 22 F.3d 1423, 1426 (8th Cir. 1994) aff'd, 118 Sup. Ct. 1633 (1999).
27 *Forbes v. Arkansas Education Television Commission*, 93 F.3d 497, 504 (8th Cir. 1996) *rev'd*, 118 Sup. Ct. 1633 (1998).
28 Ibid.
29 Jamin Raskin, "The Debate Gerrymander," *Texas Law Review* 77 (1999): 1954.
30 "Making the Rules for Presidential Debates: Who Plays and Who Wins," press conference at the National Press Club, sponsored by the Century Foundation,Washington, DC, 26 October 1999.
31 Thomas E. Patterson, *The Vanishing Voter: Public Involvement in an Age of Uncertainty,* John F. Kennedy School of Government, Harvard University (New York: Alfred A. Knopf, 2002), 171.

32 Stephen Bates, *The Future of Presidential Debates* (Washington, DC: The Annenberg Washington Program in Communications Policy Studies of Northwestern University, 1993).

33 *Congressional Record,* National Presidential Debates Act of 1991, House, 26 February 1991.

34 *Congressional Record,* Senate Elections Ethics Act, Senate, 17 May 1991.

35 Sidney Kraus, *Televised Presidential Debates and Public Policy,* 253.

36 *Congressional Record,* The Democracy in Presidential Debates Act, House, 4 February 1991.

37 Debate Requirements for Presidential Candidates, Amendment Offered by Mr. Paul to Amendment in the Nature of a Substitute No. 13 Offered by Mr. Shays.

38 *Congressional Record,* House, 1 July 1999.

39 Bobby Burchfield, interivew by the author, 5 April 2001.

40 House Committee on House Administration, *Presidential Debates,* 29.

41 Barbara Vucanovich, interview by the author, 23 July 2001.

42 House Committee on House Administration, *Presidential Debates,* 21.

43 John Lewis, interview by the author, 17 September 2002.

8: CITIZENS' DEBATE COMMISSION

1 Don Hazen, "The Nader Wildcard," *Christian Science Monitor,* 9 July 2000.

2 The TVs were attached to ropes and pulled out of the water in an environmentally sound manner.

3 Jeff Cohen, James Pinkerton, Jane Hall, Cal Thomas, and Eric Burns, "Why Not Open the Debates?" *Washington Times,* 24 September 2000.

4 Steve Forbes and Ralph Nader, conversation with the author, 16 May 2002.

5 Committee for a Unified Independent Party, press conference, Washington, DC, 8 May 2000.

6 George Stephanopolous, interview by the author, 20 March 2001.

7 Thomas E. Patterson, *The Vanishing Voter: Public Involvement in an Age of Uncertainty,* John F. Kennedy School of Government, Harvard University, New York (2002): 173.

8 Bob Teeter, interview by the author, 31 July 2001.

9 "Election Day in America: What's Left to Say?" *Talk Back Live,* CNN, 7 November 2000.

10 "Should Third-Party Candidates Get Seats at the Debates?" *Newsstand,* CNN, 18 September 2000.

11 Scott McLarty, "Election Reform for Two," letter to the editor, *Washington Post,* 4 April 2001.

12 Stephen Coleman, *Televised Election Debates: International Perspectives* (New York: St. Martin's Press, 2000), 133.

13　Ibid., 147.

14　Tom Brokaw, "Networks Should Sponsor Debates," in *Presidential Debates: 1988 and Beyond*, 74.

15　Ralph Nader, "Letter from Ralph Nader to Network Executives," Nader 2000 Presidential Campaign, 6 September 2000.

16　*Congressional Record*, Senate, 4 October 2000.

17　Frank Fahrenkopf, interview by the author, 27 March 2001.

18　Stephen Bates, *The Future of Presidential Debates* (Washington, DC: The Annenberg Washington Program in Communications Policy Studies of Northwestern University, 1993).

19　John Lewis, interview by the author, 17 September 2002.

20　Dennis Kucinich, responses to a presidential candidate questionnaire titled "Choosing an Independent President 2004," The Committee for a United Independent Party, http://www.cuip.org/chipResponses/kucinich.pdf.

21　John Buckley, interview by the author, 2 February 2002.

22　Newton N. Minow and Clifford Sloan, "Political Parties Should Sponsor Debates," in *Presidential Debates: 1988 and Beyond*, chapter 9.

23　Bob Dole, "Debating Our Destiny," interview by Jim Lehrer, Public Broadcasting System, 10 November 1999.

24　Frank Donatelli, interview by the author, 12 October 2001.

25　Newt Gingrich, "Who Rules America?," a debate with Ralph Nader, Portand, 12 February 2002.

26　Scott Reed, interview by the author, 2 April 2001.

27　"Let Ross Perot Debate," *New York Times*, 6 September 1996.

28　Committee for a Unified Independent Party, press conference, Washington, DC, 8 May 2000.

CONCLUSION

1　House Committee on House Administration, *Presidential Debates: Hearing Before the Subcommittee on Elections of the House Committee on House Administration*, 24.

2　Theo Lippman Jr., "Keep Debates Democratic," *Baltimore Sun*, 28 July 2000.

3　Janet Brown, interview by the author, 1 August 2001.

Index

About the Author

George Farah is the founder and executive director of Open Debates, a Washington-based nonprofit committed to reforming the presidential debate process. He is also a student at Harvard Law School. His articles have appeared in *Extra! Magazine* and *The Philadelphia Inquirer*, among other publications. He has appeared on C-Span and has been interviewed on several radio stations.

About Open Debates

Open Debates (www.opendebates.org) is a new nonprofit, nonpartisan organization that works to reform the presidential debate process. Open Debates works to inform the public and policymakers about the fundamental problems with the bipartisan Commission on Presidential Debates. It also promotes an alternative presidential debate sponsor—the nonpartisan Citizens' Debate Commission—comprising national civic leaders committed to maximizing voter education. Open Debates possesses a politically diverse board of directors, a large volunteer corps, and substantial support from other civic organizations.